A NAVAL HISTORY

OF THE

AMERICAN REVOLUTION

IN TWO VOLUMES

VOLUME II

THE BONHOMME RICHARD AND THE SERAPIS

A NAVAL HISTORY OF THE AMERICAN REVOLUTION

BY

GARDNER W. ALLEN

VOL. II

NEW YORK

RUSSELL & RUSSELL · INC

CONTENTS

ILLUSTRATIONS

A NAVAL HISTORY

OF THE

AMERICAN REVOLUTION

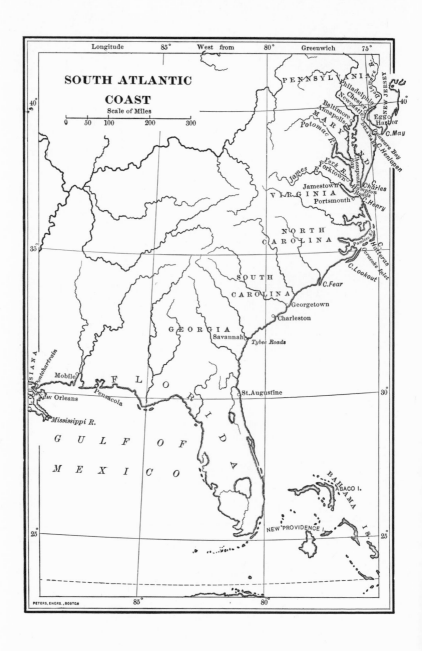

SOUTH ATLANTIC
COAST
Scale of Miles
0   50   100   200   300

A NAVAL HISTORY OF THE AMERICAN REVOLUTION

CHAPTER XI

NAVAL OPERATIONS IN 1779

TAKING into account the heavy losses of the last two years, the Continental navy still showed vigor at the opening of 1779 and rendered valuable service during the year. The British, in spite of their naval superiority, were not free from solicitude as to the possibilities of the American sea forces. Admiral Gambier reported that there were at Boston December 6, 1778, fifteen vessels of war, including five Continental frigates, and January 10, 1779, he wrote: "A Report prevails that one 40, four 32, one 28, and two 20 Gun Ships of the Rebels sailed about ten days ago from Boston; this Circumstance if true is very alarming, not only on Account of the probability of their falling in with our victuallers, but on Account of the present reduced numbers of our Ships, and they much divided, the Coppered Frigates could not without the greatest danger from Ice have been kept on this part of the Coast during the Winter Season." He wrote later, on the authority of a privateer, that three frigates had sailed from Boston January 18, " in order to Cruise off the Chesepeak," and that they had been seen ten days later, off the Delaware capes.[1] His information in regard to both these sailings was obviously incorrect.

A few new Continental vessels went into commission or into active service, the most important of which were the frigates Alliance and Confederacy, of thirty-two guns each ; the first was built in Massachusetts, the other in Connecticut. The Confederacy was a hundred and thirty-three feet long, with an extreme breadth of thirty-five feet, six inches, and was designed to carry twenty-eight guns on the main deck, six on the quarter deck, and two on the forecastle. These ships, which had been authorized by Congress two years or more before, encountered the usual difficulties and delays in getting ready for sea. The Marine Committee in their efforts to expedite matters issued many orders which, owing to slow communication and uncertainty as to the condition of vessels and the state of affairs in distant ports, were frequently modified or changed. February 10, it was arranged that the Confederacy, Captain Harding, then at New London, should make a short cruise in Long Island Sound with two vessels of the Connecticut navy. Later she was to join the Queen of France in a cruise along the Atlantic coast, in which the Ranger was to take part.

[1] *Brit. Adm. Rec., A. D. 489,* Nos. 19, 22, 25, December 20, 1778, January 10, February 3, 1779.

Captain Olney of the Queen of France, the senior
officer, was ordered to " sweep in the first place this
coast from the Southward of Cape May to the Bar
of Charles Town and afterwards to Cruize in such
Latitudes and Longitudes which are best calculated
to give the greatest aid and protection to the Trade
of Delaware, Chesapeake and Charles Town, and
as often as circumstances and the safety of your
Ships will admit of it, you are to enter the mouths
of Delaware and Chesapeake for the purpose of
destroying the small Armed Vessels from New York
that lurk about the Capes to the certain destruction
of almost every Merchantman that sails ; you are
at the same time to be extreamly cautious in continuing in any of these places so long as to render
yourself a certain Object for the pursuit of the
enemy. If in the Course of this Cruize you should
meet with the Deane or the Confederacy or both
of them, it is our orders that you and they proceed
on this Cruize in Company, under the command of
the Superior Officer, to execute these Orders ; and
least you should be seperated by Storms or other
circumstances, it would be advisable to establish
such Private Signals that when the Ships meet
again they may be known to each other as friends.
The great delay, expence and trouble in manning
the Ships for Sea has induced this committee to
direct and Order you to continue this Cruize as long
as your Provisions and other circumstances will
admit. . . . The superiority of the Naval force of

the enemy on this Coast and the misfortunes that have heretofore happened to some of our Ships will, we trust, make you extreamly vigilant and active; the confidence we repose in your fidility, courage and good conduct gives us every reason to hope for a successful Cruize. Most of the Armed Vessels from New York are inferior in force to yourself, which will put it in your power to aid the Trade of the Southern States by destroying many of them and thereby to render not only essential service to the Public, but to add to the honor and reputation of your own character. You are to keep these Instructions a profound secret and when the state of your Provisions requires, you will return into the Port of Philadelphia or some convenient one in the Bay of Chesapeake." [1]

A little later, orders were sent to the Navy Board at Boston to get the frigate Providence ready for sea immediately and again for her to cruise on the Atlantic coast. Then these orders were transferred to the Warren, and later still the committee decided to hold the Warren in port and fit out the Providence for a four months' cruise; and then to send the Boston to the southern coast. Apparently in accordance with this last order, the Navy Board at Boston instructed Captain Tucker, April 6, to proceed with his ship, the frigate Boston, in com-

---

[1] *Mar. Com. Letter Book*, 195, 196, 197 (to Olney, to Governor Trumbull, to Harding, and to Navy Board, Boston, all dated February 10, 1779). The measurements of the Confederacy are taken from *Wolcott MSS.*, February 12, 1777.

pany with the sloop Providence, on a ten days' cruise in Massachusetts Bay and along the Maine shore and then to go south. It does not appear that any of these instructions were, at the time at least, carried out precisely according to the intentions of the Marine Committee. The delay in fitting out the Confederacy was so great that the committee determined to relieve Captain Harding from command, should he be found responsible. That frigate did not get to sea until the end of April.[1]

Meanwhile the frigates Deane, Captain Nicholson, and Alliance, Captain Landais, sailed together from Boston January 14. Pierre Landais was a French naval officer of experience, having sailed around the world with the famous navigator Bougainville; he had embarked in the American cause and on the recommendation of Silas Deane had been appointed a captain in the Continental navy. The Alliance was bound to France and parted with her consort on the third day out.[2] The Deane soon captured an armed ship of the enemy which was sent back to Boston. "Last Thursday," February 4, a newspaper announces, "arrived in this Harbour the ship Viper, taken by Capt. Samuel Nicholson, in the Continental Frigate Deane; she is a letter

[1] *Mar. Com. Letter Book*, 200, 201, 204, 206, 210 (February 21, 26, March 9, 21, 26, April 27, 1779, to Navy Board, Boston), 207 (April 17, 1779, to Harding), 211 (April 27, 1779, to Deshon); *Tucker MSS.*, April 6, 1779; *Boston Post*, May 8, 1779.

[2] *Publ. R. I. Hist. Soc.,* viii, 258; *Wharton*, ii, 387; *Stevens*, 1552.

of Marque fitted out at Liverpool, mounting 16 Guns and 75 Men. . . . Capt. Nicholson took and burnt a ship belonging to London in ballast from New York to Cadiz." The Deane cruised about four months, most of the time in the West Indies. While there she fell in with the Continental ship General Gates, which had sailed from Boston in December and had taken several prizes. The Deane returned to the United States and went into Philadelphia April 17.[1]

The Ranger sailed from Portsmouth for Boston February 24 and the same evening anchored in Nantasket Roads. The frigates Warren, Commodore John B. Hopkins, and Queen of France, Captain Olney, and the Ranger, Captain Simpson, having finally got ready for sea, sailed from Boston March 13. The log of the Ranger, under date of April 6, says: " At 6 A.M.," being sixteen miles east of Cape Henry, " saw 2 sails, gave Chase to one of them; at ½ past 6 the Warren and Queen of France hois'd English Colours and fired a gun to Leeward, as did we, which she answered and bro't too at 7. We brought too, found her to be the Hibernia, a Schooner of 10 guns, a british Privatier; sent 2 of Our People on Board to help man her and now She remains in Concord with us." The next morning, " at ½ past 5 saw a Fleet of 9 sails to the N. E., at 6 made sail and gave Chase, at 8 Tack'd Ship [by] Signal

<hr>

[1] *Publ. R. I. Hist. Soc.*, viii, 258, 259; *Boston Post*, February 6, May 1, 1779; *Adams MSS.*, April 10, 1779, Vernon to Adams.

and made all the Sail we could, alow and aloft;
found we gained on the Fleet, our Consort the
Warren out sailing us all." In the afternoon:
" Pleasant gales and fair weather. The Warren,
Queen of France & Our Selves in Chase of the
Fleet; at 4 P.M. came up with" them. Hopkins
reported to the Marine Committee April 18 that
on the 6th " we fell in with the armed schooner
Hibernia from New York, with 45 men, which we
took ; and on the 7th at 4 o'clock A.M. in latitude
36.40 discovered two fleets, one to leeward consisting of ten sail, the other to windward, of nine sail.
We gave chace to the windward-most, and at about
two o'clock took seven sail, consisting of the following vessels, viz. : Ship Jason, Capt. Porterfield,
mounting 20 nine and six pounders, 150 men, convoy to the fleet bound from N. York to Georgia,
having passengers on board as per the enclosed list ;
Ship Meriah, a letter of marque mounting 16 six
pounders, 84 men, very richly laden with provisions,
dry goods and accoutrements for a regiment of horse ;
Brig Patriot, brig Prince Ferdinand, brig John, brig
Batchelor, schooner Chance, laden with provisions
and goods for the army, to a very large amount. As
soon as they were manned we thought best to stand to
the eastward, having had intelligence of a large number of armed vessels being off Chesapeak and Delaware Bays." Among the passengers on board the Jason were a colonel, a lieutenant-colonel, two captains
and two lieutenants. The Ranger's log for the 9th

says: " Jogging under easy sail, to keep our little Fleet together." April 10 : " The Patriot being a heavy Sailer, the Warren at 7 took her in tow." Hopkins's report continues : " On the 16th instant I arrived in this port [Boston], having parted with the fleet on the 11th in a thick fog. The next day the Jason arrived, which is a very fine ship; also the schooner at Portsmouth, which is a very valuable vessel. Several vessels are now in sight, which I hope is some of the fleet. By the activity of Captains Olney and Simpson we manned the fleet in four hours." [1] The Queen of France arrived in Boston several days after the Warren and Jason, bringing in with her the Maria, Hibernia, and three brigs. The other two prizes were taken into Portsmouth April 21 by the Ranger. The Jason and Hibernia were afterwards fitted out as privateers and made successful cruisers. The Ranger returned to Boston harbor in June and anchored again in Nantasket Roads.[2]

The Marine Committee were greatly pleased with the results of this cruise, sent a congratulatory letter to Hopkins, and proposed to purchase the Jason and Hibernia and take them into the naval service; but a more thorough knowledge of all the circumstances caused a change of sentiment. May 20, the committee wrote to the Navy Board at Boston:

---

[1] *Penn. Gazette*, April 28, 1779.

[2] *Boston Gazette*, April 19, 26, 1779; *Boston Post*, May 22, July 31, 1779; *Log of the Ranger*.

" Since ours of the 4th instant we are favoured with yours of the 28th Ultimo, whereby we find there is reason to conclude that Captain Hopkins has violated his Orders by returning into Port when he should have continued to Cruize and by not sending the Prizes he took into the nearest Port; and we find also that Captain Olney has acted contradictory to your Orders by comeing up to Boston when you had expressly required him to remain with his Ship in [Nantasket] road. We now direct that you immediately order a Court of Inquiry to inquire into the Conduct of those Two commanders during their late Cruize, and afterward if necessary a Court Martial. If you find the prosecution of that business will produce any delay in getting the Ships again to Sea, it is our desire that you suspend the said Commanders and put in others, and in that case we recommend Captain Saltonstal and Captain Rathbourne to be appointed in their room. We deem it highly necessary for the good of the service that the orders of your Board should be obeyed by all Officers of the Navy under your direction, and we desire that you will cause Courts of enquiry to be held, when it is your Opinion the good of the service requires it, on the conduct of such Officers as may disobey your Orders or in any other manner may misbehave. We highly disaprove of Captain Hopkins sending an Officer to this place with a Letter contrary to the Orders of your Board, which disobedience of Orders in this as well as in other instances were unknown

to us when we wrote him a Letter of approbation;
and we consider it very injurious to the service for
the Officers to get themselves appointed Agents for
their men as well as dishonorable to such Officers."
As a result of this exercise of discipline Captains
Hopkins and Olney were suspended from the navy
and they seem never again to have held any command in the Continental service. Captains Saltonstall and Rathburne were appointed to command
the frigates Warren and Queen of France. The
sequel will suggest a doubt as to whether the change
in the case of the Warren was to the advantage of
the country.[1]

After a successful cruise in the West Indies the
Continental cutter Revenge, Captain Conyngham,
sailed north and arrived at Philadelphia February
21, 1779. Here the Revenge was sold, but the pur-
chaser fitted her out as a privateer and Conyngham
was put in command again, under his Continental
commission of May 2, 1777. In April the Revenge
was captured by the British frigate Galatea and
taken into New York. Conyngham was sent to
England in irons and treated with great severity.
He was accused of piracy on the ground that his
cruise in the Surprise in the spring of 1777 pre-
ceded the date of his commission. His first commission, dated March 1, 1777, had been taken from

[1] *Mar. Com. Letter Book*, 213 (to Hopkins, May 4, 1779), 210,
213, 215, 216, 222 (to Navy Board, Boston, April 27, 30, May 20,
26, June 21, 1779); *Adams MSS.*, May 25, 1779, Vernon to
Adams.

him at Dunkirk and sent to Versailles.[1] Search
was made for this earlier commission, but without
success.[2] Franklin's assurance, however, that it
had existed apparently resulted in some ameliora-
tion of Conyngham's treatment. He was removed
to Plymouth and in November, 1779, after several
unsuccessful attempts, he escaped from Mill Prison
with about fifty others. He proceeded first to London and thence found his way to Holland.[3]

About the first of the year the sloop Providence,
Captain Rathburne, took five prizes, all of which
seem to have arrived safely in port. One of these
was a ship from Glasgow which had been taken by
an American privateer, retaken by the British, and
then captured again by the Providence. Early in
April the Providence was ordered to make a short
cruise in Massachusetts Bay and along the coast of
Maine in company with the frigate Boston. Later
she was sent south of Cape Cod. May 7, at nine
o'clock in the morning, while cruising off Sandy
Hook, the Providence, now commanded by Captain
Hacker, was seen from the British brig Diligent,
whose captain, testifying at his court martial, says
that about noon, "as soon as I had taken measures

[1] See above, p. 265.

[2] This commission has come to light within a few years and is
in the possession of James Barnes, Esq., of New York.

[3] *Penn. Mag. Hist. and Biogr.*, January, 1899; *Outlook*, January
3, 1903; *Hale*, i, 342–350; *Almon*, viii, 340; *Maryland Journal*,
March 2, 1779; *Penn. Gazette*, August 4, 1779; *Mar. Com. Letter
Book*, 201, 217 (March 10, June 2, 1779); *Archives de la Marine*
B³ **16** (Avril, Novembre, 1779).

for fighting him on the Larboard side, the side his Boom was of, he Gibed & luffed across." The Diligent luffed and received two broadsides and two volleys of musketry before returning the fire of the Providence. " Not an officer except myself unhurt, being deserted by the remains of my Crew except seven, five of them wounded, . . . Masts, Rigging & Hull cut all to pieces," was forced to surrender to the Providence. The Diligent carried twelve three-pounders and fifty-four men; the Providence, according to this English captain, six six-pounders, six fours, two twos, and eighty-three men. The Americans lost four killed and ten wounded; the British, eleven killed and nineteen wounded. The Diligent was taken into the Continental naval service.[1]

In the spring the frigate Boston, Captain Tucker, in response to the instructions of March 26, came south to Chesapeake Bay and on April 27 was ordered to Delaware Bay. The Confederacy, after long delay, sailed from New London April 29, and a month later was in Delaware Bay. Meanwhile the Deane had arrived at Philadelphia from the West Indies April 17. The plans of the Marine Committee, which required frequent modification to suit the exigencies of changing circumstances, were defined

[1] *Boston Post*, January 16, 1779; *Independent Chronicle*, January 21, 1779; *Penn. Packet*, May 25, 1779; *Maryland Journal*, June 1, 1779; *Adams MSS.* April 10, May 25, 1779; *Tucker MSS.*, April 6, 1779; *Brit. Adm. Rec., Courts Martial*, No. 5311 (August 21, 1779).

SAMUEL TUCKER

for the moment in their letter of May 20 to the Navy Board at Boston. " We have lately had sufficient reason to lay asside the expedition intended against the enemys force on the Coast of Georgia, and the service the frigate Providence was intended for, is supplied by another Ship ; therefore it is now our intention to place our collected Naval force in such a manner as to accomplish the double purpose of intercepting the enemies outward bound Transports for New York from Great Britain and Ireland & the homeward bound West India Ships. But if the Providence & Ranger should be ready for Sea more than a fortnight before the other Ships, that then you order those Ships to proceed to Cruize for the above purpose, marking out to them their Cruizing ground in such a manner as there may be the greatest possible certainty of being joined by the other Ships as soon as they shall be ready." [1]

The Deane, Boston, and Confederacy being all in Delaware Bay by the end of May, a cruise along the Atlantic coast was planned for them by the Marine Committee. Instructions for the Boston and Confederacy were dated June 2. To Tucker the committee wrote : " The Ship Boston which you command and the Frigate Confederacy, Captain Harding, being now ready for Sea, they are directed to Sail in company with each other on a Cruize upon

---

[1] *Mar. Com. Letter Book*, 206, 215 (to Navy Board, Boston, March 26, May 20, 1779), 209 (April 21, 1779), 211 (to Tucker, April 27, 1779) ; *Boston Post*, May 8, 1779.

this Coast from the Latitude of Forty to thirty-five degrees and to take, burn, sink or destroy as many of the enemys Ships or Vessels of every Kind as may be in their power. The Prizes you will Order into the nearest and safest Ports, addressed to the Continental Agents in those Ports. And as this Committee have received authentic intelligence that a number of the enemys Privateers are Cruizing near the Latitude of 36, in expectation of falling in with a fleet of Merchant Vessels bound from the West Indies, . . . it is their first Object to frustrate the designs of the enemy by Capturing or destroying their Vessels and to afford every aid and assistance in their power to the inward bound Merchantmen." They were also to give their attention to two British frigates said to have been sent out from New York " to cruize upon this Coast, . . . and we need not remind you how greatly it would redound to your reputation and the honor of the American flag to capture or destroy these ships. You are to continue cruizing for the space of three weeks from your Departure from the Capes of Delaware," and then return to Delaware Bay for further orders. " As the Object of this Cruise is to take or destroy the enemys Privateers or small ships of war and give every aid and assistance to the Merchantmen, the Committee direct you to confine yourself strictly to the Latitudes above mentioned and to such Longitudes as are best calculated to answer that purpose. But if from circumstances it should happen that the Public Service necessarily requires you to exceed those Limits, then you are at liberty to do it. The Ship General Greene, Captain Montgomery, belonging to the State of Pennsylvania, now in this Bay, will have Orders from His Excellency President Reed to act in conjunction with you during this Cruize. Captain Harding will be furnished with a Copy of these Instructions and will be directed to Obey your Orders as Senior Officer. It is expected that before you put to Sea you will fix with him a proper System of Signals for the Ships under your command. The Confidence we repose in your Courage and good Conduct gives us every reason to hope for a Successful Cruize." [1] Ten days later, the frigate Deane being ready for sea, essentially the same orders were sent to Captain Nicholson. In case he should fall in with the Boston and Confederacy, he was to cruise in company with them, returning to the Delaware capes by July 1. " When joined to those Ships, you, being the Senior Officer, will have under your direction three fine frigates, which we doubt not will be judiciously managed and we recommend to you to cultivate strict harmony with the Commanders of those Ships as being essentially necessary for the Public good." [2] Few details of this short cruise have been preserved. A number of captures seem to have

[1] *Mar. Com. Letter Book*, 218 (to Tucker), 219 (to Harding, June 2, 1779).

[2] *Ibid.*, 221 (to Nicholson, June 12, 1779).

been made, the most important of which was the
British privateer ship Pole of twenty-four guns,
taken by the Boston.[1]

On the 18th of June the frigates Providence,
Commodore Whipple, and Queen of France, Captain Rathburne, and the Ranger, Captain Simpson,
sailed from Boston on a cruise to the eastward.
The log of the Ranger records the capture of a
vessel July 20 and another the next day; they were
both from Jamaica. A midshipman on the Queen
of France gives an account of falling in with a
Jamaica fleet of a hundred and fifty sail one morning about the middle of July near the Banks of
Newfoundland in a dense fog. Nothing could be
seen, but the sound of signal guns and ships' bells
indicated the presence of a fleet. When the fog
lifted, about eleven o'clock, the Queen of France
found herself close by a large merchant ship from
whom it was learned that the fleet was under convoy of a seventy-four and several frigates and sloops
of war. Under the pretense of being a British frigate the Queen of France sent a boat to the English ship and quietly took possession of her, and
then took another ship in the same manner. Commodore Whipple at first feared discovery and capture by the convoy, but was induced to remain in
the fleet all day with his squadron. No alarm was
excited among the Englishmen, and eleven ships

[1] *Tucker*, ch. vi; *Penn. Gazette*, June 16, 1779; *Boston Gazette*,
July 5, 1779; *Tucker MSS.*, June 28, 1779, Nicholson to Tucker.

ABRAHAM WHIPPLE

were taken in this way by the Americans. They succeeded in getting away at nightfall without arousing any suspicion. Andrew Sherburne, a seaman on the Ranger, gives a somewhat different account of this affair. He says : " Our little squadron was in the rear of the fleet and we had reason to fear that some of their heaviest armed ships were there also. . . . No time was to be lost. Our commodore soon brought to one of their ships, manned and sent her off. Being to windward, he edged away and spoke to our Captain. We were at this time in pursuit of a large ship. The Commodore hauled his wind again and in the course of an hour we came up with the ship, which proved to be the Holderness, a three decker mounting 22 guns. She struck, after giving her several broadsides. Although she had more guns and those of heavier metal than ourselves, her crew was not sufficiently large to manage her guns and at the same time work the ship. She was loaded with cotton, coffee, sugar, rum and alspice. While we were employed in manning her, our Commodore captured another and gave her up to us to man also. When this was accomplished it was nearly night ; we were, however, unwilling to abandon the opportunity of enriching ourselves, therefore kept along under easy sail. Some time in the night we found ourselves surrounded with ships and supposed we were discovered. We could distinctly hear their bells, on which they frequently struck a few strokes, that their ships

might not approach too near each other during the
night. We were close on board one of their largest
armed ships and from the multitude of lights which
had appeared, supposed that they had called to
quarters. It being necessary to avoid their convoy,
we fell to leeward and in an hour lost sight of them
all. The next day the sky was overcast and at times
we had a thick fog. In the afternoon the sun shone
for a short time and enabled us to see a numerous
fleet a few miles to windward, in such compact
order that we thought it not best to approach them.
We were however in hopes that we might pick up
some single ship. We knew nothing of our consorts,
but were entirely alone. Towards night we took
and manned out a brig. On the third morning we
gained sight of three ships, to which we gave chase
and called all hands to quarters. When they discovered us in chase, they huddled together, intend-
ing as we supposed to fight us. They however soon
made sail and ran from us ; after a short lapse of
time we overhauled and took one of them, which
we soon found to be a dull sailer. Another, while
we were manning our prize, attempted to escape,
but we soon found that we gained upon her. While
in chase a circumstance occurred which excited
some alarm. Two large ships hove in sight to windward running directly for us under a press of sail.
One of them shaped her course for the prize we had
just manned. We were unwilling to give up our
chase, as we had ascertained from our prize that the

two other ships were . . . unarmed. We soon came up with the hindmost, brought her to and ordered her to keep under our stern, while we might pursue the other, as our situation was too critical to allow us to heave to and get out our boat. The stranger in chase of us was under English colors; we however soon ascertained by her signal that she was the Providence frigate, on board of which was our commodore. This joyful intelligence relieved us from all fear of the enemy and we soon came up with our chase. . . . We now ascertained that the strange ship, which was in chase of our first prize, was another of our consorts, the Queen of France." Three of the eleven prizes taken from the Jamaica fleet were afterwards recaptured, but the other eight, worth with their cargoes over a million dollars, were brought safely into port when the squadron returned to Boston about a month later. Whipple received the congratulations of the Marine Committee.[1]

The Massachusetts brigs Tyrannicide, Captain Hallet, and Hazard, Captain Williams, did most of the cruising on behalf of their state in 1779, and with some success. The Hazard was in the West Indies early in the year, and on March 12 sailed from Martinique in company with the Continental ship General Gates, Captain Waters. On

[1] *Clark*, i, 94; *Memoirs of Andrew Sherburne*, 21–23; *Boston Gazette*, September 27, 1779; *Log of the Ranger; Mar. Com. Letter Book*, 229, 233, 234 (August 24, September 7, 1779), 238 (to Whipple, September 19, 1779).

the 16th, off St. Thomas, the Hazard captured the privateer brigantine Active, from Antigua, after a "smart action for 35 minutes, yard arm and yard arm." [1] The Active carried eighteen four-pounders and ninety-five men; she lost thirteen killed and twenty wounded. The American loss was three killed and eight wounded. The prize arrived safely in port. The Hazard also fought with a British ship of fourteen guns and eighty men, but did not succeed in capturing her. After having taken several prizes in all, Captain Williams returned to Boston in April. The General Gates returned about the same time and soon afterwards was sold out of the Continental service.[2]

Meanwhile the Tyrannicide had sailed from Nantasket Roads, March 9, for Martha's Vineyard, but encountered a gale off Cape Cod and ran off to the southward. March 29, in latitude 28^b 30′ north, longitude 68° 25′ west, the British privateer brig Revenge of Grenada, carrying fourteen carriage guns, six- and four-pounders, four swivels and two coehorns, and sixty men, was seen "at 4 o'clock P.M. about 4 leagues to windward coming down upon us. Upon which," says Captain Hallet, "I cleared ship and got all hands to their quarters ready for action, then stood close upon the wind,

[1] *Independent Chronicle*, April 8, 1779.

[2] *Mass. Archives*, cli, 271, cliii, 133, 150, 167, 208; *Boston Gazette*, February 22, April 12, 1779; *Clark*, i, 90; *Publ. R. I. Hist. Soc.*, viii, 259; *Massachusetts Mag.*, July, 1908; *Mar. Com. Letter Book*, 208, 219 (April 19, June 7, 1779).

waiting for her till about half past six P.M., when she came up and hailing me, asked where I was from. I told them from Boston. I asked them where they were from and was answered, they were a British cruiser from Jamaica. I immediately reply'd that I was an American cruiser, upon which they ordered me to strike, but finding me not disposed to gratify their desires, they run up under my lee and saluted me with a broadside. Without loss of time I returned the compliment and dropping astern got under their lee, where our fires were so warm from below and from our tops and the shots so well directed, we dismounted two of their guns, drove the men from their quarters, and compelled them to strike to the American flag. The engagement lasted one hour and a quarter, during which we were not half pistol shot distant and some part of the time our yards were locked in with theirs." [1] " I had Eight men wounded, only two of which are Bad ; amongst the wounded are my first Lieut. & Master. I intended to man her and keep her as a Consort during the Cruise, but having twenty wounded Men on board, of my own men & prisoners, I thought it Best to send her home, with all the wounded men on board under the Care of the Sergeon's Mate." [2] The Revenge lost eight killed and fourteen wounded. She arrived safely in Boston and the Tyrannicide followed April 25, having cap-

[1] *Boston Gazette*, April 19, 1779.
[2] *Massachusetts Mag.*, April, 1908.

tured two other vessels, one of them a fourteen-gun ship.[1]

Captain Williams, on his return to Boston in the Hazard, was met with certain charges brought against him by the Board of War, the nature of which is not stated. He was exonerated, however, by a joint committee of the General Court, and a few days later that body passed a resolve renouncing all claim on the part of the state to the privateers Active and Revenge " in testimony of their approbation of the spirit and good conduct of the said " Williams and Hallet and their officers and men. The Active was purchased by order of the General Court and taken into the Massachusetts navy. She was put under the command of Captain Hallet and in June was ordered on a cruise.[2]

In May the Hazard and the Tyrannicide, now commanded by Captain John Cathcart, were ordered to cruise in company alongshore, "first in the Vineyard Sound, then round the Island of Nantucket . . . to clear the Coast of the Picaroons that infest them." [3] A party of British and tories had recently raided along the south shore of Cape Cod, and Martha's Vineyard and Nantucket; in September a proclamation was issued by British officers

[1] *Mass. Rev. Rolls*, xliv, 408; *Boston Gazette*, April 19, 26, 1779; *Boston Post*, May 1, 1779; *Clark*, i, 91.

[2] *Mass. Court Rec.*, April 20, 23, June 11, 1779; *Boston Gazette*, April 26, 1779; *Massachusetts Mag.*, October, 1909.

[3] *Mass. Archives*, cli, 467, 468.

threatening the people of Nantucket with hostilities if they did not observe strict neutrality. In the Sound the Massachusetts vessels fell in with the Continental sloop Providence and brig Diligent and early in June, in Buzzard's Bay, were joined by the Continental sloop Argo, Captain Talbot. June 15, Cathcart wrote to the Board of War that at half-past eight that morning the Tyrannicide and Hazard chased a ship and brig, which " hove too for us & hauld up their Courses, upon which I spoke Capt. Williams & we agreed to Engage them, he to take the Ship & I the Brig, upon which I pass'd the Ship & gave her two Broadsides & then run along-side the Brig & after exchanging 6 or 7 Broadsides she struck, the Ship in the mean time having struck to Captain Williams." [1] The brig was a letter of marque mounting twelve six-pounders; she got safely into New Bedford. The ship was a recapture, having been taken by two British privateers. Mean-while, in order to insure continuous protection, the General Court had, on June 11, directed the Board of War to arrange a series of cruises in rotation by the different vessels of the state navy along the eastern and southern shores of the state.[2]

The Connecticut navy lost its two most import-

[1] *Mass. Archives*, cliii, 229.

[2] *Mass. Court Rec.*, April 15, June 11, 1779; *Mass. Archives*, cliii, 219, 224, 229, 230; *Boston Post*, April 10, 1779; *Independent Chronicle*, April 15, 1779; *Boston Gazette*, October 11, 1779; *Almon*, viii, 268–271; *Clark*, i, 92.

ant vessels in 1779. In March the Defence was
wrecked on the shore of her native state. The Oliver
Cromwell, Captain Parker, sailed from New London June 3. On the morning of the 6th, Parker
saw a sail and gave chase. Half an hour later he
saw four other sail, three of them large ships. He
then hauled close and one of the ships chased the
Cromwell, the others soon joining in on signal from
the first. They showed English colors and gained
fast. "We found," says Parker's report, "that
Fighting would be Inevitable. Therefore ordered
the Ship to be Cleared and all hands to Quarters
in good Season. Att about half after Ten A.M. we
Began to play upon the Enemy with our Stern
Chases and as She Closed up with us verry fast, in
order the better to make use of our lee guns, we
Shortened Sail by halling Down the Stay Sails and
keeping before the wind. A pretty warm Action
Ensued for about the Space of one hour, in which
we had two men killed and one Mortally wounded,
Two Slightly wounded. The Consequence of our
keeping before the wind while Engaging (a Circumstance that could not be avoided) Brought the
Enemies other Ships Close up with us verry fast;
and as we found we had Considerably Disabled our
Antagonist By Shooting away his main Topmast,
we again halled our wind to the Northward, Thinking thereby to out sail him so much, before he could
Repair his Damages, as to bring on night and if we
could not avoid him, we hoped at least to have Sep-

erated him from his other Consorts." The Cromwell
drew away from her antagonist, but by half-past
two in the afternoon the English ship had repaired
damages and renewed the chase. She gained fast
and soon came up under the Cromwell's lee quarter.
Meanwhile the other ships had also gained. " We
were under the Necessity of Shortening our Sail
and keeping before the wind again, in order to Enable us to fight our lee guns. The Action began
again about 3 P.M. and Continued till a little after
4 Do. In this last action we had two men wounded ;
one had his Right arm and Collar bone broke by a
Splinter, the other a flesh wound in the thigh by a
nine pound shot. The Damages Done to the Ships
Hull were Inconsiderable. She had her main and
fore Stays Shott away, with one or two of her main
& Mizen Shrouds, her main and fore Braces, and
a nine pound shot through the head of her Mizen
mast. By which time the Delewar Frigate and
Union Privateer were closing up with us so fast,
we found no Possibility of avoiding a Contest with
Treble our force. Both officers and men appeared
to be Brave and undaunted. I had a short Consul-
tation with my Principal Officers. We hoped we had
Done our Duty, we hoped we had Done Enough to
Convince our Enemies as well as Others that we
Dare oppose them and, as we then thought, with
Spirit too, though on Disadvantageous Terms." [1]
The Oliver Cromwell then lowered her colors. She

[1] *Trumbull MSS.*, ix, 237.

was taken into the British service and her name was changed to Restoration.[1]

Lieutenant-Colonel Silas Talbot, after his capture of the Pigot in 1778,[2] was employed in protecting the Rhode Island coast from the ravages of the enemy's privateers, which did great damage alongshore. The Pigot was taken into the Continental service and seems to have sailed in company with Talbot, who commanded a sloop called the Argo, mounting twelve six-pounders. He captured six privateers, some of them of superior force to the Argo, and a number of merchantmen. One of his prizes was taken from him by three brigantines from Philadelphia. A letter from Providence, dated August 10, says : " This moment an express arrived from New London with an account of the gallant, intrepid Talbot's taking [the] infamous villain Stanton Hazard, in a Brig of 14 guns out of Newport, after a short action. Talbot was in a small sloop [the Argo] of 12 guns, and had an inferior number of men on board to the Tory privateer, which was fitted out on purpose to attack & take Talbot's sloop." [3] Hazard was a loyalist, a native of Rhode Island, who had made himself obnoxious to the people of that vicinity. September 17, Congress made Talbot a captain in the Continental navy.[4]

---

[1] *Trumbull MSS.*, ix, 93, 95, 237; *Papers New London Hist. Soc.*, IV, i, 39, 41, 42; *Boston Gazette*, September 20, 1779.

[2] See above, p. 335.   [3] *Boston Gazette*, August, 16, 1779.

[4] *Ibid.*, September 6, 20, 1779; *Boston Post*, October 2, 1779;

Oliver Pollock, the commercial agent of Congress at New Orleans, had supervision of naval affairs on the Mississippi River and was authorized to commission both vessels and officers for the Continental service and for privateers. In commissioning and fitting out vessels and in otherwise executing the orders of Congress, Pollock was encouraged and assisted by the Spanish governor of Louisiana, Bernardo de Galvez, who was very friendly to American interests. In 1778, Pollock purchased the ship Rebecca, one of several prizes taken on the Mississippi by a party of Americans under Captain James Willing, who had come down the river from Ohio. A year later this vessel, renamed the Morris, had been armed with twenty-four guns, fully manned, under the command of Captain William Pickles, and ready for sea, when she was unfortunately destroyed by a hurricane, August 18, 1779, and eleven of her crew were lost. Governor Galvez then provided an armed schooner for the use of the Americans; this vessel seems also to have been called the Morris, or Morris's tender. Pickles cruised in this schooner and " Captur'd in Septr. a Vessell of very superior force in Lake Ponchetrain, after a very severe conflict." [1] The prize was a British sloop called the West Florida. She was fitted out

Talbot, ch. iv; *Pap. Cont. Congr.*, 37, 193, 197, 201, 209 (November 4, 11, 1779, February 28, 1780); *Mar. Com. Letter Book*, 256 (January 25, 1779).

[1] *Pap. Cont. Congr.*, 50, 9 (September 18, 1782); *Sparks MSS.*, xli, 42.

by Pollock and under the command of Pickles cruised on Lake Pontchartrain during the fall and captured a British settlement. The surrender of the British posts on the Mississippi to Galvez soon followed. Later the West Florida assisted the governor in the capture of Mobile and then proceeded to Philadelphia, where she was sold out of the service.[1]

Through Commodore Collier, commanding a squadron in Chesapeake Bay in the spring of 1779, came the intelligence that "Capt. Henry, R. N., Senior Officer in Georgia, reports in letter dated April 16, 1779, from Savannah, Ga., that 2 Rebel Galleys, Called Congress and Lee, former of 1 18 Pounder and one 12 in her Prow, two 9 pdr and 2 Sixes in her Waste & manned with 100 Men; the other with 130 French & carrying one 12 and one 9 Pdr. in her Prow, 2 fours and 2 one Pounders besides swivels in her Waste, attacked H. M. S. Greenwich & Galleys Comet, Thunder & Hornet off Yamasee Bluff, & that action ended with Capture of Rebel galleys." This was a death-blow to the Georgia navy, and its revival was made impossible by British control of the waters of that state until the end of the war.[2]

[1] *Pap. Cont. Congr.*, 19, 5, 193 (July 10, 1780), 37, 251, 535, 537, 541 (January 20, June 7, November 20, December 5, 1780), 50, 1–13, 66, 77–81, 97, 120–125; *Jour. Cont. Congr.*, July 10, December 8, 1780; *Sparks MSS.*, xli, 7, 10, 16, 22, 23, 36, 41, 42; *Penn. Gazette*, June 7, 1780; *Almon*, ix, 359–365; *Stopford-Sackville MSS.*, 122; *Paullin*, 307–311.

[2] *Brit. Adm. Rec.*, *Captains' Letters*, No. 1612, 2 (May 22, 1779); *Almon*, viii, 298; *Paullin*, 461.

Admiral Gambier sailed for England April 5, and the day before his departure, Collier "received a commission as Commodore and Commander-in-Chief of the King's fleet in America." Of the condition of this fleet he complained, saying that "the weak enfeebled state of the ships, both in point of numbers and of men, give me the most painful sensations. I ardently wish to prove myself deserving of the great trust I am honoured with, by the most spirited exertions." These exertions were first directed towards Virginia, "the province which of all others gives sinews to the rebellion from its extensive traffick."[1] The British fleet, which sailed May 5 from New York for Chesapeake Bay under Collier's command, consisted of the sixty-four-gun ship Raisonable, the Rainbow of forty-four guns, "the Otter, Diligent and Haerlem, sloops, and Cornwallis galley, together with several private ships of war and twenty-two transports having on board" about two thousand troops under General Mathew. The Diligent must have been captured before the squadron arrived in Chesapeake Bay.[2] "At sunrise" on the 10th, says Collier, "we saw some rebel ships and vessels in Hampton Road with their sails loose, who, as soon as the tide admitted of it, got under weigh and ran up Elizabeth and James rivers; our fleet also weighed and the Raisonable anchored shortly after

[1] *Stopford-Sackville MSS.*, 125, 126 (Collier to Germain.)
[2] See above, pp. 377, 378.

in Hampton Road, her great draught of water not admitting of her going further with conveniency. I immediately shifted my broad pendant to the Rainbow and proceeded with the fleet up Elizabeth river, till a contrary wind and the ebb tide obliged us to anchor. The next morning being calm prevented the ships from moving with the flood, on account of the narrowness and intricacy of the channel." The troops advanced, however, nearly to Portsmouth, supported by a galley and two gunboats; and a breeze springing up, the ships soon followed. The American fort on the river was evacuated. Much property was destroyed and many vessels were seized by the British, others being saved from the same fate by destruction at the hands of the Americans. The Otter and a number of other small vessels were sent up the Chesapeake. " The movements of this little squadron were so judicious that the enemy were much harrassed and distressed ; they destroyed many vessels and captured others." [1] In a later report Collier says : " The fort was raz'd, the season'd timber for ship building burnt, the buildings and storehouses of the finest yard on this continent underwent the same fate ; the sufferings of individuals I endeavoured to prevent all in my power and in general happily succeeded, and by it I hope have procured many friends to the royal cause." [2]

[1] *Almon*, viii, 290, 291, 293 (Collier to Clinton, May 16, and to Stephens, May 17, 1779).
[2] *Stopford-Sackville MSS.*, 129.

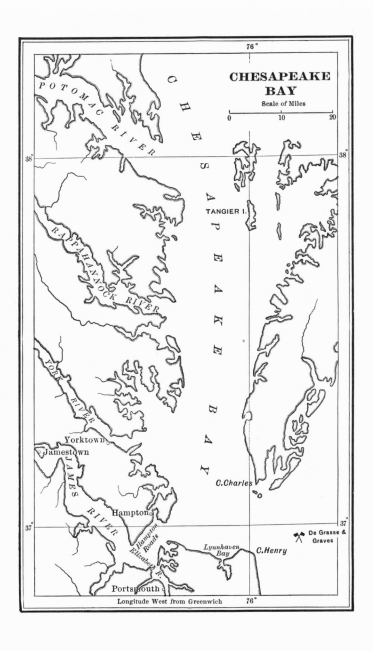

CHESAPEAKE
BAY

Scale of Miles

0   10   20

POTOMAC RIVER

C H E S A P E A K E   B A Y

TANGIER I.

RAPPAHANNOCK RIVER

YORK RIVER

Yorktown

Jamestown

JAMES RIVER

Hampton

Hampton Roads

Elizabeth R.

Portsmouth

Lynnhaven Bay

C. Charles

C. Henry

De Grasse & Graves

Longitude West from Greenwich   76°

Collier wished to remain longer and to keep possession of this valuable naval station, but General Mathew insisted that their orders required their return to New York. The two large men-of-war and the transports thereupon sailed out of the bay, leaving the others to continue their depredations. A hundred and thirty American vessels were destroyed or taken as well as a vast amount of property on shore.[1]

Richard Henry Lee, writing June 26 to William Whipple of the Marine Committee, says of the operations of these smaller vessels, left in the bay: " They have already burnt several private houses and one public warehouse with between 2 & 300 hhds of Tobo. and carried off much plunder & many negroes. Soon as they see the Militia gathering they embark and go to another unguarded place. They have 6 Vessels: Otter, 16, Harlem, 12 Guns, King's Vessels; Dunmore, 16, Schooner Hammond, 14, Lord North, 12 Guns, & Fin Castle, 2 three pounders. The 4 last are [Goodrich's] Pirates. They say the orders are to burn and destroy all before them; an Eastern Man whom they had captured . . . escaped from them when they were burning the Warehouse and gave us the above account of their force, which is confirmed by others. They land between 60 & 70 men when they mean to do mischief." [2] Lee requests the Marine Com-

---

[1] *Almon*, viii, 289–295; *Penn. Gazette*, June 9, 1779; Town's *Detail of Particular Services in America*, 76–87.

[2] *Penn. Mag. Hist. and Biogr.*, January, 1899.

mittee to send two frigates into the bay, a force sufficient, he says, to destroy the enemy's fleet. The Marine Committee had already issued orders for the purpose. As early as the previous November and again in January they had expressed a desire to capture or destroy " the infamous Goodrich," and June 25, Captain Nicholson of the Deane was " directed to proceed in company with the Frigate Boston from the Capes of Delaware into Chesapeake Bay and on your arrival there, at Hampton or any Other way, endeavour to Obtain the best intelligence if any of the enemies Ships of war or Privateers are in the Bay, and if you find there are and of such force as you are able to encounter, you are to proceed up and attack them, . . . taking or destroying as many of the said Vessels as may be in your power." [1] The Confederacy was ordered up to Chester to prepare for other service, but on July 2 was directed to cruise ten days longer with the Deane and Boston. Accounts of this service in Chesapeake Bay are lacking, but that it was performed may be inferred from Lee's letter of August 8 to Whipple, saying: " We are much obliged to the Marine Committee for their attention. I see the frigates have taken and sent in two prizes, vessels of war." [2]

[1] *Mar. Com. Letter Book*, 223.

[2] *Penn. Mag. Hist. and Biogr.*, January, 1899; *Mar. Com. Letter Book*, 187, 193 (to Navy Board, Boston, November 16, 1778, January 9, 1779), 223, 224, 225 (to Nicholson and to Harding, June 25, July 2, 1779); *Penn. Gazette*, August 4, 1779.

Upon the return to New York, May 29, of the British fleet from Chesapeake Bay, says Collier, " I found Sir Henry Clinton on the point of setting off on an expedition up the North River and I immediately determin'd on assisting in it, carrying with me the Raisonable, Camilla, Vulture, three row galleys and two gunboats with the transports and troops." This excursion up the Hudson resulted in the capture of Stony Point and other successes, which induced Collier to observe: " I hope I may now say with some confidence that rebellion is thrown on its back and that this campaign will be the last of this unnatural civil war." [1] Stony Point, however, was very soon recaptured by the Americans. About this time also the British sloop Haerlem was captured by an American privateer. The attention of the British was next directed towards Connecticut, where their trade in Long Island Sound was harassed by small privateers and armed boats. " The land forces," says Collier's report of his expedition against them, " consisting of 2600 men commanded by Major-general Tryon, I caused to be embarked in transports, and sending the Renown, Thames, Otter and two armed vessels to block up New-London and the East entrance of the Sound, I proceeded on the 3d [of July] from New York by the way of Hell Gates with his Majesty's ships Camilla, Scorpion, Halifax brig and Hussar

[1] *Stopford-Sackville MSS.*, 129 (Collier to Germain, June 15, 1779).

galley, together with the transports, and on the 5th landed the army in two divisions at the town of Newhaven, which after an irregular resistance from the rebels, was taken possession of by us together with a small fort at the entrance of the harbour, which latter we destroyed, after spiking up the guns, as also many warehouses filled with stores &c. together with several vessels and whale boats. The number of killed, wounded and missing on our side amounted to fifty-six; that of the rebels we are unacquainted with, but suppose the numbers considerable. We embarked the troops without loss and two days afterwards our flat boats, covered by the galley and gun boats, landed near Fairfield, though opposed by the militia and some continental troops; the rebels firing from the windows and tops of houses occasioned the band of loyal refugees to set several of them on fire, which communicating to others, burnt the whole town and also several whale boats. The troops embarked from thence without molestation and the third day following they were landed again in three divisions at the town of Norwalk, which, for the treacherous conduct of the rebels in murdering the troops from windows of houses after safeguards were granted them, was destroyed, together with five large vessels, two privateer brigs on the stocks and twenty whale boats." The small town of Greenfield was treated in the same manner.[1]

[1] *Almon*, viii, 295, 296, 299, 355, 356; *Town*, 90–98; *Clark*, i, 110.

The instructions of the Marine Committee, of June 25, required Nicholson, after disposing of the enemy in Chesapeake Bay, to sail at once with the Deane and Boston "on a Cruize in which you are to Choose such Station as you think will be best to Accomplish the double purpose of intercepting the enemies outward bound Transports for New York from Great Britain and Ireland and the homeward bound West India Ships. We are of Opinion that between the Latitudes of 36 and 41, and 100 Leagues to the Eastward of the Island of Bermuda will be your best Cruizing ground, but in this we do not mean to restrict you, leaving you to exercise your own Judgment, which probably may be assisted by information Obtained in your Cruise." This was to continue until the middle of September, or longer if their provisions lasted, and then they were to return to Boston "We have ordered the Continental frigates at the Eastward to Cruise for the same purposes you are now going on and we think it very probable that you will fall in with them. In that case you or they or any of them are hereby directed to Cruise in Company under the command of the Senior officer, and should you be joined by any of those frigates and find by any intelligence you may Receive of the situation of the enemys Sea force at Bermuda that it will be adviseable to make an attempt on their Shipping, we recommend your undertaking it. . . . We now wish to draw your attention to the execution of the

business before you. The great Expence and difi-
culty that attends the fitting and manning of our
Ships must make you and every Commander in Our
service fully sensible how much they Should exert
themselves to employ them usefully while at Sea.
This consideration we hope will have due weight in
your mind and will call forth such active and prudent behavior as will be of Essential Service to
your Country and add to your own reputation and
the honor of our Flag."[1]

The Deane and Boston sailed out of Chesapeake
Bay, July 29, in company with two ships of the
Virginia navy and a convoy of merchantmen, from
whom they soon parted. A successful cruise of
about five weeks was made by the two frigates,
during which they captured eight prizes, including
four New York privateers; but the most important
were the ships Sandwich and Thorn, each of sixteen guns. The former was a packet carrying as
passengers a number of army officers; the Thorn
was a sloop of war. The frigates arrived at Boston,
September 6, with two hundred and fifty prisoners,
including a lieutenant-colonel, a major, and three
naval captains. Nicholson received the congratulations of the Marine Committee.[2]

On September 21 and 22, the Marine Commit-

---

[1] *Mar. Com. Letter Book*, 223.

[2] *Boston Post*, September 11, 1779; *Boston Gazette*, September
13, 1779; *Penn. Gazette*, September 22, 1779; *Tucker*, 119–121;
Mar. Com. Letter Book, 237, 238 (to Navy Board, Boston, and to
Nicholson, September, 18, 19, 1779).

tee instructed the Navy Board at Boston to fit out the Deane, Boston, and Queen of France as quickly as possible for important service at Charleston, South Carolina. Shortly afterwards Admiral Arbuthnot at New York received information from Boston which led him to believe that these vessels were fitting out for an attack on the British post in Penobscot Bay.[1] November 10, orders were sent for the frigates to sail at once. The Deane, perhaps because she could not be made ready in time, was subsequently detached from this duty, and the squadron, as finally made up under the orders of the Eastern Navy Board, November 20, consisted of the frigates Providence, Boston and Queen of France, and the Ranger, with Commodore Whipple in command. They set sail from Nantasket Roads, November 23, and cruised to the eastward of Bermuda. An officer on board the Providence wrote home that three days out from Boston they "met with a severe gale of wind, which lasted about 30 hours, in which time we sprang our mizen-mast; the Ranger shared the same fate and the Boston sprang the head of her mainmast. On the 5th [of December] we took a privateer brig of 12 guns called the Dolphin."[2] The destination of the squadron was not made known until they had passed Bermuda. They finally arrived at Charleston December 23.[3]

[1] *Stopford-Sackville MSS.*, 147 (Arbuthnot to Germain, October 10, 1779).

[2] *Independent Chronicle*, February 24, 1780.

[3] *Mar. Com. Letter Book*, 239, 245 (to Navy Board, Boston, Sep-

On August 24 the frigate Confederacy was ordered on a short Cruise off the Delaware capes, keeping a lookout for the privateer Eagle of Philadelphia, expected from St. Eustatius. September 3 the Confederacy was again ordered up to Chester, and on the 17th received instructions for a voyage to France, taking as passenger the French minister, Gérard. The Eagle was a ten-gun brigantine sailing under a Continental commission in the West Indies. Whether or not she returned to Philadelphia at this time is perhaps uncertain, but she was in the West Indies in November and on attempting to get into St. Eustatius was headed off and chased by six British privateers. She took refuge under a fort on the Dutch island of Saba, but was cut out and captured by the privateers, taken to Nevis and condemned by a British admiralty court, in violation of the neutrality of Saba.[1]

In the orders of September 17, sending the Confederacy to France, Captain Harding was instructed to make the best of his "way to any Port which the Minister may think proper to direct and on your passage you are carefully to avoid coming to action with any vessel of equal or superior force. Your

tember 21, 22, November 10, 1779); *Tucker MSS.*, November 20, 1779; *Log of Ranger; Penn. Mag. Hist. and Biogr.*, April 1891, journal of Lieutenant Jennison; *Tucker*, ch. vii.

[1] *Mar. Com. Letter Book*, 230, 231, 235 (to Harding, August 24, September 3, 17, 1779); *Pap. Cont. Congr.*, 44, 325–397 (June 12, November 13, 16, 25, 30, December 14, 1779, January 18, 20, March 21, 23, 1780); *Massachusetts Spy*, February 10, 1780.

Ship being entirely designed for the Accomodation of the Minister, you are in all things, as far as may be, to comply with his wishes and to treat him with the respect due to his character." On his arrival in France he was to report to "his Excellency Benjamin Franklin, Esqr., Minister Plenipotentiary of the United States at the Court of Versailles." After refitting his ship, he was to take on board "such Stores for the use of these States as may be offered by the Agents in France, so as not to incommode your vessel as a Ship of war, and when you have received the Orders of our Minister, you are immediately to make the best of your way back to this port or into Chesapeake Bay. . . . If you can procure A Set of good 18 Pounders when in France and you are of Opinion that the Confederacy can bear them, you are at liberty to mount them and put those you have now on Deck into your hold. We desire you will be careful of the Confederacy, her Materials and Stores and that you will not delay any time unnecessarily in France, but be diligent for dispatch." Under the same date the committee wrote to Franklin of the expected visit of the Confederacy to France.[1] October 17, the Confederacy still lying at Chester, Harding received orders to take on board another distinguished passenger, John Jay, with his family. Jay had been appointed minister to Spain.[2]

The Confederacy sailed soon after this and cleared

---

[1] *Mar. Com. Letter Book*, 235, 236.   [2] *Ibid.*, 242.

the Delaware capes October 26. In relating the story of this eventful voyage, Harding says that on November 7 at five o'clock in the morning, in latitude 41° 3′ longitude 50° 39′, " the ship unfortunately lost her Bow Sprit, Fore Mast, Main Mast and Mizen Mast," in a gale. Six hours were passed in cutting away the wreck of spars, sails, and rigging, " after which all hands were imployed in clearing the Ship and preparing to get up Jury Masts, which would have been done with the Assistance of my Officers, who behaved themselves exceedingly well on the Occasion, in a Very short time, but the next day about 7 Oclock A.M. in addition to our misfortune found the Rudder to be gone, at least the head of it Wrung in such a manner that rendered it entirely useless, in which situation we lay Tossing and Drifting with the Wind and Current, making use of every Opportunity to secure the Rudder and Refit the Ship in order to proceed on her intended Passage till the 23d November." During this time the ship had drifted eastward to longitude 48° 28′. " I, with the advice of Mr. Jay and Mr. Gérard, Call'd a Council of my Officers Relative to the Ship's proceeding on her intended passage, who unanimously agreed that it would be very imprudent to approach the Coast of Europe in the situation she was then in; that it would be impossible for the Rudder to survive a hard Gale of wind without increasing the Leake very much, which was Occationed by the Rudder's Striking against her

Stern Post; that if we should be Necessitated to part with it, should undoubtedly be thrown into Various Difficultys, in Consequence of which the Ship might Founder; that if we should be attacked by a Gale of Wind inshore, we must inevetably be Cast on Shore, and perhaps the greater part of us if not the whole fall a sacrifice to our own folly; and that if we should loose any of Sparrs or Rigging we had none to Replace them; that in the situation the ship was then in, thought it most prudent to proceed to the West Indias. After which I Consulted Mr. Jay & Mr. Gerard the latter declining to give any Opinion on the Subject, the former gave his Opinion that the sentiments of the Officers Corresponded with his and that their advice ought in his opinion to be followed." [1] Thereupon the ship was brought to Martinique, arriving at St. Pierre December 18. The two ministers continued their passage to France in a French frigate [2]

In the fall of 1779 a change was made in the administration of Continental naval affairs by placing them in charge of a smaller executive board. [3] John Brown, secretary of this new body, in a letter to the Navy Board at Boston says: " Congress having dissolved their Marine Committee did by A Resolve bearing date the 28th of October . . . Consti-

---

[1] *Pap. Cont. Congr.*, **78**, 11, 487 (Harding to President of Congress, December 30, 1779).

[2] *Boston Post*, February 19, 1780; *Boston Gazette*, February 21, 1780; *Papers New London Hist. Soc.*, IV, i, 61.

[3] See above, p. 35.

tute a Board of Admiralty and Appointed three Commissioners not members of Congress, together with two Members of Congress and A Secretary, to whose management All Affairs Relative to the Continental Navy are committed, subject nevertheless to the controul of Congress." Instructions and suggestions concerning various matters are given in the letter. "As to the Continental Armed Vessels still remaining at Boston, you are hereby authorized and directed to send them out on a cruize in such Latitudes as you may think will be most likely to annoy the enemy by Captures."[1]

Captain Manley, after his release from imprisonment and acquittal by court martial for the loss of the frigate Hancock,[2] took command of a Boston privateer, the twenty-gun ship Cumberland. In December, 1778, he sailed for the West Indies, but after a short cruise was captured by a British frigate and taken into Barbadoes. With other prisoners he soon escaped, seized a sloop, got to Martinique and thence to Boston in April, 1779. In June he took command of the ship Jason, recently captured by a Continental squadron[3] and fitted out as a privateer with eighteen six-pounders and a hundred and twenty men. The Jason sailed June 19 and off the Isles of Shoals was chased and nearly captured by a British frigate and brig. She was saved by a violent thunder squall, which, al-

[1] *Mar. Com. Letter Book*, 249 (December 10, 1779).
[2] See above, p. 313.　　　[3] See above, p. 373.

though it dismasted her, drove the British vessels out to sea. A seaman on the Jason wrote in his journal: " When the squall struck us it hove us all aback, when we clued down. In ten seconds the wind shifted on our starboard beam and shivered our sails. In a few seconds more the wind shifted on the starboard quarter and struck us with such force that hove us on our beam ends and carried away our three masts and bowsprit. She immediately righted and the squall went over."[1] The crew then insisted upon going into port to repair damages, but Manley, having quelled the mutinous, succeeded in having masts stepped and the ship completely re-rigged at sea in thirty-six hours; the new masts he procured at Portsmouth. He then continued his cruise. Off Sandy Hook, July 23, he fell in with two British privateer brigs of sixteen and eighteen guns. " The enemy hove upon the wind with his larboard tacks on board, run up his courses, hoisted his colours and gave us a broadside. Our Captain ordered the sailing master to get the best bower anchor out, so that the bill of it should take into the fore shrouds of the enemy. It was quickly done. The Captain ordered the helm hard a-port, which brought us along side. The anchor caught their fore rigging. Our Captain then said: 'fire away, my boys.' We then gave them a broadside which tore her off side very much and killed and wounded some of them. The rest all ran below,

[1] *Narrative of Joshua Davis*, 4.

except their captain who stood on the deck like a man amazed." The brig was then boarded and quickly captured. "When we got disentangled we bore away for the other privateer, that began to run from us. We gave her a few shot from our bow chasers and she hove too."[1] The second brig then also surrendered. The British lost thirty killed and wounded; the Jason three wounded, one of them mortally. The prizes were brought safely into Boston Harbor. Fearing that his men would desert if he went up to the town, Manley procured stores at Hull and then continued his cruise. After escaping a British frigate off Nantucket Shoals with a large fleet of merchantmen under convoy, which he ran into in a fog, Manley cruised to the eastward. Off Newfoundland he captured an English brig. Here the Jason was chased by the British frigate Surprise, of twenty-eight guns and two hundred and thirty men. The frigate overhauled the Jason about eleven o'clock in the evening of September 30 and fired a broadside. "Our captain would not let us fire until they got abreast of us. They gave us another broadside, which cut away some of our running rigging and drove some of our men from the tops. We gave them a broadside which silenced two of her bow guns. The next we gave her cut away her maintopsail and drove her maintop-men out of it. Both sides continued the fire until one o'clock. Our studding sails and booms, our sails, rigging, yards,

[1] *Narrative of Joshua Davis*, 6, 7.

&c. were so cut away that they were useless. Lanterns were hung at the ship's side, between the guns, on nails, but they soon fell on deck at the shaking of the guns; which made it so dark that the men could not see to load the guns. They broke the fore hatches open and ran below. Our captain sent the sailing master forward to see why the bow guns did not keep the fire up, but he never returned. The captain then sent the master's mate on the same errand and he never returned. It was therefore thought needless to stand it any longer and the captain took the trumpet and called out for quarters."[1] The Surprise lost fifteen killed and thirty wounded, the Jason five killed and a few wounded. Manley was taken to St. John's, Newfoundland, and afterwards sent to Mill Prison, England, where he remained more than two years.[2]

The private armed ship Hampden, of twenty-two guns, Captain Thomas Pickering, of Portsmouth, New Hampshire, in the early spring of 1779 was returning from a cruise in European waters, having sent four prizes into France, when on March 7, at ten o'clock in the morning, in latitude 47° 15' north, longitude 28° 31' west, a sail was sighted. The Hampden gave chase. At five in the afternoon both vessels showed their colors. The stranger was a large ship carrying twenty-six nine-pounders and

[1] *Davis*, 11, 12.

[2] *Independent Chronicle*, March 4, 1779; *Boston Gazette*, March 8, November 29, 1779; *Boston Post*, July 31, 1779; *Essex Inst. Coll.*, January, 1909.

eight fours; at dusk she was lost sight of, but at daylight was seen again. "At 7 A.M. came under her lee quarter within hail, hoisted continental colours and gave her a broadside. She kept all her guns hous'd till just before we fired, altho' we could tell her ports thirteen of a side, a very great distance apart; she return'd the broadside without any damage, with twenty-four nine pounders and eight four pounders and had the advantage of a spar deck to cover her men. Being a beautiful large ship with two tier of cabin windows we knew her to be an East Indiaman and of much superior force, but supposing they were badly mann'd, were determined to fight her as long as we could. The engagement continued till half past Ten, close alongside, when finding our three masts and bowsprit very badly wounded, our starboard main shrouds totally gone, our rigging and sails cut to pieces, our double headed shott expended, and near twenty of our men killed and wounded, were obliged to our grief to leave her a mere wreck, her masts, yards, sails and rigging cut to pieces. Having ourselves only the foresail which we could set to get off with, the sheets being cut away, were obliged to use our tacks. During the action our brave and worthy commander, Capt. Pickering, was killed." One other man was killed and seventeen wounded, two of them mortally. The Hampden arrived at Portsmouth April 20.[1]

[1] *Continental Journal,* April 22, 1779; *Independent Chronicle,* April 22, 1779.

The ship General Mifflin, Captain McNeill, after cruising more than a year in European waters, returned in February to Boston, having taken thirteen prizes. She was also successful in home waters during the year and fought an engagement with a sloop of war.[1] The sixteen-gun ship General Pickering, Captain Haraden, of Salem, cruised successfully all the year, many of her prizes being armed vessels ; among them a fourteen-gun brig named the Hope. In a letter to Timothy Pickering, dated Cape Henlopen, October 1, 1779, Haraden says : " I left the Capes at Sundown on Tuesday last and at Sunrising on Wednesday Morning I discovered Two sail to the windward. The Winds being light I hove out two Draggs to keep my Ship from going ahead and made all the Sail I could, as though I was running from them. They both gave Chace and at 5 P.M. they got nigh enough to discover that I was a Cruising Vessel. They both hove about and haul'd their Wind, I immediately hove about after them, they crowded all the Sail they could and Rowed at the same time. At sundown the Wind breezed up a little and as Night came on, I kept Sight of them with my Night Glass; at 8 P.M. they parted, one stood to the Northward & the other to the Southward. I kept in chace of the largest and at 9 P.M. She Hove about, being to the Windward ; as she past me I hail'd her, but had no answer. Then I

<hr/>

[1] *Boston Gazette*, February 15, October 25, 1779; *Boston Post*, February 20, 1779.

gave her a Broadside, but without any effect that I could perceive; then I Tackt Ship and gave her another Broadside and hail'd her. She answered from N. York. I Order'd her to haul down the Colours, which they Obey'd instantly; very peaceable people, like the Hope, though they Had 14 6 & 4 pounders and 38 Men. She proves to be the Royal George Cutter, a Letter of Marque out of New York last Tuesday Morning bound to the West Indies and was in Company with a Sloop of 8 Carriage Guns from the same place, she being Clean & a Fast Sailor got off clear, while I was in Chase of the Cutter." [1] In October, off Sandy Hook, the Pickering engaged three letters of marque at once — a fourteen-gun ship, a ten-gun brig, and an eight-gun sloop. After an action of an hour and a half she captured all three and took them into port. [2]

The sloop Eagle of New London with other privateers captured three vessels early in the year and in May she took several more. Having manned these prizes, the prisoners on board the Eagle outnumbered her crew and took possession of her. They then murdered all the crew, except two boys, and took her into Newport. [3]

The British sloop of war Thorn, brought into

---

[1] *Pickering MSS.*, xxxix, 179.

[2] *Penn. Gazette*, September 29, 1779; *Maryland Journal*, December 7, 1779; *Boston Post*, December 18, 1779; *Boston Gazette*, December 20, 1779.

[3] *Boston Gazette*, May 17, 31, 1779; *Boston Post*, May 22, 1779; *Papers New London Hist. Soc.*, IV, i, 10.

JONATHAN HARADEN

Boston as a prize by the frigates Deane and Boston in September,[1] was fitted out as a privateer; she was ship rigged and carried eighteen six-pounders. Captain Daniel Waters of the Continental navy, who had served in Washington's fleet in 1776, was put in command of the Thorn; there were too few regular ships to give employment to all the Continental officers and it was common for them to sail in privateers. The Thorn sailed on a cruise in December. The journal of the first lieutenant relates that on the 24th at four o'clock in the afternoon, the wind being light, two armed brigantines were seen about four miles to windward. The Thorn stood off " in order to draw them within shot. At 7 P.M. almost calm, our ship in order, men at their quarters and in high spirits for engaging. Calm all night. The next morning, December 25, at 6 A.M. the two brigs were on our larboard beam about two miles distant, light breezes from the west; they, to appearance, were making preparations for engaging. At 9 A.M. the wind sprung up from the S. W.; made sail for them in as good order as circumstances would admit. At 10 A.M. came up with the sternmost, as she was the heaviest, and he hailed: From White Hall, and ask'd Capt. Waters what right he had to wear the 13 stars in his pendant. Capt. Waters answered: I 'll let you know presently; then shifted our ensign and gave her a broadside within pistol shot, which

[1] See above, p. 402.

she returned, as did the other brig on our weather bow. A warm engagement commenced on both sides for about two glasses, when the largest brig laid us on board on our weather quarter, whilst the other amused us on our weather bow, who kept up a regular fire; but she upon our quarter was soon convinced of her error, receiving such a warm and well directed fire from our marines and seeing his men running about deck with pikes in their backs instead of their hands, were undoubtedly glad to get off again. But soon shot alongside again and renew'd his cannonade with surprising spirit, but after two or three broadsides, was obliged to haul down what remained of his colours. There must have been great slaughter, as the blood was seen to run out of the scuppers. The other brig seeing her consort had struck, made what sail she could to make her escape, but they found us as ready to follow as she was to run, after Capt. Waters had ordered the captured brig to follow. This engagement lasted about four glasses. Capt. Waters received a wound in his right knee about one glass before the first struck. At 3 P.M. came up with the other, after firing several chace shot thro' her quarter, when with reluctance they hauled down their colours. Capt. Waters ordered me on board to send the officers on board the Thorn & immediately make sail for the other brig, which was making from us. Fresh breezes and cloudy weather. At 8 P.M. the Thorn hove to, losing sight of the chace." [1] The next morning she was nowhere to be seen, but many oars, spars, and other wreckage were discovered floating and it was supposed that she had sunk. Subsequently it was learned that under cover of the night she had managed to escape. These two brigs were privateers from New York; one, the Governor Tryon, which escaped, carried sixteen guns — twelves, sixes, and fours — and eighty-six men; the other, the Sir William Erskine, carried eighteen six- and four-pounders, and eighty-five men. The Thorn lost eighteen killed and wounded, the Erskine twenty. Upon learning of this exploit, John Adams, then in Paris, sent to the French "minister a Boston Gazette of 21st February, in which is a relation of a glorious combat and cruise of my countryman Captain Waters, of the Thorn. . . . There has not been a more memorable action this war, and the feats of our American frigates and privateers have not been sufficiently published in Europe. It would answer valuable purposes, both by encouraging their honest and brave hearts and by exciting emulations elsewhere, to give them a little more than they have had of the fame they have deserved. Some of the most skillful, determined, persevering and successful engagements that have ever happened upon the seas have been performed by American privateers against the privateers from New York, . . . and have seldom been properly described

[1] *Boston Gazette*, February 21, 1780.

and published even there." [1] January 13, 1780, the
Thorn fell in with the British ship Sparlin of
eighteen guns, bound from Liverpool to New York,
and captured her after an action of forty minutes.
The American loss was one killed and two wounded,
the British lost three killed and ten wounded. The
Thorn brought the Erskine and Sparlin safely into
Boston, arriving in Nantasket Roads February 17,
1780. [2]

[1] *Wharton*, iii, 650, Adams to Genet, May 3, 1780.

[2] *Boston Post*, February 19, 1780 ; *Boston Gazette*, February 21,
1780. For further information about privateers and their prizes
in 1779, see *Boston Gazette*, January 18, February 15, March 8,
22, April 26, June 14, August 2, September 27, October 4, 18, November 29, December 13, 20, 1779 ; *Boston Post*, February 6,
April 10, May 1, 22, July 3, 10, October 2, 1779 ; *Independent
Ledger*, May 10, October 11, 1779 ; *Penn. Gazette*, May 12, September 29, October 6, 1779 ; *Penn. Packet*, May 20, August 10,
October 14, December 25, 1779 ; *Maryland Journal*, January 12,
1779 ; *New York Packet*, October 21, 1779 ; *Papers New London
Hist. Soc.*, IV, i, 9–16 ; *Proc. U. S. Nav. Inst.*, June, 1911 ; Maclay's *Moses Brown*, chs. vi, vii, viii ; *Barney*, 77–80 ; *Clark*, i, ch.
vii ; *Williams*, 245 ; *Pickering MSS.*, xvii, 267. For cruise of a
New York privateer, see *Amer. Hist. Rev.*, January, 1902.

CHAPTER XII

FOR the third time within a century a military expedition of importance and magnitude, considering the resources of the community, was fitted out at Boston for service against a foreign enemy. In 1690 the forces of the colony under Phips attempted the conquest of Quebec; in 1745, led by Pepperell, they captured Louisburg;[1] and now in 1779 the citizens of Massachusetts assumed, practically alone, the burden of a new enterprise, an effort to repel an invasion of their territory. About the middle of June eight hundred or more British troops from Halifax, convoyed by three sloops of war under the command of Captain Mowatt, entered Penobscot Bay and took possession of the peninsula of Majabagaduce or Bagaduce, now called Castine. The object of this move was the establishment of a new province, furnishing a home for many of the numerous loyalists under British protection in Nova Scotia and elsewhere and at the same time serving as a bulwark for British possessions farther east and as an advanced military post convenient for operating against New England.[2]

[1] Expeditions against Acadia under Colonels Church and March in 1704 and 1707 might also be mentioned.

[2] *Hist. Man. Com., Amer. MSS. in Royal Inst.*, i, 284 (Germain

When the news of the British occupation reached Boston the General Court was in session, and it was soon determined to drive out the enemy if possible, before he had had time to strengthen his position. Preparations were made with energy and a military and naval force was soon organized, although the full number of militia called for could not be obtained. Application was made to the Continental Congress for the services of three national vessels at that time in Boston Harbor and they accompanied the expedition. New Hampshire contributed one vessel. All the rest of the force was made up and the expense borne by Massachusetts.[1]

The fleet organized for this enterprise consisted of nineteen armed vessels and twenty or more transports. The Continental vessels were the frigate Warren, 32, Commodore Saltonstall, the brig Diligent, 14, Captain Brown, and the sloop Providence,

to Clinton, September 2, 1778), 381 (Clinton to General McLean, February 11, 1779), 393, 415, 436, 440 (correspondence relating to proposed seizure of Penobscot), 452–462 (letters of McLean, Mowatt, etc., from Penobscot, June, 1779).

[1] The principal original authorities for the Penobscot Expedition are : Mass. Archives and Rev. Rolls ; General Lovell's Journal, published by Weymouth Hist. Soc., 1881 ; Journal of the Privateer Ship Hunter, printed in Hist. Mag., February, 1864 ; various papers in Wheeler's History of Castine; letters published by the State of Massachusetts in Proceedings of the General Assembly relating to the Penobscot Expedition, 1780; contemporary newspapers, e.g., Boston Gazette, August 9, September 27, December 27, 1779, March 18, 25, April 1, 8, 15, 1782 ; Boston Post, July 10, 1779 ; Continental Journal, January 6, 1780 ; London Chronicle, September 25, 28, 1779 ; Brit. Adm. Records, Captains' Letters and Captains' Logs; Almon, viii, 352–359. See also Town, 102–115.

12, Captain Hacker. The state navy furnished the
brigs Hazard, Active and Tyrannicide of fourteen
guns each, commanded by Captains Williams, Hallet,
and Cathcart. The Diligent and the Active had recently been taken from the British. In addition to
these six vessels, twelve privateers were taken into
the service of the state, the owners being guaran-
teed against loss. Four of these privateers carried
twenty guns each and four others eighteen guns,
while of the remaining four there was one sixteen,
two fourteens, and one eight. Eight of the privateers were ship-rigged. One vessel was furnished
by New Hampshire, the twenty-gun ship Hampden,
a privateer temporarily taken into the service of
that state. The fleet carried over two hundred guns,
a large proportion of them probably light ones, and
more than two thousand men ; Saltonstall was in
command. The military force on board the transports it had been intended to recruit to the number
of fifteen hundred men, but owing to hurried preparations, less than a thousand apparently embarked
on the fleet ; and they, according to the testimony
of the officers, were a very inferior set of men, even
for militia. These troops were under the orders of
General Solomon Lovell, with General Peleg Wadsworth second in command and Lieutenant-Colonel
Paul Revere in charge of the artillery.[1]

On June 25, the General Court made provision
for " Nine tons of Flour or Bread, Nine Tons of

[1] *Court Records*, June 24, 1779.

Rice, Eighteen Tons of Salt Beef, six hundred Gallons of Rum, six hundred Gallons of Molasses, Five hundred stand of Fire Arms." [1] July 13, Commodore Saltonstall was instructed by the Board of War " to take every measure & use your utmost Endeavours to Captivate, Kill or destroy the Enemies whole Force both by Sea & Land, & the more effectually to answer that purpose, you are to Consult measures & preserve the greatest harmony with the Commander of the Land Forces, that the navy & army may Coöperate & assist each other." [2] It would have been well if this injunction had been strictly heeded. Lack of coöperation between army and navy, a cause that has brought disaster upon many a joint expedition, was to have its baleful effect on this. Another source of weakness was Saltonstall's incompetency. It was also unfortunate that the necessity for prompt action, with a view to forestalling reinforcements of the enemy, made it impracticable to enlist the number of men that had been considered essential for the success of the enterprise. Moreover, for the important and difficult work in prospect, that of assaulting fortifications, a fair proportion at least of regular troops should have been incorporated with the force. The fleet sailed from Boston July 19. They proceeded first to Townsend (Boothbay Harbor), the appointed rendezvous, where it had been expected that the full complement of men would be made up, but the

[1] *Court Records.*   [2] *Mass. Archives,* cxlv, 39.

general was disappointed. Unwilling to delay, he set sail again on the 24th.[1]

Information of the departure of this expedition reached English ears no earlier perhaps than might have been expected. Commodore Collier wrote from New York July 28: " I received this morning certain intelligence that an armament sailed from Boston on the 21st instant to attack his Majesty's new settlement in Penobscot River. . . . I intend putting to sea at daylight tomorrow," [2] in pursuit. While the sloop Providence was fitting out at Boston, Lieutenant Trevett, who had long served on board that vessel, decided to remain at home and attend to his private business, saying that he had " no particular inclination to go to Penobscot, for I think the British will get information either at New York or Newport before our fleet can get ready to sail and if they do, I know that three or four large British ships can block them in and that will be the last of all our shipping." [3]

The fleet arrived in Penobscot Bay July 25, in the afternoon. There were three British sloops of war in the harbor, the North, of twenty, and the Albany and Nautilus of eighteen guns each. Nine of the American ships, in three divisions, stood towards these vessels, hove to and engaged them. There was a brisk fire for two hours without much effect. In a report to the President of the Massachusetts Coun-

---

[1] *Weymouth Hist. Soc.*, 1881, *Sketch of Lovell*, ch. vii.
[2] *Almon*, viii, 356.   [3] *R. I. Hist. Mag.*, October, 1886.

cil, dated three days later, General Lovell says:
" I the same evening attempted to make a lodgment
on Majorbagaduce, but the wind springing up very
strong, I was obliged to desist, lest the first division
might suffer before they could be supported by the
second. On the 26th I took possession with the
marines, supported by General Wadsworth's division, of an island in the harbour, beat them off, took
4 pieces of artillery and some ammunition." [1] The
landing was made on Nautilus Island, also known
as Banks Island. Captain Cathcart of the Tyrannicide says of this affair that "on the 26th July a
Council was held on board the Warren, where it was
agreed that each Ship or Armed Vessel should furnish such a Number of Marines to take possession
of Banks's Island on the South side of the Entrance
of Bagaduce River under cover of the Sloop Providence, Brig Pallas & Defence." [2] An officer on board
the ordnance brig, presumably Revere, gives another account of this episode, dated July 29, saying that "the marines attacked an island where the
enemy had a battery of 2 guns; they were commanded by Captain Welsh of the Warren. I sent
one field piece to support them; they landed under
cover of three vessels. The enemy quitted it with
precipitation, left their colours flying and four pieces
of cannon, two of them not mounted. We immediately built a battery there and mounted two 18 and
one 12 pounder. This island is directly opposite to

[1] *Boston Gazette*, August 9, 1779.   [2] *Rev. Rolls*, xxxix, 113.

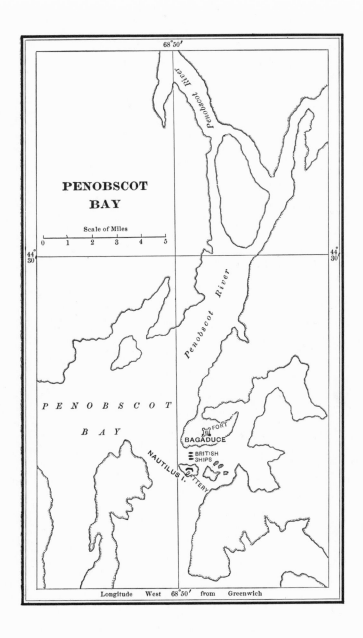

68°50'

Penobscot River

PENOBSCOT
BAY

Scale of Miles

0   1   2   3   4   5

44°
30'   44°
30'

Penobscot River

PENOBSCOT

BAY

FORT
BAGADUCE

BRITISH
SHIPS

NAUTILUS I.

BATTERY

Longitude   West   68°50'   from   Greenwich

the enemy and commands the mouth of the harbour." [1] This battery forced the British ships to
shift their anchorage further up the harbor.[2]

On the 27th there seems to have been lack of
harmony between the military and naval commanders and a misunderstanding about the landing of
the marines in an attack on the peninsula of Bagaduce. The importance of prompt and energetic action was appreciated by some of the subordinate
naval officers, who presented to the commodore on
that day a petition in which they " Would Repre-
sent to your Honour that the most spedy Exertions
should be used to accomplish the design we came
upon. We think Delays in the present Case are
extremely dangerous, as our Enemies are daily For-
tifying and Strengthening themselves & are stimu-
lated so to do, being in daily Expectation of Reinforcement"; they did not wish to advise or censure,
but only " to express our desire of improving the
present Opportunity to go Immediately into the
Harbour & Attack the Enemy's Ships." [3] It was
the opinion of these officers that the capture of the
British post at Bagaduce would be greatly facilitated and hastened by removing the ships which supported it. By evening arrangements had been made
for landing the marines on the peninsula. At three

[1] *Boston Gazette*, August 9, 1779.

[2] *Hist. Mag.*, February, 1864; *Wheeler*, 293, Journal of John
Calef; *Brit. Adm. Rec., Captains' Logs*, Nos. 23 and 630, logs of
the Albany and Nautilus.

[3] *Mass. Archives*, cxlv, 50.

the next morning the commodore ordered Cathcart "to begin to fire into the Woods with an Intent to scower them of the Enemy, which was Immediately obey'd." [1]

Early on July 28 the attack was made on Bagaduce. The Warren engaged the British ships at long range and they moved still farther up the harbor, to escape the fire of the battery on Nautilus Island. Lovell says: "This morning I have made my landing good on the S. W. head of a Peninsula which is 100 feet high and almost perpendicular, very thickly covered with bush and trees. The men ascended the precipice with alacrity and after a very smart conflict we put them to the rout. They left in the woods a number killed and wounded and we took a few prisoners; our loss is about 30 killed and wounded. We are within 100 rods of the enemies main fort, on a commanding piece of ground. I hope soon to have the satisfaction of informing you of the capture of the whole army." [2] "We landed in three divisions," says Colonel Revere, "the marines on the right, Col. Mitchell on the left, and Col. Mc. Cobb, the volunteers and my corps in the centre. The land being so mountainous and full of wood that our cannon could not play, I landed with my small arms, the whole force under cover of two ships and three brigs, who drew near the shore and kept up a constant fire into the woods till we began to land. The enemy's greatest strength lay upon

<hr>

[1] *Rev. Rolls*, xxxix, 113.   [2] *Boston Gazette*, August 9, 1779.

our right, where the marines landed ; they had three hundred in the woods. As soon as the right landed they were briskly attacked. The enemy had the most advantageous place I ever saw; it is a bank above three hundred feet high and so steep that no person can get up it but by pushing himself up by bushes and trees, with which it is covered. In less than 20 minutes the enemy gave way and we pursued them. They left twelve dead on the spot, 8 wounded and about 10 prisoners. We lost about 35 killed and wounded. We took possession of a height near their fort and are now building a battery to play upon them. I expect to put two 18 pounders, one 12, two 4, and a howitz on shore this day. I am in hopes that if the ships go into the harbour today [July 29], as it is said they will, and take their ships, we shall have an easy conquest. In the afternoon we took another battery of three 6 pounders, upon which they abandoned it and went into their fortress." [1] Another officer puts the American loss at ten killed and twenty wounded.[2]

On the 29th, according to Cathcart, it was agreed that the ships should go in and attack the enemy's squadron, but the next day, at a council of war on board the Warren, Saltonstall said there was no sufficient reason for the ships' going in. At this time, July 30, a galley arrived from Boston and three days later was sent back with Lovell's dispatches.

[1] *Boston Gazette*, August 9, 1779.
[2] *Ibid.; Wheeler*, 295 ; *Hist. Mag.*, February, 1864.

Frequent councils were held on the Warren, but with little result. The marines gave some assistance to the army, but with this exception the navy was of little service. The commodore, upheld by the privateer captains, remained inactive day after day, apparently incapable of coming to a decision. He seems to have feared the exposure of his ships to the fire of the fort while attacking the enemy's ships and to have insisted that the fort should be captured first; whereas Lovell's force was insufficient to justify an assault on the stronghold supported as it was by the British ships. Meanwhile the army erected batteries at different points for the reduction of the fort, if possible, and for the annoyance of the little squadron, which it would seem might easily have been captured, destroyed, or driven away at the outset of operations by the vastly superior American fleet. August 6, Lovell notes in his journal: "I wrote a Letter to the Commodore desiring an answer whether he wou'd or whether he wou'd not go in with his Ships & destroy the Shipping of the Enemy, which consist only of three Sloops of war, when he returned for answer, if I wou'd storm the fort he wou'd go in with his Ships, upon which I called a Council, the result of which was that in our present situation it was impracticable, with any prospect of Success." A simultaneous attack by army and navy might have succeeded. Lovell himself, perhaps, was moved by excess of prudence; but he lacked confidence in his men.

Notwithstanding the steadiness with which the militia with the help of the marines, carried the precipitous heights of Bagaduce on July 28, part of their subsequent behavior convinced the general of their unreliable character. He continued to urge more naval activity and wrote to the commodore August 11: "The destruction of the Enemy's ships must be effected at any rate, although it might cost us half our own." [1]

Meanwhile the commodore had had a somewhat ridiculous adventure August 7, described in Lovell's journal: "A Boat from the Hazard with Comr Saltonstall, Capts Waters, Williams, Salter, Holmes & Burke were a reconnoitering up a Cove nigh the Enemy's Ships; on their discovering them they immediately sent 8 Boats armed, to hem them in. They so far succeeded that they made a prize of the Boat, but the Gentlemen took to the Bush and escaped being made prisoners." After a circuitous tramp through the woods the naval officers rejoined their friends.

Immediately after the council of war on August 6 another express had been sent to Boston with dispatches from the general, but with no report from the commodore. The Navy Board of the Eastern District noticed this omission in a letter to Saltonstall dated August 12, in which they went on to say: "We have for sometime been at a loss

---

[1] *Wheeler*, 310; *Lovell's Journal*; *Rev. Rolls*, xxxix, 113; *Hist. Mag.*, February, 1864.

to know why the enemy's ships have not been attacked, nor does the result of this Council give us any satisfaction on that head; it is agreed on all hands that they are at all times in your power. If, therefore, your own security or the more advantageous operations of the army did not require it, why should any business be delayed to another day, that may as well be done this? Our apprehensions of your danger have ever been from a reinforcement to the enemy; you can't expect to remain much longer without one. Whatever, therefore, is to be done, should be done immediately, both to prevent advantages to the enemy and delays if you are obliged to retreat. As we presume you would avoid having these ships in your rear while a reinforcement appears in front, or the necessity of leaving them behind when you retire yourself; with these sentiments we think it our duty to direct you to attack and take or destroy them without delay, in doing which no time is to be lost, as a reinforcement are probably on their passage at this time. It is therefore our orders that as soon as you receive this you take the most effectual measures for the capture or destruction of the enemy's ships, and with the greatest dispatch the nature and situation of things will admit of."[1] These urgent instructions, signed by William Vernon and James Warren, might possibly have produced some effect, had they been issued and forwarded several days earlier;

[1] *Proc. of Gen. Assembly*, 26.

but it was too late, as was also an application to General Gates for aid, which had recently been made by the Massachusetts Council.

By the time the American forces had been in Penobscot Bay between two and three weeks the fort on Bagaduce peninsula, which at first had been a mere breastwork, was becoming stronger every day and was already a formidable structure. At last, August 13, when General Lovell, hoping for succor from Boston, was still besieging this work and preparing for a possible assault, the enemy's reinforcements appeared. The Active and Diligent since July 30 had been cruising off "the Mouth of the Bay in order to make the earliest Discoveries of an Enemy's Approach," when "on the 13th Inst. 2 P.M. Discovered five Sail Standing into the Bay."[1] Two others came in sight, making a force of one ship of the line, five frigates and a sloop of war. The Diligent ran in at once to notify the commodore and the Active joined the fleet the next day. There was a disposition at first, no doubt encouraged by the more resolute commanders, to make a stand with the fleet, and the ships were drawn up in the form of a crescent, but at another council it was decided that the British fleet was too strong to engage and that the only alternative must be adopted, which was to run up the river. The captains evidently had no confidence in their leader and little hope of his making a determined resistance.

[1] *Mass. Archives,* cxlv, 207.

Meanwhile, upon first receiving information of the approach of British reinforcements, the army had hastily embarked on the transports and the whole fleet made every effort to get as far up the river as possible. All but two of the vessels escaped capture, yet only to be destroyed by their crews after landing, to prevent their falling into the enemy's hands. The New Hampshire privateer Hampden and the ship Hunter, one of the largest and best of the Massachusetts privateers, were taken by the British. The Hunter was run ashore and her crew escaped before capture. Captain Salter of the Hampden says that when the fleet got under way the enemy was a league and a half astern and that he set all sail, but "my Ship Sailing heavey the enemy Soon came up With me, three frigetes, and fiered upon [me] one after ye outher, & cutt away my rigen & Stages &c, and huld me Sundrey times & wounded Sum of my men. I found it Emposable to Joyane our fleet again; was obliged to Strik, all thou Contray to my well."[1]

The British squadron, that caused this reverse of fortune for the American arms, consisted of the sixty-four-gun ship Raisonable, two thirty-two-gun frigates, the Blonde and Virginia, the Greyhound of twenty-eight guns, and the Camilla and Galatea of twenty guns each, and the fourteen-gun sloop Otter, and was under the command of Commodore Collier. He received information of the expedition,

[1] *Mass. Archives*, cxlv, 44; *Wheeler*, 302 (Calef's journal).

July 28, and sailed from Sandy Hook, August 3.
According to the log of the Blonde, at half-past
twelve in the afternoon of August 15, " the Rebel
fleet got under weigh & formed a Line of Battle,
we, the Galatea & Virginia being the Headmost
ships, the Reisonable, Greyhound & Camilla about
6 or 7 miles a starn." At half-past one " saw the
Rebels forming a Line of Battle ; us together with
the Virginia & Galatea pursued the 21 sail of Rebels & Drove them before us without the Return of
a single shot. At 3 two Ships & a Brigg hauld
round to the S. W., trying to get Down the western
passage of Long Island ; us & the Galatea hauld
close to the North End & cut off their Retrait.
They then wore & stood after the Body of the fleet;
the Galatea Pursued the Brigg & Drove her on shore,
we then standing after the Ships & fired several
shot at them. At 4 one of the Ships run on shore,
ye Galatea sent her 2 Boats to Board her, but finding the Rebels to be armed on the Beach, returned
on bd & made sail after us, leaveing them to the
Command of our Rere, the Albany, Nautilus &
North Just Coming out of Magebacduce River. At
$\frac{1}{2}$ past 4 fired several shot at the other ship & Huld
Her, as did the Virginia. At 5 she struck to us ;
sent a Boat with an Officer to board Her, which
she did, & made sail after us. At 6 upewards of 20
sail of small Vessels run on shore, the most of them
they set fire to, which Oblig'd us to anchor." At
seven o'clock the Greyhound got into shoal water

and anchored. About the same time the Americans set fire to a sloop and sent her down the river. " Sent 2 Boats man & armed, Cut her Loose & twod Her on shore; sent 3 Boats to Board a schooner & bring her to Anchor, she proved to be Laden with provisions. At 10 saw the Skyrocket on fire, at $\frac{1}{2}$ pst saw the Greyhound afloat again; Virginia anchord with the Greyhd $\frac{1}{2}$ a mile below us. At 8 Discovered Numbr of small boats passing to & fro from the small Craft to the shore Forts; a Broadside of Round & Grape shot at them. At 9 the Boats returned from ye prize Hamdon of 22 Guns. At 5 A.M. made sigl for all Lieuts that the Boats mand & armed to attack the small Vessels. At 11 made the Signal & weighd, But the wind falling cam, . . . sent the pinnace to Reconnitre the Enemys Vessels." The next day the Blonde with other British vessels continued the pursuit up the river; they saw the Warren on fire two miles above, " heard the Explosation & saw the smoke of several Vessels on fire above her." The loss on board the Albany, North, and Nautilus during the siege was trifling: four killed, nine wounded, and eight missing.[1]

The British fleet, although carrying fewer men and fewer but doubtless much heavier guns than the American, was far too powerful for an irregular,

[1] *Brit. Adm. Rec., Captains' Letters*, No. 1612, 2 (Collier, August 20, 1779), No. 2121, 16 (Mowatt, September 19, 1779), *Captains' Logs*, Nos. 23, 118, 157, 420, 630 (logs of the Albany, Blonde, Camilla, Greyhound and Nautilus).

heterogeneous armament, made up mostly of undisciplined privateers to engage, with any hope of success. Unity of action and mutual support in an emergency could not be expected of such a force. The committee of the Massachusetts General Court, which inquired into the affair, reported, October 7, that the total destruction of the fleet was occasioned principally by "the Commodore's not exerting himself at all at the time of the retreat in opposing the enemy's foremost ships in pursuit." With the pursuing British extended over a long line, a resolute and skillful commander, backed by disciplined and subordinate captains, might have struck a blow of some effect at the enemy; but probably under the circumstances the best course was followed in depriving them of a number of valuable prizes. The fault lay in the earlier, inexcusable inaction. Collier sailed from Sandy Hook August 3. Before that date, if the small British squadron in the bay had been disposed of at the outset and if proper support had been given to the army, General Lovell should have been able to carry the half-finished fort and would probably have been in possession of the whole region, even with his inadequate force. The legislative committee of inquiry expressed the opinion that if Lovell had "been furnished with all the men ordered for the service or been properly supported by the Commodore, he would probably have reduced the enemy"; and added that the naval commanders in the service of the state "behaved like brave, experienced, good officers throughout the whole expedition." [1]

The need of reinforcing Lovell had been appreciated and when the Massachusetts Council applied to General Gates, August 8, a regiment of the Continental army, of four hundred men, was detailed for this service. They did not get away from Boston, however, until after the disaster at Penobscot. Upon receiving information of this, August 19, they at once put into Portsmouth in the fear of falling in with some of Collier's ships. [2] If the inadequacy of Lovell's force had been realized in the beginning and the reinforcement had been asked for at once, it would have reached the Penobscot in time. The whole affair is a record of blunders and lack of foresight.

Leaving the wrecks of their fleet strewn along the banks of the river, the unhappy soldiers and sailors of the Penobscot expedition found their way back to Boston through the wilderness. The disaster had a depressing effect in Massachusetts. A heavy debt, estimated at seven million dollars, was imposed upon the state, but the humiliation of the affair was felt even more keenly. As General Sullivan said of it, the expense was "not so distressing as the disgrace." [3] It has been held that this enterprise was not only mismanaged and doomed to failure,

[1] *Boston Gazette*, December 27, 1779; *Proc. of Gen. Assembly*, 27–29.

[2] *Ibid.*, 21; Thacher's *Military Journal*, 166–168.

[3] *Sparks MSS.*, xx, 2.

but was ill-conceived and would have been comparatively useless, at least not justifying the cost, even
if successful; but another view may perhaps with
some reason be entertained. In the first place the
establishment of a hostile post within striking distance of Boston naturally caused apprehension and
its removal was an object worth considering. Moreover, success justifies much, and more than material
advantage is to be considered. In this case victory
would have brought prestige to the American arms
and would in some degree have inspired confidence
in the ultimate happy conclusion of the war, with
animating effect on the supporters of the patriotic
cause, who had met with much discouragement.

The end of Saltonstall's career in the Continental
service was near. The committee of inquiry reported
that the principal reason for the disaster was " want
of proper spirit and energy on the part of the Commodore." [1] It is an interesting question for specu-
lation whether a more " proper spirit and energy "
would have been displayed by Captain Hopkins,
who had recently been displaced by Saltonstall in
command of the frigate Warren,[2] and who otherwise would doubtless have led the American fleet
into Penobscot Bay. A few weeks after the report
of the committee, Saltonstall was tried by court
martial on board the frigate Deane in Boston Harbor and was dismissed from the navy.

The British held Bagaduce until the end of the

[1] *Boston Gazette*, December 27, 1779.   [2] See above, p. 376.

war, but they were not entirely unmolested. Just within a year the sting of defeat was in a slight measure alleviated, according to the following account of a small but successful expedition: " A few days ago a detachment from the troops under General Wadsworth went up Penobscot-river, having pass'd the fort in whale-boats in the night, and took two sloops which had been weighing up some of the cannon lately belonging to our privateers which were burnt there. They had got 8 cannon on board and were coming down the river, little expecting to be conducted by our people; but Capt. Mowat had the mortification to see them passing down by the fort, out of his reach however, in triumph. They fired at the fort to vex the enemy and got safe away. Mowat followed them to Campden, but General Wadsworth having drawn up his men and made a breastwork to frighten the enemy, he and his ship were obliged to meach back again, and we are in full possession of the vessels which were intended to invest our coasts. General Wadsworth has taken 40 prisoners, including the men who were on board these vessels." [1]

[1] *Boston Gazette*, July 10, 1780; *Almon*, x, 227.

CHAPTER XIII

A CRUISE AROUND THE BRITISH ISLES, 1779

THE frigate Alliance, Captain Landais, with Lafayette on board, arrived at Brest February 6, 1779, after a passage of twenty-three days from Boston. The voyage had not been without incident. Two vessels were captured and the frigate lost her main topmast in a storm. February 2 a mutiny was discovered among the English and Irish sailors on board. The difficulty of recruiting ships' crews for the regular naval service, chiefly due to the superior attractions of privateering, had led to the practice in some cases of enlisting British prisoners, who were willing in this manner to escape confinement. In the case of the Alliance the disinclination of Americans to sail under a French captain had increased the difficulty and accordingly many British subjects were taken. The unreliable character of such crews is illustrated in this instance. Among the ringleaders of the conspiracy were John Savage, master-at-arms, and William Murray, sergeant of marines. Murray confessed, saying "that Savage and he, with 70 more, had agreed to take the ship and carry her into some part of England or Ireland, and force one of the Lieutenants to take command of her. He said the plan they had laid to take her was, that they were to divide themselves into four divisions, the first to take the magazine, the other three at the same time to force the cabbin, wardroom, and quarter deck, then to take command of the arm-chests, and in case of opposition, they were to point the fore-castle guns aft and fire them, the guns being 9 pounders and all loaded. The party that was to go to the magazine were to kill the Gunner, Carpenter and Boat-swain; the other punishments for the other officers and French gentlemen were thus: Captain Landais was to be put in irons and sent in the cutter, without victuals or drink; the Lieutenants were to walk overboard on a plank from the ship side, unless they would take charge of her and navigate the ship into England; the marine officers and the Doctor were to be hanged, quartered, and hove overboard; the sailing Master was to be tied up to the mizzen-mast, scarrified all over, cut to pieces, and hove overboard." [1] Lafayette was to be put in irons and sent to England. Thirty-eight of the mutineers were confined in irons on shore to await trial. The disposition of these prisoners caused embarrassment, for there were not enough American naval captains in France to organize a court martial for their trial and it would be inconvenient and expensive to send them back to America. Franklin suggested exchanging them for Americans as prisoners of war. The Mar-

[1] *Independent Chronicle*, April 29, 1779, Murray's testimony under oath, vouched for by an officer of the ship.

ine Committee, however, could "think of no better method of disposing of them than Sending them out to this Continent by different Vessels, proportioning the number to each Vessel, so as not to render it dangerous or inconvenient : and upon their Arrival, if Sufficient evidence can be had, it is our intention to bring them to trial by Court Martial." [1]

After his return to Brest in May, 1778, with his prize the Drake, Captain Jones spent more than a year on shore, perhaps the most trying year of his life, beset with every sort of vexation and disappointment. To begin with, his drafts on the American Commissioners, for the support of his crew and prisoners and the refitting of his ship, were dishonored for lack of funds. Jones had never received any pay for his own services and he now made himself personally responsible for these necessary expenses. There was great and apparently unnecessary delay in disposing of the Ranger's prizes, so that the officers and men were kept waiting indefinitely for their prize money. At this time, too, began the long and weary wait for another and larger ship. There still seemed a chance that through the French Minister of Marine, de Sartine, Jones would get the Indien after all, and it was proposed by Franklin that he should man her partly

[1] *Mar. Com. Letter Book*, 236 (September 17, 1779, letter to Franklin) ; *Wharton*, iii, 188; *Boston Gazette*, April 19, 26, 1779 ; *Independent Chronicle*, April 22, 29, 1779 ; *Archives de la Marine*, B⁸ 16 (Février, 1779.)

with French and partly with American prisoners received in exchange for those he had taken on his cruise. But on account of the outbreak of hostilities between France and England, which soon followed, the Dutch government, anxious to maintain neutrality, would not allow the Indien to leave Holland. Other schemes were proposed, among them the command of a squadron of French ships under the American flag to cruise in the Baltic, but owing to the natural jealousy of French officers, and other causes, every plan fell through. After nearly endless correspondence without result, Jones determined to go himself to Versailles and personally urge his claims, taking the advice, it is said, given in " Poor Richard's Almanac," and hoping that by direct solicitation something might be accomplished. This hope was realized, for Sartine took more interest in his affairs and the result was the purchase, in January, 1779, of an East Indiaman called the Duc de Duras.[1]

This vessel was fourteen years old, unsound, and a dull sailer, but though Jones had insisted on the necessity for his purpose of a fast-sailing ship, he accepted the Duras and at once entered upon the work of converting her into a man-of-war. With the consent of Sartine and in honor of Poor Richard and of his faithful friend and benefactor, Franklin, Jones called his ship the Bonhomme Richard. She

[1] *Sands*, 96–149; *Sherburne*, 66–86; *Archives de la Marine*, B[1] 89, 179, 183, 185, 203, 207.

JOHN PAUL JONES

was at L'Orient and several American seamen were enlisted there. Months were spent in preparation for a cruise against the enemy. The Alliance, which was to have returned directly to America, was detained by Franklin and put under Jones's orders; and three French vessels also, making in all a respectable squadron. The agent of the French government in the arrangements was M. de Chaumont, a zealous adherent of the American cause who had given his house at Passy free of rent to the American Commissioners. It was intended that Lafayette should accompany the expedition with a considerable military force and an attack on Liverpool, Lancaster, Bristol, Bath, and Whitehaven was contemplated ; it was proposed to take nearly fifteen hundred infantry besides a small body of cavalry and six pieces of light artillery. This project, however, was abandoned and Lafayette did not go. Later, an invasion of England was planned, for which a large French and Spanish fleet was collected, and Jones was to make a diversion in the north, but the main part of this scheme also was given up. It remained now for the American squadron to cruise independently. The ships were finally ready for sea about the middle of June, 1779. There was trouble on board the Alliance which caused Jones annoyance and perplexity, not knowing at first where to place the blame. It was owing to lack of harmony between the captain of the frigate and his officers and crew. Landais had a temperament which made impossible

anything like efficient coöperation between himself
and either superiors or inferiors.[1]

The Bonhomme Richard was not well adapted
for purposes of war, being clumsily built, slow-sail-
ing, and structurally weak. There was discussion
as to the number and weight of guns she should
carry. Jones wished a main battery of twenty-eight
eighteen-pounders and they were ordered to be
cast, but the ship was not strong enough to bear
the strain and lighter guns were deemed necessary.
The only ones that could be obtained in time for
the cruise were old French guns, many of which
had been condemned. On the gun-deck were mounted
twenty-eight twelve-pounders, and on the forecastle
and quarter deck six or eight nines, while in the
gun-room on the after part of the deck under the
main battery six eighteen-pounders were placed,
ports having been cut for them, too close to the sur-
face of the water to be of use in a moderately rough
sea. Jones had as first lieutenant, at the outset,
Robert Robinson, who was soon succeeded, however,
by Richard Dale, an excellent officer who had served
in the Virginia navy and the Continental navy and
had twice escaped from Mill Prison. The crew of
the ship was heterogeneous. Out of two hundred
and twenty-seven officers and men[2] there were

[1] *Sands*, 149–158; *Sherburne*, 86–94; *Archives de la Marine*, B⁴
172, 99–102, 128.

[2] This list of 227 in *Sherburne* is of a later date and evidently
incomplete, some of the French officers and all the marines being
omitted. A reprint of the original muster-roll, dated July 26,

seventy-nine Americans, mostly exchanged prisoners, eighty-three English, Irish, and Scotch, including Jones himself, a few Scandinavians, and nearly thirty Portuguese; the nationality of most of the others is not stated. Besides these there were a hundred and thirty-seven French soldiers acting as marines. The Alliance, by far the best ship in the squadron, carried twenty-eight twelve-pounders and eight nines, and rather more than two hundred men. The Pallas, Captain Cottineau, was a merchantman or privateer fitted out as a thirty-two-gun frigate; her battery consisted of twenty-six nines and six fours, and her crew of about two hundred and fifty men. The Cerf, Captain Varage, was an eighteen-gun cutter and a fine vessel of her class. The Vengeance, Captain Ricot, was a twelve-gun brigantine. [1]

Jones's ideas about the kind of service he was now to enter upon are expressed in a memorandum he had drawn up January 21, 1779, while waiting for the orders of the minister to take command of the Bonhomme Richard. "I am but a young Student in the Science of Arms and therefore wish to receive instruction from Men of riper Judgement and greater

1779, is contained in *The Logs of the Serapis, Alliance, Ariel*, edited by Captain John S. Barnes, New York, 1911; this list, comprising 254 names, differs considerably from Sherburne's, which is accounted for by many changes soon afterwards made in the personnel.

[1] *Sherburne*, 95, 100, 133–144, 221; *Sands*, 156, 157; *Archives de la Marine*, B¹ **89**, 215, 225–239, B¹ **91**, 51, B⁴ **158**, 143, 184, B⁴ **172**, 128.

experience, but to me the grand Object of Partizan War is, when a fair opening presents itself, to strike an unexpected Blow, which being well directed must in the nature of things be severly felt. The Man who is to be entrusted with the Chief Command of such enterprizes, ought to be worthy of confidence, and if he is, too much cannot be shown him. It seems to be his province to adopt such enterprizes as circumstances may throw him in the way of, with a prospect of success, and which being effected will tend the most to distress and distract the Enemy. A principal object or Enterprize may with propriety be thought of long before it is executed, but ought not to be committed to writing nor communicated to any person other than the commander in chief, and by him only to his Officers and Men at a proper time and Place. To effect anything of consequence, it may be necessary to embark a Body of 400 heigh Spirited and well disciplined Troops exclusive of the compliment of Seamen and Marines. Five Ships may be of infinite Service. I would recommend two small ones rather than one larger size, as more objects than one may present themselves. But Tho' in some cases large Vessels may not be necessary for Five Ships, yet the small ones ought to sail very fast, that they may hold way with the Principal Ship or Ships on which they are to attend. The passage will thus be performed in the shortest space of time that is possible and these five Ships may be made useful as light

Cruizers, should a Variety of the Enemies Ships be met with at any one time on the Passage. One fast sailing Cutter or other Vessel of Eight or Ten Guns might be of much Utility, as well in a Partizan War to cover the Troops in landing and in retreat as in Cruizing against the Enemies Commerce on the Ocean. No Cruizing Frigate with unlimited orders ought to be sent to Sea without being attended by one of these Vessels, and the Bottoms should be sheathed with Copper. If I have the Ministers Authority, I will send a trusty person or two to enquire into on the spot and view the exact strength & Situation of a place or two of great Importance. It will be proper to be provided with Two light Field pieces and a number of Scaling Ladders, &ca. . . . But the Commanding Officer of the Troops will be better able to Judge of the Articles necessary for any land Operation, and his Opinion may easily be obtained without telling him why it is Asked. It will be a necessary caution to Suffer no person concerned in the preparation of the Five Ships to know for what services they are prepared and with which Ships they are to act. Some false Idea may be whispered to them as a Secret."[1]

Jones had general instructions from Franklin, who was always moved by humane considerations. The concluding passages are: "As many of your officers and people have lately escaped from English

[1] *Jones MSS.*

prisons, either in Europe or America, you are to be particularly attentive to their conduct towards the prisoners which the fortune of war may throw into your hands, lest the resentment of the more than barbarous usage by the English in many places towards the Americans should occasion a retaliation and imitation of what ought rather to be detested and avoided for the sake of humanity and for the honour of our country. In the same view, although the English have wantonly burnt many defenceless towns in America, you are not to follow this example, unless when a reasonable ransom is refused, in which case your own generous feelings as well as this instruction will induce you to give timely notice of your intention, that sick and ancient persons, women and children may be first removed." [1] Shortly before sailing, de Chaumont, who seems not always to have been discreet, required Jones and the other captains to sign an agreement or concordat, which gave the subordinate commanders a degree of independence and freedom of action incompatible with strict discipline and efficient coöperation.[2]

The squadron sailed, June 19, from Groix Roads, near L'Orient, with a convoy, which was escorted to Bordeaux and other ports. On the night of the 20th the Bonhomme Richard and Alliance fouled each other, carrying away the Richard's jib-boom

[1] *Sands*, 152–154 (April 27, 1779).

[2] *Ibid.*, 165; *Sherburne*, 94; Mackenzie's *Life of Paul Jones*, i, 153. For the Concordat, see *Archives de la Marine*, B⁴ 158, 144, *Sherburne*, 200, and Appendix VIII.

and the Alliance's mizzen-mast. Jones considered
Landais responsible for this accident, but Lieutenant Robinson of the Richard was court-martialed
and dismissed.[1] The next evening the Cerf captured
a fourteen-gun sloop, but was obliged to abandon
the prize on the approach of a superior force. June
29, the Bonhomme Richard fell in with two frigates. Jones says: "They appeared at first earnest
to engage, but their courage failed and they fled
with precipitation, and to my mortification outsailed
the Bon homme Richard and got clear. I had, however, a flattering proof of the martial spirit of my
crew and am confident that had I been able to get
between the two, which was my intention, we should
have beaten them both together." [2] In spite of
Jones's good opinion of his crew, serious mischief
on board his ship was brewing at this time. An
incipient mutiny among the British sailors was discovered, the design being to take possession of the
ship and send Jones a prisoner to England. Many
of these undesirable persons were discharged early
in August and forty-three Americans, who had recently arrived in a cartel from English prisons,
were recruited. The Portuguese contingent in the
crew was also enlisted at this period. Most of the
month of July seems to have been spent in preparing for an extended cruise. According to the instructions of Franklin, dated June 30, 1779, which
had been virtually dictated by Sartine, the squad-

[1] *Jones MSS.*, August 8, 1779.   [2] *Sherburne*, 96.

ron was to cruise to the north of the British Isles and at the end of about six weeks put into the Texel, whence it was to convoy vessels from Holland to France.[1]

A few days before sailing, Commodore Jones issued instructions to his captains requiring careful attention to his signals and obedience to his orders. They were to keep their stations and "never to chase so as to lose company with the squadron." Sealed orders were given them appointing rendezvous at different places in case of separation. The squadron sailed from Groix Roads August 14, 1779, on a cruise which became famous. Two French privateers, Le Monsieur, 38, and La Grandville, 12, had joined the expedition, but they soon dropped out. On the 23d, the squadron was off Cape Clear. Two prizes had been taken since leaving port and sent back to L'Orient. A third was now taken by boats, there being no wind. In the evening, as it was still calm, Jones sent his barge ahead to tow the Bonhomme Richard, fearing she might be swept by the tide into a dangerous position. " Soon after sunset," says the commodore, " the villains who towed the ship, cut the tow rope and decamped with my barge. Sundry shots were fired to bring them to without effect; in the meantime the master of the Bon homme Richard, without orders, manned

---

[1] *Sands*, 158–163; *Sherburne*, 94–102; *Jones MSS.*, July 28, 29, 1779, Jones to Gourlade & Moylan and to Lieutenant Lunt, and courts martial of Robert Towers and others; *Archives de la Marine*, B¹ **89**, 270, B¹ **91**, 178, B⁴ **158**, 132, 184.

one of the ships boats and with four soldiers pursued the barge, in order to stop the deserters. The evening was clear and serene, but the zeal of that officer, Mr. Cutting Lunt, induced him to pursue too far, and a fog which came on soon afterwards prevented the boats from rejoining the ship, although I caused signal guns to be frequently fired. The fog and calm continued the next day till towards evening. In the afternoon Capt. Landais came on board the Bon homme Richard and behaved towards me with great disrespect, affirming in the most indelicate manner and language that I had lost my boats and people through my imprudence in sending boats to take a prize. He persisted in his reproaches, though he was assured . . . that the barge was towing the ship at the time of elopement and that she had not been sent in pursuit of the prize. He was affronted because I would not the day before suffer him to chase without my orders and to approach the dangerous shore I have already mentioned, where he was an entire stranger and when there was not sufficient wind to govern a ship. He told me he was the only American in the squadron and was determined to follow his own opinion in chasing when and where he thought proper, and in every other matter that concerned the service, and that if I continued in that situation three days longer, the squadron would be taken." [1]

[1] *Sherburne*, 109, 110; *Sands*, 166–168.

The Cerf was sent in to look for the lost boats, but she too disappeared. She was unable to overtake the boats, lost sight of the squadron, sprung her mainmast in a gale a few days later, was chased by a vessel of superior force, and finally returned to France, arriving at Paimbœuf September 4. Meanwhile the Bonhomme Richard remained a short time near the place where these occurrences had taken place. It was afterwards learned that Lunt was taken prisoner. Besides him the Richard lost by this mishap another officer and twenty of her best seamen. A gale on the night of the 26th compelled the flagship to stand off and the next morning only the Vengeance was in sight. Jones thought that Landais purposely kept out of the way. The Bonhomme Richard and Vengeance kept to the northward and on September 1 were off Cape Wrath, where they fell in with the Alliance and a prize she had taken. The same day a British letter of marque was captured. Contrary to Jones's orders these two prizes were sent by Landais to Bergen in Norway, where they were given up to the British consul by the Danish authorities; they became a loss to the captors for which Denmark refused to make restitution. Landais continued to behave in an insubordinate manner. September 2, the Pallas appeared. The squadron cruised a few days between the Orkney and Shetland Islands and some unimportant prizes were taken. September 5, a gale came on which blew four days and was followed by contrary

winds, so that land was not again seen until the
13th, when the Cheviot Hills were sighted. Jones
had with him the Pallas and Vengeance, the Alliance having again disappeared. Two colliers were
taken on the 14th.[1]

Jones now planned an important enterprise. In
his report to Franklin, dated October 3, 1779, he
says: "Knowing that there lay at anchor in Leith
road an armed ship of 20 guns, with two or three fine
cutters, I formed an expedition against Leith, which
I purposed to lay under a large contribution, or
otherwise to reduce it to ashes."[2] He prepared a
summons addressed to the magistrates of Leith, in
which he tells them: "I do not wish to distress the
poor inhabitants; my intention is only to demand
your contribution towards the reimbursement which
Britain owes to the much injured citizens of America."[3] This is an allusion to the depredations committed by the British in Chesapeake Bay, Long
Island Sound, and elsewhere.

His report continues: "Had I been alone, the
wind being favorable, I would have proceeded
directly up the Firth and must have succeeded, as
they lay there in a state of perfect indolence and
security, which would have proved their ruin. Unfortunately for me, the Pallas and Vengeance were

---

[1] *Sands*, 169–171, 245–247; *Sherburne*, 110–112; *Archives de la
Marine*, B¹ **89**, 274, B⁴ **158**, 150, 186, B⁸ **16** (Août, Septembre,
1779).

[2] *Sherburne*, 112.

[3] *Ibid.*, 106.

both at a considerable distance in the offing, they having chased to the southward; this obliged us to steer out of the Firth again to meet them. The captains of the Pallas and Vengeance being come on board the Bon homme Richard, I communicated to them my project, to which many difficulties and objections were made by them; at last, however, they appeared to think better of the design, after I had assured them that I hoped to raise a contribution of 200000 pounds sterling on Leith, and that there was no battery of cannon there to oppose our landing. So much time, however, was unavoidably spent in pointed remarks and sage deliberation that night, that the wind became contrary in the morning. We continued working to windward up the Firth without being able to reach the road of Leith, till on the morning of the 17th, when being almost within cannon shot of the town, having everything in readiness for a descent, a very severe gale of wind came on, and being directly contrary, obliged us to bear away, after having in vain endeavored for some time to withstand its violence. The gale was so severe that one of the prizes that had been taken on the 14th sunk to the bottom, the crew being with difficulty saved. As the alarm by this time had reached Leith by means of a cutter that had watched our motions that morning, and as the wind continued contrary (though more moderate in the evening), I thought it impossible to pursue the enterprise with a good prospect of success, especially as Edinburgh, where there is always a number of troops, is only a mile distant from Leith; therefore I gave up the project." [1]

The cutter spoken of by Jones, as having watched his motions, was one of several revenue cutters specially fitted out and armed for service against the American squadron, some of them having been placed under the orders of the admirals commanding various naval stations. As early as August 19 the alarm excited by the approach of Jones had caused orders for hasty preparations to watch his movements and to check them as far as possible. This particular cutter, having been sent out to reconnoitre, sailed at daybreak, September 17. The captain reported that he "found himself within Pistol Shot of the fifty Gun French Ship, upon which he tacked about and afterwards retook a prize they had taken in the Mouth of the Firth, but a French twenty four Gun Frigate immediately made up and obliged him to abandon the Prize. . . . The French Squadron consists of a fifty Gun Ship, a twenty four Gun Frigate and a Brig mounting ten Guns. The Ships sail ill and they say they are determined to come up to Leith Road. The Commander of the fifty Gun Ship is said to be acquainted with the Coast. Both the fifty Gun Ship and Frigate are painted Black. The fifty Gun Ship has a White Bottom and very clumsy mast head." [2] This infor-

[1] *Sherburne*, 112 ; *Sands*, 171–175.
[2] *Minutes of the Scottish Board of Customs*, 197.

mation was immediately sent to the Commissioners of the Treasury.[1]

Jones could not excite the interest of his French captains in other plans. They were getting uneasy at his remaining so long on the coast and threatened to desert him. Therefore the squadron sailed south and in the course of a few days several prizes were taken. September 21, they were off Flamborough Head. Two brigs were captured and a fleet of vessels was chased, one of which ran ashore, but night put an end to operations. The next day a fleet appeared coming up from the south, but put back upon seeing the Bonhomme Richard. On signal two pilots came aboard the Richard and informed Jones that " a king's frigate lay there in sight, at anchor within the Humber, waiting to take under convoy a number of merchant ships bound to the northward. The pilots imagined the Bon homme Richard to be an English ship of war and consequently communicated to me the private signal which they had been required to make. I endeavored by this means to decoy the ships out of the port, but the wind then changing and with the tide becoming unfavorable for them, the deception had not the desired effect and they wisely put back. The entrance of the Humber is exceedingly difficult and dangerous and, as the

[1] *Minutes of the Scottish Board of Customs*, 191–198, 205, 206; *Minutes of the Irish Board of Customs*, 23, 24, 33, 36. See also *Sands*, 173, 174, *notes*; *London Chronicle*, September 14, 18, 1779; *British Admiralty Records, Captains' Letters*, No. 2305, 1 (September 20, 23, 1779).

Pallas was not in sight, I thought it not prudent to remain off the entrance; I therefore steered out again to join the Pallas off Flamborough Head. In the night we saw and chased two ships until three o'clock in the morning, when being at a very small distance from them, I made the private signal of recognizance which I had given to each captain before I sailed from Groaix; one half of the answer only was returned. In this position both sides lay to till daylight, when the ships proved to be the Alliance and the Pallas." [1]

The events of the memorable day that followed are best told in the words of Jones himself: "On the morning of that day, the 23d, . . . we chased a brigantine that appeared laying to to windward. About noon we saw and chased a large ship that appeared coming round Flamborough Head from the northward, and at the same time I manned and armed one of the pilot boats to send in pursuit of the brigantine, which now appeared to be the vessel that I had forced ashore. Soon after this a fleet of forty-one sail appeared off Flamborough Head, bearing N. N. E. This induced me to abandon the single ship, which had then anchored in [Bridlington] Bay; I also called back the pilot boat and hoisted a signal for a general chase. When the fleet discovered us bearing down, all the merchant ships crowded sail towards the shore. The two ships of

[1] *Sherburne*, 113, 114; *Sands*, 176–180. For another account of the cruise up to this time, see *Life of Nathaniel Fanning*, 33–43.

war that protected the fleet, at the same time steered from the land and made the disposition for the battle. In approaching the enemy I crowded every possible sail and made the signal for the line of battle, to which the Alliance showed no attention. Earnest as I was for the action, I could not reach the commodore's ship until seven in the evening, being then within pistol shot, when he hailed the Bon homme Richard; we answered him by firing a whole broadside." The English ships were the Serapis and Countess of Scarborough. Jones says that at dusk they had tacked with a view to running under Scarborough Castle, but that he had headed them off. The pilot boat, which had been sent away and then recalled, contained sixteen of the Richard's best men under the second lieutenant, Henry Lunt. The boat was unable to get back before dark and Lunt then deemed it imprudent to go alongside. So the ship lost the services of these men when they were most needed.[1]

Jones took his station on the quarter-deck, while on the poop was a French volunteer officer with twenty marines. Richard Dale, first lieutenant, was in charge of the gun-deck. The tops, commanded by midshipmen, were manned by marines and sailors, twenty in the main, fourteen in the fore, and nine in the mizzen-top. They were armed with

---

· [1] *Sherburne*, 114; *Sands*, 180, 181. Jones's report to Franklin, dated October 3, 1779, is supplemented by the journal of his campaigns presented to Louis XVI, *Jones MSS.*, January 1, 1786 (quoted in *Sands*).

swivels, coehorns, and muskets and were ordered to
clear the enemy's tops before turning their fire
upon his decks.[1]

The report goes on: "The battle being thus begun was continued with unremitting fury. Every
method was practised on both sides to gain an ad-

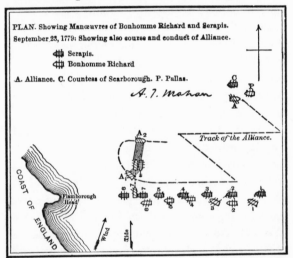

PLAN. Showing Manœuvres of Bonhomme Richard and Serapis.
September 23, 1779: Showing also course and conduct of Alliance.

⚓ Serapis.
⚓ Bonhomme Richard

A. Alliance. C. Countess of Scarborough. P. Pallas.

A. J. Mahan

Track of the Alliance.

COAST OF ENGLAND

Plainborough Head

Wind Tide

vantage and rake each other, and I must confess
that the enemy's ship, being much more manageable
than the Bon homme Richard, gained thereby several times an advantageous situation, in spite of my
best endeavors to prevent it. As I had to deal with
an enemy of greatly superior force, I was under
the necessity of closing with him, to prevent the
advantage which he had over me in point of man-

[1] *Fanning*, 43, 45.

œuvre. It was my intention to lay the Bon homme Richard athwart the enemy's bow, but as that operation required great dexterity in the management of both sails and helm and some of our braces being shot away, it did not exactly succeed to my wishes. The enemy's bowsprit, however, came over the Bon homme Richard's poop by the mizen mast and I made both ships fast together in that situation, which by the action of the wind on the enemy's sails, forced her stern close to the Bon homme Richard's bow, so that the ships lay square alongside of each other, the yards being all entangled and the cannon of each ship touching the opponent's side.

" When this position took place it was eight o'clock, previous to which the Bon homme Richard had received sundry eighteen pounds shot below the water and leaked very much. My battery of 12-pounders, on which I had placed my chief dependance, being commanded by Lieut. Dale and Col. Weibert and manned principally with American seamen and French volunteers, were entirely silenced and abandoned. As to the six old 18-pounders that formed the battery of the lower gun-deck, they did no service whatever; two out of three of them burst at the first fire and killed almost all the men who were stationed to manage them. Before this time too, Col. De Chamillard, who commanded a party of twenty soldiers on the poop, had abandoned that station after having lost some of his men; these men deserted their quarters. I had now only two pieces of cannon, 9-pounders on the quarter deck, that were not silenced, and not one of the heavier cannon was fired during the rest of the action. The purser, Mr. Mease, who commanded the guns on the quarter deck, being dangerously wounded in the head, I was obliged to fill his place and with great difficulty rallied a few men and shifted over one of the lee quarter-deck guns, so that we afterwards played three pieces of 9-pounders upon the enemy. The tops alone seconded the fire of this little battery and held out bravely during the whole of the action, especially the main top where Lieut. Stack commanded. I directed the fire of one of the three cannon against the main-mast with double-headed shot, while the other two were exceedingly well served with grape and canister-shot to silence the enemy's musketry and clear her decks, which was at last effected.

"The enemy were, as I have since understood, on the instant of calling for quarters, when the cowardice or treachery of three of my under officers induced them to call to the enemy. The English commodore asked me if I demanded quarters and, I having answered him in the most determined negative, they renewed the battle with double fury. They were unable to stand the deck, but the fire of their cannon, especially the lower battery, which was entirely formed of 18-pounders, was incessant. Both ships were set on fire in various places and the scene was dreadful beyond the reach of language.

To account for the timidity of my three under officers, I mean the gunner, the carpenter, and the master-at-arms, I must observe that the two first were slightly wounded, and as the ship had received various shots under water, and one of the pumps being shot away, the carpenter expressed his fear that she would sink and the other two concluded that she was sinking, which occasioned the gunner to run aft on the poop, without my knowledge, to strike the colors. Fortunately for me, a cannon ball had done that before by carrying away the ensign-staff; he was therefore reduced to the necessity of sinking, as he supposed, or of calling for quarter and he preferred the latter.

" All this time the Bon homme Richard had sustained the action alone and the enemy, though much superior in force, would have been very glad to have got clear, as appears by their own acknowledgments and their having let go an anchor the instant that I laid them on board, by which means they would have escaped, had I not made them well fast to the Bon homme Richard. At last, at half past nine o'clock, the Alliance appeared and I now thought the battle at an end, but to my utter astonishment he discharged a broadside full into the stern of the Bon homme Richard. We called to him for God's sake to forbear firing into the Bon homme Richard, yet he passed along the off side of the ship and continued firing. There was no possibility of his mistaking the enemy's ship for the Bon homme Richard, there being the most essential difference in their appearance and construction; besides, it was then full moonlight and the sides of the Bon homme Richard were all black, while the sides of the prizes were yellow. Yet, for the greater security, I showed the signal of our reconnoissance by putting out three lanthorns, one at the head (bow), another at the stern (quarter), and the third in the middle, in a horizontal line. Every tongue cried that he was firing into the wrong ship, but nothing availed; he passed round firing into the Bon homme Richard's head, stern, and broadside, and by one of his vollies killed several of my best men and mortally wounded a good officer on the forecastle.

"My situation was really deplorable. The Bon homme Richard received various shots under water from the Alliance, the leak gained on the pumps, and the fire increased much on board both ships. Some officers persuaded me to strike, of whose courage and good sense I entertain a high opinion. My treacherous master-at-arms let loose all my prisoners without my knowledge and my prospect became gloomy indeed." The prisoners were much frightened, believing that the ship was sinking, and were at once put to work at the pumps; otherwise, by reinforcing the enemy, they would surely have turned the scale in his favor. "I would not, however, give up the point. The enemy's main-mast began to shake, their firing decreased, ours rather increased, and the British colors were struck at half an hour past ten o'clock." [1]

Lieutenant Dale, who was in command of the gun-deck, gives further details. He says that the Bonhomme Richard's first broadside was instantly returned by the Serapis. "Our position being to windward of the Serapis, we passed ahead of her and the Serapis coming up on our larboard [starboard?] quarter, the action commenced abreast of each other. The Serapis soon passed ahead of the Bon homme Richard and when he thought he had gained a distance sufficient to go down athwart the fore foot to rake us, found he had not enough distance and that the Bon homme Richard would be aboard him, put his helm a-lee, which brought the two ships on a line, and the Bon homme Richard having headway, ran her bows into the stern of the Serapis. . . . As we were unable to bring a single gun to bear upon the Serapis, our topsails were backed, while those of the Serapis being filled, the ships separated. The Serapis wore short round upon her heel and her jibboom ran into the mizen rigging of the Bon homme Richard; in this situation the ships were made fast together with a hawser, the bowsprit of the Serapis to the mizenmast of the Bon homme Richard, and the action recommenced

[1] *Sherburne*, 115–117 ; *Sands*, 181–186 ; *Mémoires de Paul Jones*, 76–104, which differs in details from the report of October 3 ; *MacKenzie*, i, ch. viii ; *Scribner's Magazine*, August, 1898, article by Captain Mahan ; *Jones MSS.*, September 24, 1779 ; *Log of Bonhomme Richard ; Independent Chronicle*, February 17, 1780.

from the starboard sides of the two ships. With a view of separating the ships, the Serapis let go her anchor, which manœuvre brought her head and the stern of the Bon homme Richard to the wind, while the ships lay closely pressed against each other. A novelty in naval combats was now presented to many witnesses, but to few admirers. The rammers were run into the respective ships to enable the men to load, after the lower ports of the Serapis had been blown away to make room for running out their guns. . . . Neither the repeated broadsides of the Alliance, given with the view of sinking or disabling the Bon homme Richard, the frequent necessity of suspending the combat to extinguish the flames which several times were within a few inches of the magazine, nor the liberation by the master-at-arms of nearly 500 prisoners,[1] could change or weaken the purpose of the American commander. At the moment of the liberation of the prisoners, one of them, a commander of a 20 gun ship taken a few days before, passed through the ports on board the Serapis and informed Captain Pearson that if he would hold out only a little while longer, the ship alongside would either strike or sink, and that all the prisoners had been released to save their lives."[2]

[1] As there were but four hundred and seventy-two prisoners altogether, after the cruise (*Pap. Cont., Congr.*, **193**, 211, December 16, 1779), there were probably less than two hundred on board the Bonhomme Richard at the time of the battle.

[2] *Sherburne*, 121, 122 ; *Sands*, 190–194. See also *Fanning*, 46–56.

Nathaniel Fanning, a midshipman on the Bon-homme Richard stationed in the maintop, says that the enemy's tops had been silenced within an hour, and it was not long after that before "the topmen in our tops had taken possession of the enemy's tops, which was done by reason of the Serapis's yards being locked together with ours, that we could with ease go from our main top into the enemy's fore top; and so on, from our fore top into the Serapis's main top. Having knowledge of this, we transported from our own into the enemy's tops, . . . hand granadoes, &c, which we threw in among the enemy whenever they made their appearance." [1] In the course of time the quarter-deck of the Serapis was entirely cleared, largely by this fire from the tops; and their execution extended below decks. In serving the main battery of the Serapis, many eighteen-pounder cartridges had accumulated on the gun-deck, which led to a catastrophe. Fanning says: " A single hand granado having been thrown by one of our men out of the main top of the enemy, designing it to go among the enemy who were huddled together between her gun decks, it on its way struck on one side of the combings of her upper hatch-way and rebounding from that, it took a direction and fell between their decks, where it communicated to a quantity of loose powder scattered about the enemy's cannon." The hand grenade, upon bursting, ignited the powder and the car-

[1] *Fanning*, 50.

tridges, the fire running from one to another, and
" made a dreadful explosion." [1] " The effect," says
Dale, " was tremendous; more than twenty of the
enemy were blown to pieces, and many stood with
only the collars of their shirts upon their bodies." [2]
This disaster doubtless hastened the end of the
battle.

In his report of October 6, 1779, to the British
Admiralty, Captain Pearson of the Serapis says,
" that on the 23d. ult. being close in with Scarborough, about eleven o'clock, a boat came on board
with a letter from the Bailiffs of that corporation,
giving information of a flying squadron of the enemy's ships being on the coast and of a part of the
said squadron having been seen from thence the
day before, standing to the southward. As soon as
I received this intelligence I made the signal for
the convoy to bear down under my lee and repeated
it with two guns; notwithstanding which, the van
of the convoy kept their wind, with all sail stretch-
ing out to the southward from under Flamborough
head, till between twelve and one, when the headmost
of them got sight of the enemy's ships, which were
then in chace of them. They then tacked and made
the best of their way under shore for Scarborough
&c., letting fly their top-gallant sheets and firing
guns; upon which I made all the sail I could to
windward, to get between the enemy's ships and
the convoy, which I soon effected. At one o'clock

[1] *Fanning*, 53.   [2] *Sherburne*, 122.

we got sight of the enemy's ships from the mast-
head and about four we made them plain from the
deck to be three large ships and a brig; upon which
I made the Countess of Scarborough's signal to join
me, she being in shore with the convoy. At the
same time I made the signal for the convoy to make
the best of their way. . . .

"At half past five, the Countess of Scarborough
joined me, the enemy's ships then bearing down
upon us with a light breeze at S. S. W. At six,
tacked and laid our head in shore, in order to keep
our ground the better between the enemy's ships
and the convoy, soon after which we perceived the
ships bearing down upon us to be a two-decked ship
and two frigates, but from their keeping end on
upon us, on bearing down, we could not discern what
colours they were under. At about 20 minutes past
seven, the largest ship of the three brought to on
our larboard bow, within musket shot. I hailed him
and asked what ship it was; they answered in
English, the Princess Royal. I then asked where
they belonged to; they answered evasively, on which
I told them, if they did not answer directly I would
fire into them. They then answered with a shot
which was instantly returned with a broadside, and
after exchanging two or three broadsides, he
backed his topsails and dropped upon our quarter
within pistol shot, then filled again, put his helm
a-weather, and run us on board upon our weather
quarter and attempted to board us, but being re-

pulsed he sheered off; upon which I backed our
topsails in order to get square with him again, which
as soon as he observed, he then filled, put his helm
a-weather and laid us athwart hawse. His mizen
shrouds took our jib boom, which hung him for
some time, till at last gave way and we dropt along
side of each other head and stern, when the fluke
of our spare anchor hooking his quarter, we became
so close fore and aft, that the muzzles of our guns
touched each others sides. In this position we engaged from half past eight till half past ten, during
which time, from the quantity and variety of com-
bustible matters which they threw in upon our decks,
chains, and in short into every part of the ship, we
were on fire not less than ten or twelve times in
different parts of the ship and it was with the
greatest difficulty and exertion imaginable at times
that we were able to get it extinguished. At the
same time the largest of the two frigates kept sailing round us the whole action and [raking] us fore
and aft, by which means she killed or wounded almost every man on the quarter and main decks.

" About half past nine, either from a hand grenade being thrown in at one of our lower deck ports,
or from some other accident, a cartridge of powder
was set on fire, the flames of which running from
cartridge to cartridge all the way aft, blew up the
whole of the people and officers that were quartered
abaft the main-mast, from which unfortunate circumstance all those guns were rendered useless for

the remainder of the action, and I fear the greatest part of the people will lose their lives. At ten o'clock, they called for quarters from the ship alongside and said they had struck. Hearing this, I called upon the Captain to know if they had struck, or if he asked for quarters, but no answer being made, after repeating my words two or three times, I called for the boarders and ordered them to board, which they did; but the moment they were on board her, they discovered a superior number laying under cover with pikes in their hands, ready to receive them; on which our people instantly retreated into our own ship and returned to their guns again until half past ten, when the frigate coming across our stern and pouring her broadside into us again, without our being able to bring a gun to bear on her, I found it in vain and in short impracticable, from the situation we were in, to stand out any longer with the least prospect of success. I therefore struck."[1]

The Bonhomme Richard carried eight nine-pounders on her quarter-deck and forecastle, twenty-eight twelve-pounders on the gun-deck and six eighteens on the lower deck. Her broadside weight of metal, therefore, was two hundred and fifty-eight pounds. The loss of her eighteens at the very outset at once reduced this to two hundred and four pounds. The Serapis was a fine, new, double decked ship, rated

---

[1] *Almon*, ix, 46; *Sherburne*, 124; *British Admiralty Records, Captains' Letters*, No. 2305.1 (October 6, 1779).

a forty-four, but carrying fifty guns : twenty eighteens on the lower gun-deck, twenty nines above,
and ten sixes on the quarter-deck and forecastle,
giving her a broadside of three hundred pounds to
the Richard's two hundred and four. This state-
ment, however, does not fully express her superiority, as heavy guns are far more effective in proportion than light ones ; that is to say, two eighteens
can do much more execution than three twelves.
The number of men on board the Bonhomme
Richard at the time of the battle, allowing for de-
sertions and those absent in prizes and in the two
boats of Henry and Cutting Lunt, was probably
not much over three hundred ; Jones makes it three
hundred and twenty-two and thinks that a further
deduction should be made on account of the men
blown up by the bursting of the eighteen-pounders
at the first fire.[1] The crew of the Serapis appears
to have been of very nearly the same size, but more
homogeneous and reliable in character. The number of casualties was very large in both ships.
Jones estimates his loss at a hundred and fifty
killed and wounded, without specifying the proportion of each.[2] Pearson states that the Serapis had
forty-nine killed and sixty-eight wounded, but that
the list is incomplete.[3] Both ships suffered severely.
" With respect to the situation of the Bon homme
Richard," says her commander, "the rudder was

[1] *Mem. de Paul Jones*, 97.   [2] *Sherburne*, 174.
[3] *Almon*, ix, 48.

cut entirely off the stern frame and the transums were almost entirely cut away; the timbers, by the lower deck especially, from the mainmast to the stern, being greatly decayed with age, were mangled beyond my power of description." Both sides of the ship for a great distance were wholly shot away, leaving little support for the upper deck, and projectiles passed through without hitting anything. Dead and wounded were lying in heaps. "A person must have been an eyewitness to form a just idea of the tremendous scene of carnage, wreck and ruin that everywhere appeared. Humanity cannot but recoil from the prospect of such finished horror and lament that war should produce such fatal consequences." [1] The mainmast and mizzen-topmast of the Serapis fell overboard immediately after her surrender and she was otherwise much injured.

It was Jones's indomitable determination not to yield that won this battle. Pearson, in surrendering to what he considered a superior force, did so before that force, through the added weight of the Alliance, had become more than a merely potential one. That the Serapis, moreover, so greatly superior in sailing qualities, so much more manageable, even with the disadvantage of her leeward position, should have allowed the clumsy Bonhomme Richard to get alongside and grapple her, does not indicate the best seamanship.

There seems to have been a prevalent belief in

[1] *Sherburne,* 117.

England just after the battle, expressed in a letter
of Lord North, that the Serapis succeeded in beating off the Bonhomme Richard and was then obliged
to strike to the Alliance.[1] It is certain that Pearson greatly exaggerated the part taken by Landais
in the engagement. It is established by the over-
whelming weight of testimony that the Alliance
fired just three broadsides, all of them after the two
chief contestants were lashed together; and that
these broadsides damaged the Bonhomme Richard
more than they did the Serapis. Many shot-holes
found on the port side of the Richard must have
been made by the fire of the Alliance, for that side
was never turned towards the Serapis. Many officers
of the squadron, both American and French, sus-
pected Landais of treachery, and according to their
testimony he admitted that he would have been
well pleased at the surrender of the Richard, which
would have given him an opportunity to enter the
contest, capture both ships and reap the glory.[2]

Meanwhile the Pallas and the Countess of Scarborough had fought an engagement. It was supposed on board the Bonhomme Richard at the time
that it was the Alliance that engaged the Scarborough.[3] Of this action Jones says in his report
of October 3 : " Captain Cottineau engaged the
Countess of Scarborough and took her after an
hour's action, while the Bon homme Richard en-

---

[1] *Stopford-Sackville MSS.*, 145.   [2] *Sherburne*, 156–171.
[3] *Log of the Bonhomme Richard.*

gaged the Serapis. The Countess of Scarborough is an armed ship of 20 six-pounders and was commanded by a King's officer. In the action the Countess of Scarborough and the Serapis were at a considerable distance asunder, and the Alliance, as I am informed, fired into the Pallas and killed some men. If it should be asked why the convoy was suffered to escape, I must answer that I was myself in no condition to pursue and that none of the rest showed any inclination, not even Mr. Ricot [in the Vengeance], who had held off at a distance to windward during the whole action. . . . The Alliance too was in a state to pursue the fleet, not having had a single man wounded or a single shot fired at her from the Serapis, and only three that did execution from the Countess of Scarborough at such a distance that one stuck in the side and the other two just touched and then dropped into the water. The Alliance killed one man only on board the Serapis. As Captain de Cottineau charged himself with manning and securing the prisoners of the Countess of Scarborough, I think the escape of the Baltic fleet cannot so well be charged to his account." [1]

Captain Piercy of the Countess of Scarborough, in his report to Captain Pearson, has left the only detailed account of the fight between his ship and the Pallas. "About two minutes," he says, "after you began to engage with the largest ships of the

[1] *Sherburne*, 119.

DENIS COTTINEAU

enemy's squadron, I received a broadside from one of the frigates, which I instantly returned and continued engaging her for about twenty minutes, when she dropt astern. I then made sail up to the Serapis, to see if I could give you any assistance, but upon coming near you I found you and the enemy so close together and covered with smoke that I could not distinguish one ship from the other; and for fear I might fire into the Serapis instead of the enemy, I backed the main-top-sail in order to engage the attention of one of the frigates that was then coming up. When she got on my starboard quarter she gave me her broadside, which, as soon as I could get my guns to bear (which was very soon done), I returned and continued engaging her for near two hours, when I was so unfortunate as to have all my braces, great part of the running rigging, main and mizen top-sail sheets shot away, seven of the guns dismounted, four men killed and twenty wounded, and another frigate coming up on my larboard quarter." Piercy then surrendered.[1]

Captains Pearson and Piercy were subsequently tried by a court martial, the verdict of which was that they and their officers and men " have not only acquitted themselves of their duty to their country, but have in the execution of such duty done infinite credit to themselves by a very obstinate defence against a superior force." [2]

[1] *Almon*, ix, 48.
[2] *Brit. Adm. Rec., Courts Martial*, No. 5315 (March 10, 1780).

These contests attracted much attention on shore and many spectators viewed the scene from Flamborough Head and Scarborough. Bright moonlight made objects visible at a distance and the spectacle must have been impressive. A letter from Scarborough says: " Soon after our arrival on Thursday evening we were told there was an engagement at sea; I immediately threw up the sash of the room I was in and we had a fair view of the engagement, which appeared very severe, for the firing was frequently so quick that we could scarce count the shots." [1]

After the battle the Bonhomme Richard was on fire in several places and was leaking rapidly. There was five feet of water in the hold, one pump had been shot away, and the three others were barely able to keep the water from gaining, in a smooth sea. "The fire broke out in various parts of the ship," says Jones, "in spite of all the water that could be thrown to quench it and at length broke out as low as the powder magazine and within a few inches of the powder. In that dilemma I took out the powder upon deck, ready to be thrown overboard at the last extremity, and it was 10 o'clock the next day, the 24th, before the fire was entirely extinguished. . . . After the carpenters, as well as Capt. de Cottineau and other men of sense, had well examined and surveyed the ship (which was not finished before five in the evening), I found

[1] *London Chronicle*, September 30, 1779. See also *Hist. Man. Com.*, Report xiv, App. i, 21.

every person to be convinced that it was impossible
to keep the Bon homme Richard afloat so as to
reach a port if the wind should increase, it being
then only a moderate breeze. I had but little time
to remove my wounded, which now became unavoidable and which was effected in the course of the night
and next morning. I was determined to keep the
Bon homme Richard afloat and if possible to bring
her into port. For that purpose the first lieutenant
of the Pallas continued on board with a party of
men to attend the pumps, with boats in waiting
ready to take them on board in case the water
should gain on them too fast. The wind augmented
in the night and the next day, on the 25th, so that
it was impossible to prevent the good old ship from
sinking. They did not abandon her till after 9
o'clock; the water was then up to the lower deck
and a little after ten I saw with inexpressible grief
the last glimpse of the Bon homme Richard. No
lives were lost with the ship, but it was impossible
to save the stores of any sort whatever. I lost even
the best part of my clothes, books and papers; and
several of my officers lost all their clothes and
effects."[1]

Just after the action seven Englishmen of the
Richard's crew stole a boat from the Serapis and
escaped ashore, where they gave an account of the
cruise and battle and of Jones's intentions as they

[1] *Sherburne*, 117, 118; *Sands*, 186-189. See *Fanning*, 61, for a
description of the sinking of the Bonhomme Richard.

understood them.[1] The eye-witness at Scarborough says that the day after the engagement "six sail were seen about two leagues off at sea, much shattered, one of which, a large ship, had lost her mainmast; they kept their station all that day. Yesterday morning [September 25] they were gone to the northward, as is supposed, for the wind would not suit for any other quarter."[2] They had apparently drifted off before the wind, as they were not yet in a condition to make sail.

The situation of the squadron on the British coast was becoming dangerous, and yet before flight was possible a vast amount of work was to be done in repairing the injuries to the Serapis sufficiently to make her seaworthy. Jones took command of her when the Bonhomme Richard sank and after strenuous exertions, at 1 A.M. September 28, according to her journal, "Gott up a Jury Main Mast." By evening the squadron was ready to sail and the commodore signalled to stand to the westward, and a few hours later, to the eastward. Meanwhile on the very day of the battle Admiral Hardy, commanding the Channel fleet, who had received orders to send a strong force in search of the American squadron, dispatched five ships on that duty.[3] A letter from Bridlington, September 24, says that in the opinion of the sailors who had

[1] *London Chronicle*, September, 28, 30, 1779; *Boston Gazette*, January 3, 1780.

[2] *London Chronicle*, September 30, 1779.

[3] *Brit. Adm. Rec., A. D. 95*, September 23, 1779.

escaped ashore " Jones's plan was to destroy Scarborough, Bridlington and Hull, with some other places; and that he intended landing at Flamborough yesterday morning, but the sea ran too high." [1] It was reported from Hull, September 26, that the squadron was still visible from Flamborough Head that morning steering north, and that it was scarcely out of sight when four British vessels appeared in pursuit.[2] The correspondent who had been watching events from Scarborough says that on the same morning " eight of our ships of war appeared in sight, and which are gone in search of Jones."

The state of mind along the east coast of England at the time is reflected in a letter of the Marquis of Rockingham, written to Lord Weymouth September 28. Speaking of the defenses of Hull he says: " I shall not hesitate to say that from an Attack by Frigates or Ships of War it was entirely without defence; the Artillery in the Fort — its only defence — were unserviceable both from the Carriages being entirely rotten and also from most of the Guns which carried any Weight of Metal being honeycombed and dangerous to Use. . . . A ship of 60 Guns can lay, even at low Water, within less than 400 Yards of the Town. In Paul Jones's Squadron the largest Vessel was a 40 Gun Ship, so that whatever Force he had could have come up. It appeared to me that not only from the Information

[1] *London Chronicle*, September 30, 1779.   [2] *Ibid.*   [3] *Ibid.*

of a Man who had been put by Paul Jones into a prize and who had assisted very principally in securing the men and bringing her in with the Assistance of a Hull Pilot, but also from the Size and Number of Ships in Paul Jones's Squadron, that there could not be any Number of Soldiers or Marines on Board," or that any force could be landed which could not be repelled by the militia of the neighborhood, insuring the safety of Hull and its shipping. "I conceived very differently in regard to an attempt being made by the Squadron coming up Humber. I therefore pressed as much as I possibly could that every Effort should be made to prepare Batteries and get what Artillery could be had. . . . At the Meeting on Friday Morning Intelligence came that the Serapis and Countess of Scarborough had been seen shortening sail, covering the Baltic Fleet and waiting for Paul Jones"; and later "that the Engagement was begun, but it growing dark, the Event of a very Warm Action was not known. . . . The Unfortunate Event of their being Captured after a most Severe Engagement came to our Knowledge at Hull on Friday Evening, when the Mayor immediately called a Meeting, and at which the Proposition of preparing Batteries was unanimously adopted." [1]

The British ships in search of Jones did not find him, although he was " tossing about to and fro in the North Sea for ten days in contrary winds and

[1] *Amer. Hist. Review*, April, 1910.

bad weather, in order to gain the port of Dunkirk, on account of the prisoners." Notwithstanding the instructions governing the cruise named the Texel as the port of destination, Jones wished to put into Dunkirk, so as to place his prizes and prisoners at once under French jurisdiction, and it would have saved him much annoyance had this been possible. The other captains, however, insisted upon carrying out the letter of the instructions and bore away for the Texel. Jones was forced to follow or to proceed alone to Dunkirk and he chose the former alternative. The squadron anchored off the Texel October 3, 1779.[1]

The commodore spent nearly three months at the Texel refitting his ships and then waiting for an opportunity to get away, being blockaded by a British squadron cruising outside. The purpose of the French Minister of Marine in making the Texel the objective point of the cruise was that a convoy might be furnished for a number of vessels loaded with naval and military stores which it was desired to bring to France. Also it was hoped that the Indien might be taken into a French port, and the French ambassador to Holland, to whom Jones reported on his arrival, wished to obtain from the Dutch government authority for the sale of the ship to some merchant who could place her under a

---

[1] *Sands*, 200; *Sherburne*, 120. *Fanning*, 64–66, says they were chased into the Texel by a British squadron, which remained outside the bar.

neutral flag. Nothing of this sort, however, was accomplished, and the only useful purpose served by the presence of the squadron in neutral waters was increasing the estrangement between England and Holland which ultimately led to war, manifestly to the advantage of the United States. If Jones could have gone directly to the French port of Dunkirk, much vexation and embarrassment would have been saved and he could readily have disposed of his prizes and prisoners. The British ambassador at the Hague, upon the arrival of the squadron, made a vehement protest to the Dutch government, and demanded " that these ships and their crews may be stopped and delivered up, which the pirate Paul Jones of Scotland, who is a rebel subject and criminal of the state, has taken."[1] The Dutch, however, moved slowly in the matter and refused to commit themselves as to the legality of the captures. Jones was allowed time to refit his ships and was permitted to land his wounded, so that they might be cared for in a fort which was placed at his disposal. He entered into an agreement with Captain Pearson, according to which the wounded prisoners were to be guarded and cared for at the expense of the United States and later exchanged for Americans.[2]

In consequence of the charges against him Cap-

[1] *Sherburne*, 129.
[2] *Ibid.*, 128–133, 174; *Sands*, 200–218; *Wharton*, iii, 356, 397; *Archives de la Marine*, B[1] 91, 188, B[4] 158, 175.

tain Landais was ordered back to Paris by Franklin,
October 15. With respect to these charges, twenty-
five in number, and formally drawn up October 30,
there was a practical unanimity of opinion among
the officers of the squadron as to the reprehensible
conduct of Landais during the cruise. Four officers
of the Alliance, including the first lieutenant, attested that several people on board that ship " told
Captain Landais at different times that he fired
upon the wrong ship; others refused to fire." [1]
Sometime after the departure of Landais, Jones
took command of the Alliance, all the other vessels
having been put under the French flag to avoid
complications with Holland. Arrangements were
made for the exchange of prisoners and the disposal of prizes. The squadron had taken more than
enough prisoners to procure the release by exchange
of all the Americans confined in England. The
plan adopted was to exchange Jones's prisoners for
French at the Texel, France agreeing to give the
same number of English in France for the Americans in England. Jones was offered a French commission, which would further have facilitated matters,
but he resolutely refused it and saved the Alliance
from being also placed under the French flag. His
situation was daily growing more uncomfortable,
as the Dutch were unwilling longer to disregard
the importunity of the British ambassador. He
was at last peremptorily ordered by the Dutch ad-

[1] *Sherburne*, 156–171.

miral to depart with the first favorable wind. He
was ready to sail December 1, and then waited
nearly four weeks for an opportunity. On the 13th,
he wrote to Franklin: "We hear that the enemy
still keeps a squadron cruising off here, but this
shall not prevent my attempts to depart whenever
the wind will permit. I hope we have recovered
the trim of this ship, which was entirely lost during
the last cruise, and I do not much fear the enemy
in the long and dark nights of this season. The
ship is well manned and shall not be given away.
I need not tell you I will do my utmost to take
prisoners and prizes in my way from hence." [1]
About this time Captain Conyngham, who had escaped from prison in England and had crossed over
to Holland, [2] came aboard the Alliance. At last,
with a favoring east wind, the ship got away from
the Texel December 27, 1779, and succeeded in
running the blockade of the British squadron outside. [3]

With her best American colors flying, the Alliance "passed along the Flemish banks and getting
to windward of the enemy's fleets of observation in
the North Sea," ran through the Straits of Dover
in full view of the British fleet in the Downs.
During the night of December 28 several vessels

[1] *Sands*, 239; *Wharton*, iii, 425.

[2] See above, p. 377.

[3] *Sands*, 218–243; *Sherburne*, 145–152, 174–184, 219; *Wharton*,
iii, 378, 379, 424, 425, 430, 431, 535; *Archives de la Marine*, B[4]
172, 140.

were seen and the next morning the frigate passed
" the Isle of Wight, in view of the enemy's fleet
at Spithead, and in two days more got safe through
the channel, having passed by windward in sight
of several of the enemy's large two-decked cruising
ships." [1] Jones then cruised a week or more to the
southward and off Cape Finisterre. January 8, 1780,
he captured a brig which he sent to America. He
went into Coruna January 16, where he was well
received by the Spanish. Conyngham left the Alliance here and joined a ship bound to America.
Jones sailed again, January 28, for another cruise
off Cape Finisterre, but meeting with no success,
put into Groix Roads February 10. At L'Orient,
Jones found the Serapis awaiting condemnation.
She and the Countess of Scarborough and Pallas
had gone from the Texel to Dunkirk, whence the
Serapis had proceeded to L'Orient. She was eventually sold there, and the Countess of Scarborough
at Dunkirk. [2]

The situation of the United States respecting
naval conditions at the end of 1779 was relatively
better than in the two previous years ; the falling-
off was proportionately less. The heavy annual loss

---

[1] *Sands*, 243, 244.
[2] *Sherburne*, 184–190, 219 ; *Fanning*, 76–79 ; *Log of the Alliance ;
Penn. Mag. Hist. and Biogr.*, January, 1899 ; *Jones MSS.*, February
10, 12, 1780, Jones to Gourlade & Moylan and to Franklin ;
Archives de la Marine, B[1] **93**, 33, 36, 97, 99, B[4] **172**, 145, 152, B[8]
16 (Janvier, 1780).

in frigates was less heavy; there were fewer frigates to lose, and the Warren was the only one
dropped from the list. The loss of the sloop Providence was keenly felt because of her very useful
and successful career. Other small vessels that
passed away were the sloop of war General Gates,
the brig Diligent, the cutter Revenge and the sloop
Argo. Of the original thirteen frigates there still
remained the Providence, Trumbull, and Boston;
the Trumbull had at last made her escape from the
Connecticut River, but was not yet ready for sea.
The Deane, Queen of France, and Ranger also remained; and two prime thirty-two-gun frigates, the
Alliance and Confederacy, first went into active
service in 1779. Vessels still under construction
were slowly progressing towards completion. The
four vessels fitted out in France to cruise under the
American flag were for temporary service only. Unfortunately the prize ship Serapis was not procured
for the Continental navy; no money was available
for her purchase. The achievements of the navy
during the year were gratifying. The several successful cruises in American waters and the brilliant
exploits of Jones added reputation to the service.
The Penobscot expedition was chiefly a local affair
and the gloom produced by the disaster did not,
in its full intensity at least, overspread the whole
country.

In 1779, privateering played a still more important part in naval warfare than before. Two hun-

dred and nine commissions were granted by the Continental Congress to private armed vessels, eighty more than the number of the previous year. The enterprise of the separate states also in this mode of sea-service continued to develop and increase. Greater activity was likewise displayed by the English. From August, 1778, to April, 1779, one hundred privateers were fitted out in Liverpool, aggregating more than twenty-four thousand tons, mounting sixteen hundred and fifty guns and with crews numbering more than seventy-four hundred men. A list of British privateers fitted out at New York, published in April, comprised one hundred and twenty-one vessels, including two of thirty-six guns each, one thirty, one twenty-eight, and thirty others of twenty or more guns, the whole manned by about ninety-six hundred men. Another list, compiled for Admiral Gambier, February 27, " of Private Ships and Vessels of War belonging to the Port of New York, now at Sea," contains sixty-nine names. Many American vessels were taken by these privateers, of which, however, many in turn were captured.[1]

During the year 1779, the British navy increased, in the total number of ships, from four hundred and thirty-two to four hundred and eighty-one; ships

[1] *Naval Records* (calendar), 217–495, list of Continental letters of marque; *London Chronicle*, April 1, 29, 1779; *Massachusetts Spy*, April 29, June 3, 1779; *Boston Post*, March 13, 27, 1779; *Brit. Adm. Rec.*, *A. D. 489*, February 27, 1779. The first New York list is presumably the same as that cited on p. 364.

in commission, from three hundred and seventeen to three hundred and sixty-four. Seventy thousand men manned the navy. On the North American station a smaller fleet was maintained than during the two preceding years. With enemies on the continent of Europe to provide against, a larger part of the naval force was kept at home or employed in other seas. Only about sixty vessels were stationed in North America and less than half of these were frigates or larger ships. A powerful fleet was held in the West Indies.[1]

It is stated that in 1779, five hundred and sixteen vessels, of which twenty-nine were privateers and the others merchantmen, were captured from the British by their enemies; how many of them by Americans does not appear. One hundred and eleven of these were retaken or ransomed. During the same time the British took two hundred and sixty-nine vessels from their enemies, of which thirty-one were privateers, and five were recaptured.[2] Other lists cover too short a period of time to be of value and presumably have been included in the above compilation.[3] The Continental navy captured forty-four vessels, including three regular men-of-war and several privateers, letters of marque, and armed transports.[4]

[1] Hannay, 211; Schomberg, i, 453; Almon, viii, 314, 315, Brit. Adm. Rec., A. D. 489, April 3, A. D. 486, August 30, 1779, lists of ships employed under Admirals Gambier and Arbuthnot.

[2] Clowes, iii, 396.   [3] Almon, ix, 343, 350, 351, 354, 358.

[4] Neeser, ii, 28, 30, 288.

CHAPTER XIV

SOUTH CAROLINA and Georgia, far from the seat
of the Continental government and from the head-
quarters of the army, were peculiarly exposed to
attack, yet for more than two years after the unsuccessful attempt of the British to take Charleston in 1776, they were not seriously menaced. In
December, 1778, however, the English got possession of Savannah, and during the next year they
determined upon another effort to capture the
whole lower South. Admiral D'Estaing spent more
than half of 1779 in the West Indies, where, with
the exception of the conquest of Grenada, he reaped
little glory in his encounters with the British. Up
to this time the actual assistance he had rendered
to the American cause was slight and there was
general dissatisfaction with the meagre results thus
far derived from the French alliance. D'Estaing's
aid being now requested in frustrating the British
designs on the South, he appeared off the coast of
Georgia, September 1, 1779, with a powerful fleet,
although he had been ordered back to France, and
joined General Lincoln in an attempt to recapture
Savannah. Through delay, however, the opportunity
was lost and their assault when made was unsuc-

cessful. D'Estaing then sailed for France and Lincoln fell back on Charleston. General Clinton sailed from New York for South Carolina late in December, 1779.[1]

The full extent of the benefit derived from the French alliance was not appreciated at that early day in America. Its effect on the British imagination and the potential weight of the French fleet, its mere presence on the ocean, were not inconsiderable. An intercepted letter from General Clinton to Lord George Germain, dated Savannah, January 30, 1780, captured on a British packet by an American privateer, gives a view of the military situation as seen by English eyes and discloses a state of mind not free from apprehension. Clinton seems to have been impressed by the strength of Washington's army and of its position and devoted his energies before going South to strengthening the defenses of New York. " The violent demonstrations of the rebels," he wrote, " which threatened a determined attack on the post at New York in conjunction with a large naval and land armament under Count d'Estaing, then directing itself against the garrison at Savannah, necessarily turned our whole endeavours to defeat so alarming a combination. . . . Not a moment was to be lost in such a critical conjuncture, for every moment was import-

[1] *Mahan*, 365–376; *Narr. and Crit. Hist.*, vi, 519–524; *Stevens*, 1203, 1238, 1246, 1247, 2010, 2011, 2023; *Almon*, vii, 244–248, viii, 182, 298, ix, 65; *Stopford-Sackville MSS.*, 146–149; *Channing*, iii, 300.

ant and expected to come with the account of d'Estaing's appearance before our harbour." Washington not only had a superior position in the Highlands, but likewise along the shore to the east, where "every advantage of water was also in his power by the Sound and, under protection of the French fleet, exposed us to the most perplexing embarrassments. Assailable in so many points and every instant expecting d'Estaing, we had but time to look towards and take measures for our own defence and the occasion required us to put forward our best exertions. I do not reckon among the lesser misfortunes of the last year the operations of d'Estaing on the American coast, the vast relief thereby given to the Rebel trade and the injury which it brought upon our's, the impression it carried home to the minds of the people, of our lost dominion of the sea, and the disposition of the French to give them every assistance reconcileable with the general objects of the war, to compleat our ruin on the Continent." [1]

Commodore Whipple's squadron, consisting of the frigates Providence, Boston, and Queen of France, and the Ranger, arrived at Charleston December 23, 1779. An officer of the Providence wrote home: " On our arrival here we found our designs against the enemy frustrated, as they had not attempted nor is it probable they will attempt any-

[1] *Almon*, x, 36, 37, reprinted from *Pennsylvania Journal*, April 8, 1780. See *Channing*, iii, 300, 301.

thing against this town this season." This was written January 8, 1780. Three days later he added: " Since writing the above, we have received an account that the enemy are building flat boats and making preparations for another expedition against this town, which they say is to commence as soon as their reinforcement arrives from New-York. If they should attempt it, I believe it will terminate as much to their dishonour as their cause and actions deserve, as the town and river are well fortified." [1] January 24, the Providence and Ranger went to sea for a short cruise. The same officer says: "On our way to Tybee in Georgia we captured 3 transports, a brig of 14 guns and two armed sloops, which were loaded with cloathing, some military stores, a few infantry, about forty light dragoons of Lord Cathcart's legion, 7 or 8 officers, as many passengers, two horses, and military furniture for forty others, which they were obliged to throw overboard in some heavy gales on their passage. By these vessels we learn that 140 sail left New-York about 4 weeks before, under convoy of 6 or 7 ships of the line and several frigates, with troops destined for Savannah. Then we proceeded to Tybee, at the bar of which we saw a very considerable number of ships at anchor (five of them appeared to be above 36 guns) and a variety of smaller vessels, &c. The object of our voyage was to take some of their transports, that we might

[1] *Independent Chronicle*, February 24, 1780.

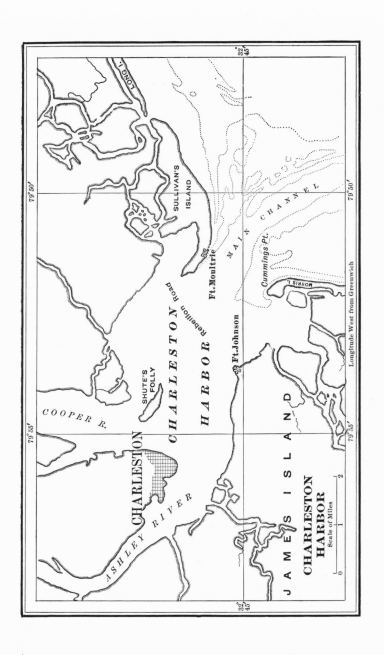

CHARLESTON HARBOR

Scale of Miles

0   1   2

gain intelligence of their strength and make what discoveries we could with respect to their situation at Tybee; this being done we returned on Thursday [January 27]. The force of the enemy must be great, considering the number of vessels employed to transport them. Some say that Sir Henry Clinton commands in person, others Lord Cornwallis. Let it be who it may, I believe we shall have a pretty serious affair of it. There can be no doubt but their intention is to carry this town." [1]

General Lincoln had about four thousand men at Charleston and the defenses of the city were strengthened as far as possible. General Clinton landed, February 11, south of the town and advanced upon it and invested it on the land side with ten thousand troops, while a British fleet under Admiral Arbuthnot, consisting of one fifty-gun ship, two forty-fours, and four thirty-twos, with smaller vessels, lay outside. On account of shallow water inside the bar, there was no practicable anchorage from which the American vessels could operate to advantage in defense of the channel and dispute the passage of the bar by the British. To inquiries of General Lincoln on this point a board of three naval captains and five pilots replied, February 27, that there was no anchorage within three miles of the bar. " In the place where the ships can be anchored, the bar cannot be covered or annoyed. . . . Our opinion is that the ships can do most effectual

[1] *Independent Chronicle*, April 6, 1780.

service for the defence and security of the town, to act in conjunction with Fort Moultrie, which we think will best answer the purpose of the ships being sent here. . . . Our reasons are that the channel is so narrow between the fort and the middle ground, that they may be moored so as to rake the channel and prevent the enemy's troops being landed to annoy the fort."[1] The sinking of hulks or other obstructions in this narrow part of the channel was apparently not attempted. The Americans destroyed the lighthouse and ranges; also Fort Johnson, on the south side of the harbor, to prevent its falling into the hands of the enemy. This work was done by Captain Tucker of the Boston. In addition to the Continental ships the South Carolina navy furnished four vessels for the defense of Charleston, two of which, the Bricole, 44, and the Truite, 26, had been purchased from France; the other two were the General Moultrie, 20, and the Notre Dame, 16. Two French ships in the harbor, L'Aventure, 26, and Polacre, 16, also took part.

In his report of May 14 to the British Admiralty, after telling of landing the army, Admiral Arbuthnot says: " Preparations were next made for passing the squadron over Charles-town bar, where [at] high water spring tides there is only nineteen feet water. The guns, provision and water were taken out of the Renown, Roebuck, and Romulus, to lighten them, and we lay in that situation on the

[1] *Tucker*, 132–134.

open coast in the winter season of the year, exposed
to the insults of the enemy for sixteen days, before
an opportunity offered of going into the harbour,
which was effected without any accident on the 20th
of March, notwithstanding the enemy's galleys con-
tinually attempted to prevent our boats from sound-
ing the channel. . . . The rebel naval force . . .
made an appearance of disputing the passage up
the river at the narrow pass between Sullivan's
island and the middle ground, having moored their
ships and galleys in a position to make a raking
fire as we approached Fort Moultrie, but on the
squadron arriving near the bar and anchoring on
the inside, they abandoned that idea, retired to the
town, and changed their plan of defence. The Bricole, Notre Dame, Queen of France, Truite and
General Moultrie frigates, with several merchant
ships, fitted with chevaux de frize on their decks,
were sunk in the channel [of the Cooper River]
between the town and Shute's Folly; a boom was
extended across, composed of cables, chains and
spars, secured by the ship's masts, and defended
from the town by strong batteries of pimento logs,
in which were mounted upwards of forty pieces of
heavy cannon. . . . As soon as the army began to
erect their batteries against the town I took the first
favourable opportunity to pass Sullivan's Island,
upon which there is a strong fort and batteries, the
chief defence of the harbour ; accordingly I weighed
at one o'clock on the 9th [of April] with the Roe-

buck, Richmond, Romulus, Blonde, Virginia, Ra-
leigh, and Sandwich armed ship, the Renown bringing up the rear, and passing through a severe fire,
anchored in about two hours under James Island,
with the loss of twenty-seven seamen killed and
wounded." The total loss of the British fleet during the operations about Charleston was twenty-
three killed and twenty-eight wounded. " The Richmond's foretop-mast was shot away and the ships
in general sustained damage in their masts and rigging; however, not materially in their hulls. But
the Acetus transport, having on board a few naval
stores, grounded within gun-shot of Sullivan's Island and received so much damage that she was
obliged to be abandoned and burnt." [1]

To prevent the British passing up the Cooper
River the Americans sunk eleven vessels, including
those mentioned in Arbuthnot's report. Possibly
these vessels, or others less valuable than some of
them, might have been sunk to better advantage in
the channel below Fort Moultrie, before the British
crossed the bar. It might also with some reason
be maintained that the squadron should have made
a more vigorous defense of the channel at that
point in conjunction with the fort; when by a lucky
chance a few broadsides might have been able to
cripple one or more of the British ships while they
were passing through the narrowest places under
a raking fire and in a disadvantageous position.

[1] *Almon*, x, 45, 46.

Instead of that, the Americans retired up the river, which they attempted to block. The Ranger and two galleys were stationed above the obstructions while the guns and crews of the other naval vessels were sent ashore to reinforce the batteries. The British lines gradually drew closer to the town and American batteries on the north side of the Cooper River were taken. A bombardment began April 12. A few entries in the log of the Ranger tell the story of the closing days of the siege. April 15 : " Enemy Kept up A Constant Cannonading." May 7 : " At 6 A.M. we could plainly discover that Our people had Evacuated Fort Moultrie & that the enemy had taken Possession of it ; at 7 they hoisted their flag on it." May 8 : " This morning the Enemy sent in a Flag of truce, Which Caused a Total cessation of arms." May 9 : " At 9 P.M. the enemy began A most Desperate Cannonading, Throwing Shells, and firing of small arms, [which] Continued all night, with very little loss on our side." May 10 : " The enemy still Keeping A constant firing of Cannon, Throwing of Shells, Carcases, &c." Here the record abruptly ends. Lincoln capitulated May 11 and Whipple's squadron fell into the hands of the enemy. The Providence, Boston, and Ranger were taken into the British service, the two latter under the names Charlestown and Halifax. The officers were paroled and sent to Philadelphia.[1]

[1] *Tucker*, ch. vii ; *Almon*, **x**, 38–53 ; *Andrew Sherburne*, 26–29 ; *Log*

The frigate Trumbull, which was launched in 1776, remained in the Connecticut River where she was built until 1779, unable to pass over the bar at the mouth of the river. It is said that at the suggestion of Captain Hinman she was finally floated over by means of a number of casks full of water placed along her sides, held together by ropes passing under the keel and then pumped out, which lifted the ship sufficiently to carry her over the bar. She was taken to New London and fitted for sea. Meanwhile another frigate, the Bourbon, was being built on the Connecticut River. It was hoped that she would soon be at sea and Captain Thomas Read was ordered to command her, but for lack of money it was necessary to suspend work on her and she was not finished in time to take part in the war. Captain James Nicholson was appointed to command the Trumbull, September 20, 1779, but it was not until April 17, 1780, that cruising orders were sent to him. The Board of Admiralty, which had succeeded the Marine Committee in the administration of naval affairs, intended that the Trumbull should cruise in company with other Continental ships, but not with privateers; of such joint expeditions the board disapproved. Meanwhile,

of the Ranger; Stopford-Sackville MSS., 162 (Arbuthnot to Germain, May 15, 1780); *Penn. Mag. Hist. and Biogr.*, April, 1891, Journal of Lieutenant Jennison; *Mar. Com. Letter Book*, 263, 264 (February 22, 1780); *Boston Gazette*, April 17, July 10, 1780; *Independent Chronicle*, May 11, 1780; *Dawson*, ch. lix; *Narr. and Crit. Hist.*, vi, 524–527; *Channing*, iii, 317, 318.

JAMES NICHOLSON

apparently awaiting an opportunity to get a number of vessels together, the orders of April 17 were repeated May 22 ; they prescribed a cruise for the Trumbull alone until the end of June.[1]

The Trumbull sailed from New London late in May and had not been long at sea when she fell in with the British letter of marque Watt and was soon engaged in one of the hardest-fought naval actions of the war. In Nicholson's account of the battle he says : " At half past ten in the morning of June [1st], lat. 35. N. long. 64 W. we discovered a sail from the mast-head and immediately handed all our sails, in order to keep ourselves undiscovered until she came nearer to us, she being to windward. At eleven we made her to be a large ship from the deck, coming down about three points upon our quarter ; at half past eleven we thought she hauled a point more astern of us. We therefore made sail and hauled upon a wind towards her, upon which she came right down upon our beams ; we then took in our small sails, hauled the courses up, hove the maintop-sail to the mast, got all clear for action, and waited for her.

" At half past eleven we filled the main-top (the ship being then about gun-shot to windward of us) in order to try her sailing, also that by her hauling up after us we might have an opportunity of dis-

[1] *Papers New London Hist. Soc.*, IV, i, 47 ; *Mar. Com. Letter Book*, 238, 240, 241, 243, 252, 274, 276, 280, 285, 288 (September 20, October 6, 12, 21, December 18, 1779, April 7, 11, 17, May, 12, 22, 23, 1780).

covering her broadside. She immediately got her main tack out and stood after us; we then observed she had thirteen ports of a side, exclusive of her briddle ports, and eight or ten on her quarter deck and forecastle. After a very short exhortation to my people they most chearfully agreed to fight her; at twelve we found we greatly outsailed her and got to windward of her; we therefore determined to take that advantage. Upon her observing our intention she edged away, fired three shot at us and hoisted British colours as a challenge; we immediately wore after her and hoisted British colours also. This we did in order to get peaceably alongside of her, upon which she made us a private signal and upon our not answering it she gave us the first broadside, we then being under British colours and about one hundred yards distant. We immediately hoisted the Continental colours and returned her a broadside, then about eighty yards distance, when a furious and close action commenced and continued for five glasses, no time of which we were more than eighty yards asunder and the greater part of the time not above fifty; at one time our yard-arms were almost enlocked. She set us twice on fire with her wads, as we did her once; she had difficulty in extinguishing her's, being obliged to cut all her larboard quarter nettings away.

"At the expiration of the above time my first Lieutenant, after consulting and agreeing with the second, came aft to me and desired I would observe

the situation of our masts and rigging, which were
going over the side; therefore begged I would quit
her before that happened, otherwise we should certainly be taken.   I therefore most unwillingly left
her, by standing on the same course we engaged
on; I say unwillingly, as I am confident if our masts
would have admitted of our laying half an hour
longer alongside of her, she would have struck to
us, her fire having almost ceased and her pumps
both going.   Upon our going ahead of her she steered
about four points away from us.   When about mus-
quet shot asunder, we lost our main and mizen topmast and in spite of all our efforts we continued
losing our masts until we had not one left but the
foremast and that very badly wounded and sprung.
Before night shut in we saw her lose her maintop-
mast.   I was in hopes when I left her of being able
to renew the action after securing my mast, but
upon inquiry found so many of my people killed
and wounded and my ship so much of a wreck in
her masts and rigging, that it was impossible.   We
lost eight killed and thirty one wounded; amongst
the former was one lieutenant, one midshipman, one
serjeant of marines, and one quarter gunner;
amongst the latter was one lieutenant, since dead,
the captain of marines, the purser, the boatswain,
two midshipmen, the cockswain, and my clerk, the
rest were common men, nine of which in the whole
are since dead.   No people shewed more true spirit
and gallantry than mine did; I had but one hun-

dred and ninety-nine men when the action commenced, almost the whole of which, exclusive of the
officers, were green country lads, many of them not
clear of their sea-sickness, and I am well persuaded
they suffered more in seeing the masts carried away
than they did in the engagement.

"We plainly perceived the enemy throw many
of his men overboard in the action, two in particular which were not quite dead; from the frequent
cries of his wounded and the appearance of his hull,
I am convinced he must have lost many more men
than we did and suffered more in his hull. Our
damage was most remarkable and unfortunate in
our masts and rigging, which I must again say alone
saved him; for the last half hour of the action I
momently expected to see his colours down, but am
of opinion he persevered from the appearance of
our masts. You will perhaps conclude from the
above that she was a British man of war, but I beg
leave to assure you that it was not then, nor is it
now my opinion; she appeared to me like a French
East-Indiaman cut down. She fought a greater
number of marines and more men in her tops than
we did, the whole of which we either killed or drove
below. She dismounted two of our guns and silenced
two more; she fought four or six and thirty twelve
pounders, we fought twenty-four twelve and six
sixes. I beg leave to assure you that let her be what
she would, either letter of marque or privateer, I
give you my honour that was I to have my choice

tomorrow, I would sooner fight any two-and-thirty
gun frigate they have on the coast of America, than
to fight that ship over again; not that I mean to
degrade the British men of war, far be it from me,
but I think she was more formidable and was better
manned than they are in general."[1]

Some further details are given in a letter of Gilbert Saltonstall, captain of marines on the Trumbull. "As soon as she discovered us she bore down
for us. We got ready for action, at one o'clock began to engage, and continued without the least intermission for five glasses, within pistol shot. It is
beyond my power to give an adequate idea of the
carnage, slaughter, havock and destruction that ensued. Let your imagination do its best, it will fall
short. We were literally cut all to pieces; not a
shroud, stay, brace, bowling or any other of our
rigging standing. Our main top-mast shot away, our
fore, main, mizen, and jigger masts gone by the
board, two of our quarter-deck guns disabled, thro'
our ensign 62 shot, our mizen 157, main-sail 560,
foresail 180, our other sails in proportion. Not a
yard in the ship but received one or more shot, six
shot through her quarter above the quarter deck,
four in the waste, our quarter, stern, and nettings
full of langrage, grape and musket ball. We suffered more than we otherwise should on account of
the ship that engaged us being a very dull sailer.
Our ship being out of command, she kept on our

[1] *Almon*, x, 225–227.

starboard quarter the latter part of the engagement. After two and a half hours action she hauld her wind, her pumps going; we edged away, so that it fairly may be called a drawn battle."[1]

In another letter, of June 19, Saltonstall says: " Our troubles ceased not with the engagement. The next day, the 2nd, it blew a heavy gale of wind, which soon carried away our main and mizen masts by the board, the fore topmast followed them and had it not been for the greatest exertions, our foremast must have gone also, it being wounded in many places, but by fishing and propping it was saved. . . . We remained in this situation till the next day, the 3rd, our men having got a little over the fatigue of the engagement and the duty of the ship; the gale abating we got up jury masts and made the best shift. In the night the gale increased again and continued from that time till we got soundings on George's Banks in 45 fathoms of water the 11th instant. We got into Nantasket the 14th, the day following into the harbor."[2]

The Watt, greatly shattered, got into New York June 11. The accounts of her force vary somewhat. She seems to have mounted twenty-six twelve-pounders and from six to ten sixes. Her crew was reported to number two hundred and fifty, but one New York paper made it one hundred and sixty-four. Her commander, Captain Coulthard, describ-

[1] *Independent Chronicle*, July 6, 1780.
[2] *Papers New London Hist. Soc.*, IV, i, 55.

ing the action, says : " Saw a large ship under the lee bow, bearing N. W. by W., distant about three or four miles ; supposed her to be a rebel vessel bound to France and immediately bore down upon her. When she perceived we were standing for her she hauled up her courses and hove too. We then found her to be a frigate of 34 or 36 guns and full of men and immediately hoisted our colours and fired a gun ; she at the same time hoisted Saint George's colours and fired a gun to leeward. We then took her for one of his Majesty's cruizing frigates and intended speaking to her, but as soon as she saw we were getting on her weather quarter, they filled their topsails and stood to the eastward. We then fired five guns to bring her to, but she having a clean bottom and we foul and a cargo in, could not come up with her. Therefore, finding it a folly to chace, fired two guns into her and wore ship to the westward ; at the same time she fired one gun at us, loaded with grape shot and round, and wore after us. Perceiving this, we immediately hauled up our courses and hove too for her.

"She still kept English colours flying till she came within pistol shot on our weather quarter ; she then hauled down English colours and hoisted rebel colours, upon which we instantly gave her three cheers and a broadside. She returned it and we came alongside one another and for above seven glasses engaged yard arm and yard arm ; my officers and men behaved like true sons of Old England. While our braces were not shot away, we box-hauled our ship four different times and raked her through the stern, shot away her main topmast and main yard and shattered her hull, rigging and sails very much. At last all our braces and rigging were shot away and the two ships lay along-side of one another, right before the wind; she then shot a little ahead of us, got her foresail set and run. We gave her t'other broadside and stood after her; she could only return us two guns. Not having a standing shroud, stay or back-stay, our masts wounded through and through, our hull, rigging and sails cut to pieces, and being very leaky from a number of shot under water, only one pump fit to work, the other having been torn to pieces by a twelve pound shot, after chasing her for eight hours, lost sight and made the best of our way to this port. We had eleven men killed, two more died the next day, and seventy-nine wounded." [1]

The Board of Admiralty continued to develop plans for a cruise by a squadron under Nicholson, who was the senior captain of the navy. The Confederacy, Captain Harding, which had been temporarily repaired at Martinique after her dismasting and had returned to Philadelphia about May 1, the Deane, Captain Samuel Nicholson, brother of

[1] *Almon*, x, 142, 143; *Massachussetts Spy*, August 17, 1780; *Boston Gazette*, June 5, 19, July 24, August 28, 1780; *Independent Chronicle*, July 6, September 7, 1780; *Papers New London Hist. Soc.*, IV, i, 51–56; *Williams*, 273.

the commodore, and the Saratoga, a new eighteen-gun sloop of war commanded by Captain Young, were, with the Trumbull, to make up the squadron. These ships were all that remained of the Continental navy, in commission at this time, except the Alliance. The Deane had made a successful cruise early in the year, taking a number of prizes. She and the Saratoga were ready for sea in June, but the Confederacy and Trumbull were in need of extensive repairs. Nicholson received a letter from the Board of Admiralty, dated June 30, congratulating him upon "the gallantry displayed in the Defence" of his ship in his recent action with the Watt and urging "exertions in Speedily refitting" her. The long-looked-for reinforcement from France, consisting of five thousand troops under General Rochambeau, sailed from Brest May 1, convoyed by seven ships of the line commanded by Admiral de Ternay, and arrived at Newport July 12; this place had been evacuated by the British in October, 1779. It was intended by Congress that the Continental squadron should keep a lookout for an expected second division of the French fleet from Brest and warn them of the situation of the British fleet, and should also coöperate with De Ternay; this was in accordance with the wish of General Washington, but no union of these forces took place. All the French ships were blockaded by the British — the second division in Brest, and De Ternay in Newport by a superior force under Arbuthnot, who had returned from Charleston.[1]

The Mercury, a packet in the employ of Congress which had been stationed in Delaware Bay, set sail in August for Holland under the command of Captain Pickles, having on board as passenger Henry Laurens, who was sent on an important mission to the Dutch government. The Mercury was convoyed for a short distance by the Saratoga and early in September was captured by a British frigate off the Banks of Newfoundland. The dispatches, including a draft of a treaty with Holland, were thrown overboard, but unfortunately did not sink and were recovered by the British. Laurens was confined about a year in the Tower of London.[2]

Many instructions were issued for the movements of the Continental squadron. August 11, the Trumbull was ordered on a two weeks' cruise off the coast, in a letter which required of Commodore Nicholson that " all such prizes as you may take and send into this port are to be directed to the care of the Board of Admiralty, the prizes which you may be Obliged through necessity to send into Other Ports you are to direct to the care

[1] *Mar. Com. Letter Book*, 259, 262, 266, 281, 284, 285, 298, 312, 315, 322 (January 31, February 15, 28, May 2, 12, June 30, August 11, 14, 28, 1780); *Pap. Cont. Congr.*, **78**, 12, 5 (February 4, 1780), **37**, 223, 287, 311 (April 11, August 1, 6, 1780); *Boston Post*, April 20, 1780; *Boston Gazette*, May 1, 1780; *Mahan*, 382, 383.

[2] *Mar. Com. Letter Book*, 295, 311, 315 (June 19, August 11, 14, 1780); *Pap. Cont. Congr.*, **37**, 431 (July 18, 1780); *Stevens*, 930, 931.

of the Continental Agent of the district. You are always to Observe that you are to give the preference to this port as a place to which you are to direct your prizes when winds, weather and Other circumstances will admit of it without being more hazardous than elsewhere. The Deane and Saratoga will Sail in Company with you and under your Orders ; you will therefore prepare and give to the Captains or commanding Officer of each of those Ships such instructions as may be necessary for regulating the Cruize. . . . You will also when at the Capes employ some of your Crew in catching Fish, which will Afford a healthful variety of food to them and save your flesh Provisions. You are to see that the Ships company of the little fleet under your command frequently are disciplined in the exercise of the great Guns and Small Arms, to render them more expert in time of Battle, and that Œconomy, frugality, neatness and good Order are punctually Observed." [1] August 19, the Saratoga was ordered to sea with sealed instructions " of a Secret Committee of Conferrence with the Minister of France," which the Board of Admiralty surmised might take her to the West Indies. On the 29th the Trumbull was ordered on a three weeks' cruise on the Atlantic coast with the Deane, and two weeks later this cruise was extended and the Saratoga was to endeavor to join them. Renewed instructions as to coöperation with the French

[1] *Mar. Com. Letter Book*, 312.

were included in nearly all the board's letters. As late as August 31, the Confederacy was still unfit for active service, being "the only Continental frigate now within Harbour, but neither manned Or victualed for the Sea." The Deane made a three weeks' cruise off the coast of South Carolina in September, but "without taking anything worth naming," according to Richard Langdon, son of the president of Harvard College, who was on board. This caused disappointment, for success had been depended upon "to equip three quarters of our navy, which is now in this river, viz: the Confederacy, Trumbull and Deane frigates."[1] The Saratoga took four valuable prizes, at least one of which was more heavily armed than herself; they were all recaptured, however. The ships were in port a large part of the time preparing for sea under difficulties which caused endless delay. These difficulties as might be expected were mostly financial and not only hindered repairs on the vessels in commission, but prevented the completion of those under construction, the frigate Bourbon in the Connecticut River and the seventy-four-gun ship America still on the stocks at Portsmouth. The Board of Admiralty appealed to the governors of the New England States and to other persons of influence for help, but at this period of the war money had become the scarcest of all commodities. William Vernon, of the Eastern Navy Board, writ-

[1] *Independent Chronicle*, January 25, 1781.

ing, November 10, about naval matters to William
Ellery, then a member of the Board of Admiralty,
says that Captain Samuel Nicholson had recently
" arrived from Phila. having leave of absence . . .
to come to Boston, his younger Brother John Nicholson being appointed to the Command of his ship
the Deane Frigate, which he is to resume the Command of at the end of her present Cruise; he further informs that all the Continental Ships were
to sail from the Delaware in consequence. That it
was reported, when their Cruise was up, they were
to go into the Chesapeake to recruit their Stores
and Men; this message he verily believes was
agreed upon. Which if true we are extreem sorry
to hear, not that we as a Board can receive any
injury, on the contrary shall get clear of a great
deal of Trouble and Fatigue, but are fearful the
Public are in much danger of Looseing the small
remains of their Navy, at least of their being rendered useless for a Time, as it certainly cannot be
difficult for British ships of superior Force to block
up if not Capture them; moreover if this should
not be the case, can stores of every kind be supplied in Virginia or Maryland, can Men be obtained
to Mann the Deane and Trumbul, whose Time
must be expired at their Arrival in the Chesapeake? Indeed we think they were entitled to their
discharge upon their Arrival in the Delaware from
their last Cruise; they certainly were shiped for a
Cruise only, upon no other Terms have we at any

Time been able to Mann our ships. If we do not keep faith with the Seamen, our expectations are at an end of even Manning the Ships. I speak in regard to the Trumbul and Deane; perhaps it may be otherwise with the Confederacy and Saratoga, they may be shiped upon the New invitation of Entering for 12 Months. I have given you these hints not officially, meerly as my private opinion and that of my Colleage and make no doubt they will have their proper weight with you and that upon your joining the board of Admiralty at Phila., will suggest to them what shall in your judgment appear consonant to the benefit and Interest of the Public."[1] Another matter taken up by the Board of Admiralty in 1780 was the systematic attempt to obtain, through navy boards and other agents, all the information possible as to the numbers, character, and movements of the British naval forces at all points between Newfoundland and the West Indies.[2]

The Massachusetts navy, which had lost all of its vessels in commission in the ill-fated Penobscot expedition, was about this time reinforced by the largest and most powerful ship in the state service

[1] *Publ. R. I. Hist. Soc.*, viii, 268.

[2] *Mar. Com. Letter Book*, 265, 289, 290, 291, 294, 300, 303, 304, 308, 310, 312, 313, 314, 315, 317, 318, 319, 321, 322, 331 (February 22, May 30, June 16, July 7, 21, August 4, 11, 14, 19, 22, 29, 31, September 14, 1780); *Pap. Cont. Congr.*, 37, 265, 269, 273, 517 (July 21, November 6, 1780); *Penn. Packet*, October 24, 1780; *Publ. R. I. Hist. Soc.*, viii, 264–269; *Barney*, 84–86.

during the Revolution. This was the twenty-six-gun frigate Protector, which was built on the Merrimac River and launched in 1779, but not ready for sea until the spring of 1780. In December, 1779, she narrowly escaped destruction by a fire at the wharf where she was moored. March 21, 1780, the following action was taken by the Massachusetts General Court: " Whereas it is absolutely necessary to increase the Naval Force of this State to defend the Trade and Sea Coasts thereof, Therefore Resolved, that the Board of War be and they are hereby directed to procure and fit for the Sea with all possible dispatch Two Armed Vessels to carry from Twelve to Sixteen Guns each." Under this and supplementary acts a ship called the Mars was purchased in April and another was built and named the Tartar ; the latter, however, was not finished until 1782. Captain Williams was put in command of the Protector ; among her midshipmen was Edward Preble, who afterwards became famous. In January it had been intended to send her to Europe, but in May, after having made a short cruise, Williams was ordered by the Board of War on another, as far east as the Banks of Newfoundland and south to the thirty-eighth parallel and to the track of vessels from the West Indies, meanwhile making occasional visits to the coast of Maine. Captain Sampson was appointed to command the Mars, and in June was ordered to Nantes for goods needed by the army ; he sailed early in August. On

June 22, the General Court expressed disapproval of robberies said to have been committed along the Nova Scotia shore by Massachusetts privateers and resolved that in the future privateers must give bonds for the abolition of such evils.[1]

On her cruise to the eastward the Protector fought a hard battle on the Banks of Newfoundland of which the captain gives an account in his journal. "Friday, June 9, 1780, wind W. S. W. At 7 A.M. saw a large ship to windward bearing down for us under English colours; she hauled up her courses in order for action. At 11 A.M. we came along-side of her under English colours, hail'd her; she answered from Jamaica. I shifted my colours & gave her a broadside. She soon returned us another. The action was heavy for near 3 glasses, when unfortunately she took fire and soon after blew up; got out our boats to save the men, took up 55 of them. Among them was the 3d mate and the only officer sav'd; the greatest part of them very much wounded and burnt. She was called the Admiral Duff, a large ship of 32 guns, commanded by Richard Stranger, from St. Kitts and St. Eustatia laden with sugar and tobacco, bound to London." [2] The Protector lost one killed and five wounded out of her complement of two hundred.

[1] *Mass. Court Rec.*, March 15, 21, April 20, May 5, June 22; *Mass. Archives*, cli, 506, cliii, 320, 345; *Massachusetts Mag.*, July, October, 1910; *Amer. Hist. Rev.*, x, 69; *Boston Post*, April 20, 1780.

[2] *Boston Gazette*, July 24, 1780.

This event was narrated in greater detail many years later by Luther Little, a midshipman on the Protector and brother of the first lieutenant, George Little. The midshipman says that on the morning of the battle there was a fog and when it " lifted, saw large ship to windward under English colors, standing down before the wind for us, we being to leeward. Looked as large as a 74. Concluded she was not a frigate. All hands piped to quarters. Hammocks brought up and stuffed in the nettings, decks wet and sanded &c. . . . We stood on under cruising sail. She tried to go ahead of us and then hove to under fighting sail. We showed English flag. She was preparing for action. We steered down across her stern & hauled up under her lee quarter, breeching our guns aft to bring them to bear. Our first lt. hailed from the gangboard. . . . Our capt. ordered broadside and colors changed. She replied with 3 cheers and a broadside. Being higher, they overshot us, cutting our rigging. A regular fight within pistol range. In a hf hour a cannon shot came thro' our side, killing Mr. Scollay, a midshipman who commanded the 4th 12-pounder from the stern. His brains flew over my face and my gun, which was the third from the stern. In an hour all their topmen were kld by our marines, 60 in no. and all Americans. Our marines kld the man at their wheel & the ship came down on us, her cat-head staving in our quarter galley. We lashed their jib-boom to our main shrouds.

Our marines firing into their port holes kept them from charging. We were ordered to board, but the lashing broke & we were ordered back. Their ship shooting alongside nearly locked our guns & we gave a broadside, wh. cut away her mizen mast and made gt havoc. Saw her sinking and her maintopgallantsail on fire, wh run down her rigging and caught a hogshead of cartridges under her quarter deck and blew it off. A charge of grape entered my port hole. One passed between my backbone and windpipe and one thro' my jaw, lodging in the roof of my mouth & taking off a piece of my tongue, the other thro' my upper lip, taking away part, and all my upper teeth. Was carried to cockpit; my gun was fired only once after. I had fired it 19 times. Thinking I was mortally wounded they dressed first those likelier to live. Heard the surgeon say ' he will die.' The Duff sunk, on fire, colors flying. Our boats had been injured, but were repaired as well as possible & sent to pick up the swimmers; saved 55, one half wounded. Then first lt confided to me that many were drowned rather than be made captives. Some tried to jump from the boats. Our surgeons amputated limbs of 5 of them. One was sick with W. India fever and had floated out of his hammock between decks. The weather was warm and in less than 10 days 60 of our men had it. Among those saved were 2 American captains & their crews, prisoners on board the Duff. One of the Am. captains told us that Capt. Strang had hoped we were a Continental frigate, when he first saw us." [1] While cruising off Nova Scotia with a great deal of sickness on board, the Protector fell in with the Thames, a British frigate of thirty-two guns. After a running fight of several hours the Protector escaped. She returned to Boston, August 15. In the fall she made another cruise, first running to the eastward and then to the West Indies.[2]

Captain Elisha Hart, of the private armed sloop Retaliation, ten guns and fifty men, wrote from New London, September 29, 1780, to Governor Trumbull of Connecticut, that he had sailed on the 22d along the south side of Long Island to Sandy Hook and towards the Narrows, in New York Harbor. Several sloops were seen coming down from New York. The Retaliation chased them and overhauled one that was standing for Staten Island. "I discovered She Had no Guns," says Hart, "but appeared full of Men Elligantly Dressed. I then Supposed her to be a Pleasure Boat from the Fleet, which I then Saw Lying In the Narrows and was within One League of them and in full View of the City and More than a League within the Guard Ships." Captain Hart got out sweeps, came up fast on the chase and hailed her, but her commander was very suspicious and refused to come on board

[1] *Manuscript* in Harvard College Library.
[2] *Mass. Archives*, cliii, 385; *Boston Gazette*, July 17, 24, August 21, 1780; *Adventures of Ebenezer Fox*, ch. iv, v; *Clark*, i, 102, 103; Sabine's *Life of Preble*, ch. i.

the Retaliation. " I then ordered Down my English
Colours, Ran out my Bow Guns and Told him if
He did not Come on Board I would Sink Him
Immediately. He then Hove out his Boat and
Come on Board. I Immediately Man'd the Prize
and Took out the Prisoners." They were forty-seven
in number, including a captain, a lieutenant, and
two sergeants; they were a captain's guard, sent to
relieve guard at the lighthouse. An armed sloop
from near the guardship approached, but bore away
upon the Retaliation's heaving to for her. The
prize was brought safely into New London.[1]

Alexander Murray, who was afterwards a lieutenant in the Continental navy, commanded the
letter of marque Revenge in 1780; she carried
eighteen six-pounders and fifty men and was fitted
out at Baltimore for a voyage to Holland. Having
collected a convoy of fifty sail in Chesapeake Bay,
some of them armed, Murray attempted to get to
sea, but upon the appearance of a squadron of British privateers, consisting of an eighteen-gun ship,
a sixteen-gun brig, and three schooners, his convoy,
with the exception of two vessels, deserted him and
fled. The Revenge alone engaged the ship and brig
with both broadsides, lying between them, and beat
them both off after a hard-fought action of more
than an hour. The two vessels with him kept the
three schooners occupied until the convoy had time

[1] *Trumbull MSS.*, xiii, 41 ; *Continental Journal*, October 5, 1780;
Papers New London Hist. Soc., IV, i, 18.

to escape into Hampton Roads. Murray returned
to port to repair damages and then once more set
sail. On the Banks of Newfoundland he captured a
letter of marque brig. He pursued his voyage, but
unluckily fell in with a large British fleet of men-
of-war and transports, was chased by a frigate and
captured. Not long afterwards Murray was exchanged.[1]

A source of embarrassment to British naval administration during the war was jealousy and ill-
feeling among the officers of the navy. One instance was a bitter quarrel between Admirals Kep-
pel and Palliser in 1778. Admiral Rodney came
out to the West Indies early in 1780 and remained
there most of the time until 1782. His relations
with other officers seem seldom to have been pleasant, and lust of prize money interfered at times
with the discharge of duty. His first exploit was an
encounter with a French fleet under the Comte de
Guichen, which led to contentions with his captains
due to misunderstanding about signals. In September, Rodney went to New York for a short stay,

[1] *Clark*, i, 117; *Port Folio*, May, 1814. For further accounts of
privateering and prizes in 1780, see *Boston Gazette*, March 6, 20,
May 1, July 3, 24, 31, September 4, November 6, 1780; *Massachusetts Spy*, August 17, 1780; *Continental Journal*, October 19,
1780; *Penn. Gazette*, July 19, 1780; *London Post*, May 1, August
4, 1780; *Pickering MSS.*, xxxiii, 280; *Almon*, x, 55, 60, 265–267;
Clark, i, 116, 119; *Virginia Hist. Register*, July, 1853; *Tucker*, ch.
viii; *Papers New London Hist. Soc.*, IV, i, 16; *R. I. Hist. Mag.*,
July, 1884.

arriving just in time to fall into a large amount of prize money, which came to him as senior officer on the station and would otherwise have gone to Admiral Arbuthnot. This occasioned a disagreeable quarrel between them. In a letter dated October 19, 1780, Rodney says to Arbuthnot: " I am honoured with your letter of the 16th Instant and am sorry that my Conduct has given you offence; none was intended on my part. . . . It was not inclination or Choice that brought me to America; it was the Duty I owed my King and Country. I had flattered myself it would have met with your approbation. I am sorry it has not, but I own I have the vanity to think it will meet with His approbation whose it is the greatest Honor a Subject can receive. Your Anger at my partial interfering (as you term it) with the American War not a little surprises me. I came to Interfere in the American War, to Command by Sea in it and do my best Endeavours towards the putting an end thereto. I knew the Dignity of my own Rank and the power invested in me by the Commission I bear entitled me to take the supreme Command, which I ever shall do on every Station, . . . unless I meet a Superior Officer. . . . Your having detached the Raisonable to England without my knowledge, after you had received my orders to put your self under my command, is I believe unprecidented in the Annals of the British Navy." [1]

[1] *Brit. Adm. Rec., A. D. Leeward Islands*, vii.

On October 30, Rodney wrote to the Admiralty:
" Vice Admiral Arbuthnot having taken it into
his head to be highly Offended at me for doing
what I thought my duty to His Majesty and the
Public and acquainting me by letter dated the 16th
Instant that he would remonstrate to their Lordships against my Conduct, I think it a duty I owe
myself to transmit to the Admiralty Board Copies
of My Orders and Letters to Mr. Arbuthnot with
his answers to Me (His Superior officer), that their
Lordships may Judge which of us has most cause
to trouble them with Complaints. . . . That I have
been extremely tender in issuing Orders to Vice
Admiral Arbuthnot and been attentive towards pay-
ing him every respect due to his Rank, the inclos'd
letters I am sure will convince their Lordships.
If in his Answers to me his letters have not been
penn'd with that Cordiality which ought to pass
between Officers acting in the Public Service, I am
sorry for him, they effect not Me. I am ashamed
to mention what appears to Me the real cause and
from whence Mr. Arbuthnot's chagrene proceeds,
but the proofs are so plain that Prize Money is the
Occasion that I am under the necessity of trans-
mitting them. . . . On my arrival at New York
. . . I found it necessary. . . to give Mr. Arbuthnot Orders to put himself under My Command,
not only for the better carrying on the Public Service, but likewise to prevent any Litigious Suits
relative to Prize Money, which Mr. Arbuthnot had

given me but too much reason to expect. . . . I can solemnly assure their Lordships that I had not the least conception of any other Prize Money on the Coast of America but that which would be most honourably obtain'd by the destruction of the Enemy's Ships of War and Privateers, but when Prize Money appear'd predominant in the mind of my Brother Officer, I was determin'd to have my Share of that Bounty so graciously bestow'd by His Majesty and the Public. . . . I flatter'd myself I should have had the honour even of Mr. Arbuthnot's approbation of my Conduct. I am sorry I have not, but if I am so happy as to meet with that of their Lordships, it will more than fully compensate." [1] Rodney returned to the West Indies in December.

[1] *Brit. Adm. Rec., A. D. Leeward Ids.,* vii; *Mahan,* 377–382; *Hannay,* ii, 226–229, 244–251; *Belcher,* i, 293, 301, 302; *Channing,* iii, 324; *Nav. Rec. Soc.,* iii, 1, 2. For Arbuthnot's complaints against Rodney, see *Brit. Adm. Rec., A. D. 486,* September 30, October 29, 1780.

CHAPTER XV

AFTER his arrival at L'Orient in February, 1780, Captain Jones had to endure another long period of waiting on shore, but was occupied for some time in giving the Alliance a thorough overhauling; for lack of money this was less complete than he had hoped. In the first place the ship had been put out of trim by the arrangement of the ballast, which, Jones says, " Captain Landais has extended along the ceiling from the stern-post to the stem; an idea that I believe he may without vanity call his own." Besides correcting this, repairs were necessary and Jones proposed to have the ship coppered. Another object of his desire was the purchase of the Serapis, and he says in the same letter, which was written to Franklin, February 13 : " I wish she could be made the property of America." [1] He seems to have had an idea that the French government would bear the cost of repairs on the Alliance. Franklin wrote to him, February 19: " As to refitting your ship at the expense of this court, I must acquaint you that there is not the least probability of obtaining it, and therefore I cannot ask it. I hear too much already of the ex-

[1] *Sherburne,* 186.

traordinary expense you made in Holland to think of proposing an addition to it, especially as you seem to impute the damage she has sustained more to Capt. Landais's negligence than to accidents of the cruize. The whole expense will therefore fall upon me and I am ill provided to bear it, having so many unexpected calls upon me from all quarters. I therefore beg you would have mercy upon me, put me to as little charge as possible and take nothing that you can possibly do without. As to sheathing with copper, it is totally out of the question. I am not authorised to do it, if I had money; and I have not money for it, if I had orders. The purchase of the Serapis is in the same predicament. . . . Let me repeat it, for God's sake be sparing, unless you mean to make me a bankrupt or have your drafts dishonored for want of money in my hands to pay them." [1] In spite of difficulties, however, the ship was in fine condition by the middle of April. Jones took on board of her twenty-eight eighteen-pounders and twelve nines, the guns that had been made for the Bonhomme Richard, but were not ready in time; besides which it had been decided that eighteens were too heavy.[2] Jones expected to return to America in the Alliance, but wished before he left France to settle his own and his men's affairs. His prizes had not yet been

[1] *Sherburne*, 189, 190.

[2] *Ibid.*, 221; *Archives de la Marine*, B¹ 89, 225. Probably these guns were to be transported to America, not mounted on the Alliance.

sold and his crew were without wages, without prize money, and without clothes. In order to expedite matters, Jones made another trip to Paris and obtained the promise of an early sale. Franklin advanced a sum of money to supply the immediate needs of officers and men. The French government loaned the ship Ariel of twenty guns to accompany the Alliance to America and assist in transporting a large amount of clothing and military supplies for the Continental army. Many exchanged American prisoners arrived from England who would be available for her crew. Jones was received in Paris with marked distinction and was presented by the King with a gold-hilted sword and the cross of the Order of Military Merit; the latter in the following year, after having obtained the approval of Congress.[1]

About this time the project of another cruise to the north, under the command of Commodore Jones, was formed. It is outlined in the following paper drawn up by Jones and dated June 10: "It is understood that a considerable Number of the King's Frigates are likely to remain unarmed and unemployed in the Ports, through the Scarcity of French Seamen. To Man these the Government might ask of Congress the Services of Commodore Jones and of a sufficient Number of American Officers and Sailors, of which there are about 500

[1] *Sands*, 247–262; *Sherburne*, 185–197; *Archives de la Marine*, B¹ **93**, 45, 283, 285, B⁴ **172**, 176.

now Prisoners in England, whose exchange will naturally take place in two or three Months and who being arrived here might easily be engaged and retained for that purpose. Commodore Jones is now bound for America, from whence with the permission of Congress he might return in about four Months with the Alliance and probably with one or two other American Frigates, on board of which and of such Merchant Ships as would gladly put themselves under his Convoy he could embark and bring over a considerable number of chosen Supernumerary officers and Seamen to be joined with those expected from England and to such others as might be collected in France, and the whole employed in manning the French Frigates in Question, which during Commodore Jones's absence might be put in some degree of readiness. Should the Serapis be bought by the King, it would be advisable to employ her in this Service. In this way a squadron of Frigates from America and of fast sailing French Frigates, sloops &c. manned by Americans might be easily formed, capable of rendering very essential services to the Common Cause, by destroying the Enemies Commerce, alarming their Coasts, taking their Towns &c. &c. It would be expedient to embark a few hundred of good French Troops on board the different Vessels of War, to serve as Marines and to assist in making descents &c. Commodore Jones can and at any time will point out to Government many desirable undertakings for the Armament in Question, but as the utmost secrecy is necessary to render them successful and as changes of Winds and a variety of circumstances may render it expedient to change the operations of this Force, he would desire and expect to be left at full Liberty to act according as situations and circumstances may in his own opinion appear for the best." This proposition was favorably received by the French Ministry, but apparently owing to the inability of Congress to take the necessary steps on their part and to other circumstances, it came to nothing.[1]

During Jones's absence from L'Orient, Landais, instigated by Arthur Lee, encouraged a spirit of discontent almost amounting to mutiny among the crew of the Alliance. The men were led to believe that Jones was responsible for their not receiving the prize money due them, and they demanded the restoration of Landais to the command of the ship. Apparently Jones here again, as on the Ranger, suffered from the lack of a warm personal regard for him on the part of his men, who, repelled by his demeanor, never understood his devotion to their interests. The former officers and men of the Bonhomme Richard, however, stood by him. Lee expressed the opinion that as Landais's commission had not been revoked, nor had he been relieved by order of Congress, he was still legally in command of the Alliance. Jones wrote to Robert Morris:

[1] *Archives de la Marine*, B⁴ **172**, 188, 199; *Sherburne*, 208-211.

"I am convinced that Mr. Lee has acted in this matter merely because I would not become the enemy of the venerable, the wise and good Franklin, whose heart as well as head does and will always do honor to human nature."[1] In regard to the legality of Landais's commission, the Board of Admiralty in a report to Congress a few months later observed that "Captain Landais regained command of the Alliance by the advice of Mr. Lee, notwithstanding his suspension by Dr. Franklin, who by the direction of the Marine Committee had the sole management of our marine affairs in Europe."[2] John Adams, however, believed that the Marine Committee lacked authority to confer upon Franklin the power to remove the commander of a ship. Commodore Gillon of South Carolina, at that time in France, also took the part of Landais. The French ministry declined to take sides in the controversy. June 13, after Jones's return from Paris but during his temporary absence from the ship, Landais went on board and took command. To avoid trouble which might be serious and lead to bloodshed, Jones relinquished his claim to the command.[3]

About the 1st of July the Alliance sailed for America with Arthur Lee on board as passenger, but without the clothing so much needed by the

---

[1] *Wharton*, iii, 821; *Sands*, 278.   [2] *Sands*, 321.

[3] *Ibid.*, 262–280; *Sherburne*, 197–207; *Hale*, ch. xvii; *Archives de la Marine*, B⁴ 172, 166, 197, 198, 204–210, 231, 237–242, 244, 245, 248, 255, 261.

PIERRE LANDAIS

army. The conduct of Captain Landais became so
erratic during the voyage that the safety of the ship,
crew, and passengers seemed imperiled. After vain
appeals to him it became necessary to relieve him
forcibly of the command, which devolved upon the
first lieutenant. This was on August 10, in latitude
41° 30' north, longitude 59° west. The ship was
then taken into Boston, where she arrived, August
16. Captain Barry was appointed to command the
Alliance, September 5. She remained in Boston
Harbor during the rest of the year and on board of
her was convened the court martial, of which Barry
was president, for the trial of Captain Landais and
his first lieutenant, James Degge. As a result, they
were both dismissed from the navy.[1]

After the departure of the Alliance from France,
Jones was occupied in getting ready for his own return to America. "He obtained a crew for the
Ariel, that was ordered by government to be fully
armed and equipped. He embarked such a quantity
of arms and powder as with provision for only nine
weeks filled the ship even between decks. He hoped
to make the passage in a favourable season of
the year, but was detained by contrary and stormy
winds in the road of Groix from the 4th of Sep-

[1] *Pap. Cont. Congr.*, **193**, 451–595, 597, 599, 631, 639, 655, 679,
705, 757, 773 (August 10, September 22, November 10, 29, 1780,
January 5, 6, 25, 1781); *Mar. Com. Letter Book*, 328 (September
5, 1780); *Lee MSS.*, August 5, 10, December 20, 1780; *Boston
Gazette*, August 21, 1780; *Archives de la Marine*, B⁸ **16** (Juin,
1780).

tember till the 8th of October. He then sailed with
a fair wind and pleasant weather, but the next night
the Ariel was driven by a violent tempest close to the
rocks of the Penmarque, a terrible ledge between
L'Orient and Brest. The ship could show no sail, but
was almost buried under the water, not having room
to run before the wind and having several feet
water in the hold. Finding the depth of water
diminish fast, Captain Jones in the last extremity
cast anchor, but could not bring the ship's head to
the wind. Sometimes the lower yard-arms touched
the water. Captain Jones now had no remedy left
but to cut away the foremast. This had the desired
effect and the ship immediately came head to the
wind. The main-mast had got out of the step and
now reeled about like a drunken man. Foreseeing
the danger of its either breaking off below the gun-
deck or going through the ship's bottom, Captain
Jones ordered it to be cut away. But before this
could be done, the chain-plates gave way and the
main-mast breaking off by the gun-deck carried with
it the mizen-mast; and the mizen-mast carried away
the quarter-gallery. In that situation the Ariel rode
in the open ocean to windward of perhaps the most
dangerous ledge of rocks in the world for two days
and near three nights, in a tempest that covered
the shore with wrecks and dead bodies and that
drove ships ashore from their anchors even in the
port of L'Orient. It was perhaps fortunate that
the Ariel lost her masts, since no anchors could

have held her so long had the masts stood. By the help of jury-masts, erected after the gale, the Ariel returned to L'Orient."[1] It then took several weeks to refit the Ariel, and Jones made an unsuccessful effort to obtain a better ship. During this time he made further arrangements in regard to the prize money due himself and officers and men, which had not yet been paid. Franklin wrote to him, December 4: "I shall strongly solicit the payment of the prize money, which I understand is not yet received from the king. I hope soon to see an end of that affair, which has met with so many unaccountable obstructions. I enclose despatches for Congress, which are to be sunk in case of danger. I wish you to make the best of your way to America and that you may have a prosperous voyage."[2] The Ariel sailed December 18.[3]

The account of this voyage is given in Jones's journal. "After a variety of rencounters he, in the latitude 26° north and longitude of Barbadoes, met with a remarkably fast sailing frigate belonging to the enemy's navy. Captain Jones endeavoured to avoid speaking with that ship and as night approached, he hoped to succeed, notwithstanding her superior sailing. He was, however, mistaken, for the next morning the ships were at a less distance asunder than they had been the evening before, al-

[1] *Sands,* 294, journal prepared for the King.
[2] *Sands,* 299.
[3] *Ibid.,* 294–300; *Sherburne,* 211–213; *Archives de la Marine,* B⁴ 172, 271–274, 277.

though during the night the officers of the watch
had always informed Captain Jones the sail continued out of sight. An action now became unavoidable and the Ariel was prepared for it. Every thing
was thrown overboard that interfered with the defence and safety of the ship. Captain Jones took
particular care, by the management of sails and
helm, to prevent the enemy from discovering the
force of the Ariel, and worked her so well as not
to discover any warlike appearance or preparation.
In the afternoon the Ariel fired now and then a
light stern-chaser at the enemy from the quarter-
deck and continued to crowd sail as if very much
alarmed. This had the desired effect and the enemy
pursued with the greater eagerness. Captain Jones
did not suffer the enemy to come close up till the approach of night, when having well examined his
force, he shortened sail to meet his approach.

" When the two ships came within hail of each
other they both hoisted English colours. The person whose duty it was to hoist the pendant on board
the Ariel had not taken care to make the other end
of the halliards fast, to haul it down again to change
the colours. This prevented Jones from an advantageous manœuvre he had intended and obliged him
to let the enemy range up along the lee-side of the
Ariel, where he saw a battery lighted for action. A
conversation now took place between the two ships,
which lasted near an hour, by which Captain Jones
learned the situation of the enemy's affairs in Amer-

ica. The captain of the enemy's ship said his name
was John Pindar. His ship had been constructed
by the famous Mr. Peck of Boston, built at Newburyport, owned by Mr. Tracy of that place, commanded by Captain Hopkins, the son of the late
Commodore Hopkins, and had been taken and fitted
out at New York and named the Triumph by Admiral Rodney. Captain Jones told him he must
put out his boat and come on board and show his
commission, to prove whether or not he really did
belong to the British navy. To this he made some
excuses, because Captain Jones had not told him
who he was, and his boat he said was very leaky.
Captain Jones told him to consider the danger of
refusing. Captain Pindar said he would answer for
twenty guns and that he himself and every one of
his people had shown themselves Englishmen. Captain Jones said he would allow him five minutes
only to make his reflection. That time being elapsed,
Captain Jones backed a little in the weather-quarter
of the enemy, ran close under her stern, hoisted
American colours, and being within short pistol shot
on the lee-beam of the enemy, began to engage.

" It was past seven o'clock and as no equal force
ever exceeded the vigorous and regular fire of the
Ariel's battery and tops, the action while it lasted
made a glorious appearance. The enemy made a
feeble resistance for about ten minutes. He then
struck his colours. The enemy then begged for
quarter and said half his men were killed. The

Ariel's fire ceased and the crew, as usual after a victory, gave cries of joy. To 'show themselves Englishmen,' the enemy filled their sails and got on the Ariel's weather-bow, before the cries of joy had ended on board the Ariel. Captain Jones, suspecting the base design of the enemy, immediately set every sail he could to prevent her escape, but the enemy had so much advantage in sailing that the Ariel could not keep up and they soon got out of gun shot. The English captain may properly be called a knave, because after he surrendered his ship, begged for and obtained quarter, he basely ran away, contrary to the laws of naval war and the practice of civilized nations. A conspiracy was discovered among the English part of the Ariel's crew immediately after sailing from France. During the voyage every officer and even the passengers had been constantly armed and kept a regular watch, besides a constant guard with fixed bayonets. After the action with the Triumph the plot was so far discovered that Captain Jones confined twenty of the ringleaders in irons till his arrival. Captain Jones arrived at Philadelphia on the 18th February, 1781, having been absent from America three years, three months and eighteen days." [1]

Among the American privateers in France commissioned by Franklin was one owned by Frenchmen in Dunkirk named the Black Prince, a small

[1] *Sands*, 300–302; *Sherburne*, 213, 214; *Boston Gazette*, March 12, 1781.

cutter armed with sixteen three- and four-pounders
and thirty-two swivels, which proved such a prize-
taker that the owners obtained from the American minister a commission for another, which they
called the Black Princess. The latter at first carried
eighteen two-, three-, and four-pounders and twenty-
four swivels, but later a much heavier armament.
These two vessels, manned chiefly by English and
Irish smugglers with a few Americans, cruised with
remarkable success during 1779 and 1780. There
were disadvantages in giving commissions to vessels owned by foreigners and likely to be manned
by the refuse of the seafaring population, but as
Franklin said, "The prisoners brought in serve to
exchange our countrymen, which makes me more
willing to encourage such armaments, though they
occasion a good deal of trouble." [1] The Black
Prince was commanded, for a time, at least, by
Captain Stephen Merchant, who after leaving her
returned to America, arriving in Boston about
March 1, 1780. According to Merchant, "this ship
was fitted out at Dunkirk under a Continental
commission and colours. . . . She went round the
coasts of Britain and Ireland and in less than three
months took 37 prizes; three of them were retaken, 4 burnt after taking out what was valuable,
all the rest were either ransomed or arrived safe in
port, by which the lowest men have made a little fortune. By instructions from Dr. Franklin the Cap-

[1] *Wharton*, iii, 364.

tain was prohibited doing mischief above high
water mark. This generous prohibition he punctually observed, though he had it frequently in his
power to land and distress the inhabitants of Britain
on their remotest coasts. He had not heard of their
burning Fairfield in Connecticut, of which State he
is a native, or he would have been strongly tempted
to have transgressed his orders by a just retaliation. Being once in want of water and some re-
freshments on the coast of Scotland, he sent his
boat to a small town and demanded a supply, prom-
ising security to the inhabitants and their property
in case his demand was complied with. It was refused; upon which he approached the town with
his ship and saluted it with a broadside. A white
flag was immediately displayed by the inhabitants
and the Black Prince was not only supplied with
water, but with cattle, sheep, poultry and every re-
freshment the place could afford and the commander
chose to receive." [1]

The Black Prince was afterwards commanded by
Captain Dowlin, and in April, 1780, captured a
Dutch ship called the Flora with an English cargo.
Franklin at once ordered the removal and condemnation of the cargo and the release of the vessel with payment of damages, giving his reasons in
a letter to Vergennes, dated June 18. It was just
at this time that Russia and other maritime powers
were forming the Armed Neutrality for the protec-

[1] *Independent Chronicle*, March 9, 1780.

tion of their commerce from the interference of belligerents by enforcing the doctrine that "free ships make free goods," always most obnoxious to England. This principle had been incorporated in a treaty which the United States was trying to negotiate with Holland, but which the Dutch had hitherto failed to accept. Franklin, therefore, felt justified in acting under the old law of nations, although he was well known to be a strong advocate of the principles of the Armed Neutrality.

In his letter to Vergennes he explains his position on the subject of privateering and especially of vessels fitted out by Frenchmen under the American flag. " I beg leave to observe," he says, " that by the express words of the commission granted to them they are directed to submit the prizes they shall carry into any port in the dominions of a foreign state to the judgment of the admiralty courts established in such ports or states, and according to the usages there in force. Several of our first prizes brought into France were, if I mistake not, so judged; and it was not upon any request of mine that such causes were afterwards referred to me, nor am I desirous of continuing to exercise that jurisdiction. If therefore the judgment I have given in the case of the Flora is not approved and the Council of Prizes will take the trouble of re-examining and trying that cause and those of all other prizes to be brought in hereafter by American cruisers, it will be very agreeable to me and, from the very terms above mentioned of the commission, I think it will also be agreeable to the Congress. Nor do I desire to encourage the fitting out of privateers in France by the King's subjects with American commissions. I have had many applications of the kind which I have refused, advising the owners to apply for the commissions of his majesty. The case of the Black Prince was particular. She had been an old smuggler on the coasts of England and Ireland, was taken as such and carried into Dublin, where her crew found means to break prison, cut their vessel out of the harbor and escaped with her to Dunkerque. It was represented to me that the people, being all English and Irish, were afraid to continue their smuggling business, lest if they should be again taken they might be punished as British subjects for their crime at Dublin, and that they were willing to go a privateering against the English; but speaking no other language, they imagined they might, if taken, better pass as Americans if they had an American commission than as Frenchmen if under a French commission. On these grounds I was applied to for a commission, which I granted believing that such a swift vessel with a crew that knew so well all parts of the enemy's coasts might greatly molest their coasting trade. Her first success occasioned adding the Black Princess by the same owners, and between them they have taken and sent in or ransomed or destroyed an amazing number of vessels;

I think near eighty. But I shall continue to refuse granting any more commissions except to American vessels; and if, under the circumstances above represented, it is thought nevertheless inconvenient that the commissions of the Black Prince and Princess should continue, I will immediately recall them."[1]

Franklin wrote to the President of Congress, August 10, that these two vessels had taken in eighteen months nearly a hundred and twenty prizes. In the summer of 1780 the Black Prince was wrecked on the French coast, but the Princess, under the command of Captain Edward Macatter, continued cruising, and between June 20 and July 10 made twenty-eight captures. Vergennes advised the recall of these privateers' commissions. Franklin replied, August 15, that he had already recalled them and added: "I have had no other interest in those armaments than the advantage of some prisoners to exchange for my countrymen."[2] These two vessels were the only ones owned and fitted out in France that had been granted commissions by Franklin. In August it was ordered by the King that the prizes of American privateers should be judged by the French Council of Prizes.[3]

The ship Mars of the Massachusetts navy sailed

[1] *Wharton*, iii, 802.   [2] *Ibid.*, iv, 33.

[3] *Ibid.*, iii, 364, 682, 801–803, iv, 26, 33; *Continental Journal*, March 9, 1780; *London Post*, July 21, 1780; *Proc. U. S. Naval Inst.*, xxxvii (September, 1911), 954–960; *Hale*, ch. xvi; *Williams*, 278.

from Boston for Nantes about the 1st of August.
On September 13, Captain Sampson reported to
the Board of War : " I have the pleasure of informing you of my safe arrival at the Entrance of the
River Loyer in the Ship Mars the 10th Inst., after
a Passage of Forty-four days, and embrace the
earliest opportunity to acquaint you of the same.
During my Passage I had favourable Winds untill
abt the Twentieth of Augt, when I had got as far
to the Eastwd as the Long. 20.0 W., then taking
the Winds to the Southd & Eastwd & having a very
Strong Northwardly Current and my ship very foul
and after trying her trim everyway, found her to sail
very Indifferently ; was drove to the northward of
Ushant, wch greatly Retarded my Passage. During
my passage I gave Chase to several Vessels wch I
had every reason to believe them to be English,
but to my great mortification could not speak with
any of them. On the 7th Augt I spoke a Dutch
Ship from Curiso bound to Amsterdam and on the
11th with a Dean from St. Croix bound to Copen-
hagen. On the 31st, in Latt. 49.40 N., Long. 11.
W., I gave chase to a Brig, who seeing me in Chase
of her, hove too. She proved to be . . . from St.
Jube bound to Cork loaded with Salt, Commanded
by a Portugue. The Capt. came on board with his
Portugue papers and told me his cargo belonged to
himself. I sent an Officer on board him to search
for more papers, who found concealed in the Captain's State Room a number of Letters directed to

Merchants in Cork [containing] Sufficient Papers
to prove her Cargo was Consigned to [one of these
merchants] ; upon which I took the Captain &
Seven Portugue out and sent [a prize master in
her] to proceed for Boston. My Reasons for sending her to America was that her Cargo would not
have been Valuable in Europe but would be in
Great Demand in America. . . . On the 8th Inst.
at 25 Leagues to the Westward of Belle Isle at
10 A.M. I saw several Sail to the S. W. and a
Ship and a Sloop under my Lee ; I kept on my
Cruise to the S. E. The ship & sloop Standing by
the wind in order to speak to me, I perseved the
Sloop to come up with me very fast. At 5 P.M. the
Sloop, which was an English Cutter mounting
twenty-two Guns, came along side of me and at 5
minutes past 5 P.M. the action began wch lasted
One hour & 5 minutes, but my Ship being very
foul and very heavy to work and not more than
half Mand & a very large Swell running, gave the
Cutter every advantage possible during the action,
as she could sail round me at her pleasure, but after
her engaging me rather better than an hour she
thot proper to shear of to the Ship, & I having
my Crotchet yard shot away and imagining her
consort the ship to be an English Privateer and
knowing it Impossible to come up with the Cutter,
did not think proper to give her chase. During
the Action my Officers and men behaved with great
Spirit ; my loss during the action was two men

killed, viz. Mr. Nathan Haskell, Lt. Marines, and Thoms Ransford." [1] The Mars returned to Boston later in the year.

The Portuguese ambassador at Paris having complained of the seizure by the Mars of the vessel belonging to one of his countrymen and of alleged illtreatment, Franklin advised sending the claim to America, and wrote to the President of Congress, December 3, saying: "I hope the Congress may think fit to take some notice of this affair and not only forward a speedy decision, but give orders to our cruisers not to meddle with neutral ships for the future, it being a practice apt to produce ill blood and contrary to the spirit of the new league, which is approved by all Europe; and the English property found in such vessels will hardly pay the damages brought on us by the irregular proceedings of our captains in endeavoring to get at such property." [2] Congress had already, on October 5, "Resolved, That the board of admiralty prepare and report instructions for the commanders of armed vessels commanded by the United States conformable to the principles contained in the declaration of the Empress of all the Russias on the rights of neutral vessels. That the ministers plenipotentiary from the United States, if invited thereto, be and hereby are respectively empowered to accede to such

[1] *Massachusetts Mag.*, October, 1910; *Mass. Rev. Rolls*, xxxix, 215; *Mass. Archives*, cliii, 400.

[2] *Wharton*, iv, 180.

regulations conformable to the spirit of the said declaration as may be agreed upon by the Congress expected to assemble in pursuance of the invitation of her Imperial majesty." [1]

The privateer General Pickering of Salem, a ship of a hundred and eighty tons commanded by Captain Haraden, carrying sixteen six-pounders and forty-seven men, on a voyage to Spain fell in with a twenty-gun British cutter, May 29, 1780, and beat her off after an action of an hour and three quarters. Three days later, in the Bay of Biscay, the Pickering captured a schooner called the Golden Eagle with fourteen nine-pounders, eight fours, and fifty-seven men. June 4, while proceeding towards Bilbao, she fell in with the British privateer Achilles armed with twenty-two nine-pounders and eighteen other guns and with a crew of a hundred and thirty men. She was a very much larger ship than the Pickering. They fought nearly three hours at close range and the Achilles then sheered off and sailed away, the Pickering being unable to follow. This battle was fought close to the Spanish coast and was watched by a multitude of people. [2]

During the year 1780 the Continental navy suffered the loss of nearly half its fleet at the fall of Charleston: the Providence, Boston, Queen of

[1] *Wharton*, iv, 81.
[2] *Independent Chronicle*, August, 10, 17, 1780; *Hunt's Merchants' Mag.*, February, 1857; *Clark*, i, 114.

France, and Ranger. Of the thirteen frigates provided for in 1775, the Trumbull alone remained at the end of the year, and this ship with the frigates Alliance, Confederacy, and Deane and the sloop of war Saratoga comprised the whole navy in commission, except the Ariel loaned by France and only temporarily on the list. The America and Bourbon were still far from completed and were destined never to go to sea in the Continental service. Little had been accomplished by the navy during the year; few prizes of any considerable value or importance had been taken. The hotly contested action of the Trumbull with the Watt enhanced somewhat the reputation of a service that had suffered from the shortcomings of zealous and brave but untrained officers.

As the navy dwindled, privateering continued to thrive and grow. The number of private armed vessels commissioned by the different states doubtless increased considerably, though figures are not accessible. The Continental Congress issued three hundred and one letters of marque in 1780, ninety-two more than in 1779.[1] Although it is evident that privateers were increasing in numbers, there seem to be fewer accounts of their cruises than in previous years.

The increase in the total number of ships of the British navy during 1780 was from four hundred and eighty-one to five hundred and thirty-eight; of

[1] *Naval Records* (calendar), 217–495.

these, three hundred and ninety-six were in commission at the end of the year, as compared with three hundred and sixty-four twelve months earlier. The navy employed eighty-five thousand seamen and marines, an increase of fifteen thousand. In the fall there were fifty-nine vessels of all classes on the North American station, including two of ninety guns each, eleven seventy-fours, five sixty-fours, three forty-fours, and fourteen frigates. Earlier in the year the number seems to have been considerably smaller. There were eleven vessels at Newfoundland and a strong fleet in the West Indies.[1]

According to the table of losses and captures, already cited for previous years, the enemies of England in 1780 took five hundred and ninety-six of her vessels, of which fifteen were privateers and the rest merchantmen; of these, two hundred and sixty-two were retaken or ransomed. During the same time the British captured from their enemies two hundred and thirty-seven vessels including thirty-four privateers; of this total only four were recaptured.[2]

[1] *Hannay*, ii, 211; *Schomberg*, ii, 1, iv, 353–364; *Brit. Adm. Rec.*, *A. D. 486*, September 30, 1780, List of Ships and Vessels Employed under the orders of Vice-Admiral Arbuthnot.

[2] *Clowes*, iii, 396.

CHAPTER XVI

NAVAL OPERATIONS IN 1781

THE frigate Alliance, Captain Barry, was made ready at Boston for another voyage to France as soon as the court martial of Captain Landais was over. There was the usual delay and difficulty in recruiting a crew for the ship and application was made to the state government for authority to impress seamen and to enlist soldiers. The former request was denied, but permission was obtained to enroll volunteers from the guard at the castle and it was again necessary to take a considerable number of British prisoners. A turbulent ship's company was the consequence and a sanguinary brawl on Long Wharf with the crews of two French frigates was an early result. Some distinguished passengers were taken, including Colonel John Laurens and Thomas Paine. Several others obtained passage on condition that if necessary they should serve against the enemy or in quelling mutiny. Laurens was a son of Henry Laurens, still a prisoner in England, and was bound on an important mission to France. He was the bearer of a letter, dated January 15, 1781, from General Washington, addressed to himself (Laurens), discoursing on the objects of his mission; it was afterwards submitted to Vergennes. In this letter, first of all, the imperative need of money to carry on the approaching campaign was urged. Washington then says: "Next to a loan of money, a constant naval superiority on these coasts is the object most interesting. This would instantly reduce the enemy to a difficult defensive and, by removing all prospect of extending their acquisitions, would take away the motives for prosecuting the war. Indeed, it is not to be conceived how they could subsist a large force in this country, if we had the command of the seas to interrupt the regular transmission of supplies from Europe. This superiority, with an aid in money, would enable us to convert the war into a vigorous offensive. I say nothing of the advantages to the trade of both nations, nor how infinitely it would facilitate our supplies. With respect to us, it seems to be one of two deciding points, and it appears too to be the interest of our allies, abstracted from the immediate benefits to this country, to transfer the naval war to America. The number of ports friendly to them, hostile to the British, the materials for repairing their disabled ships, the extensive supplies towards the subsistence of their fleet, are circumstances which would give them a palpable advantage in the contest of these seas."[1] The Alliance sailed from Boston, February 11, 1781. On the voyage a small British privateer was taken and her prize, a Vene-

[1] *Washington*, ix, 106.

tian ship, was released. The frigate arrived at L'Orient, March 9.[1]

The two main objects of Washington's desire, indispensable at this critical period, were realized. Money was obtained and a French fleet soon set sail for America. March 29, the Alliance got under way for her return voyage in company with a large French letter of marque called the Marquis de Lafayette, loaded with military stores. Soon after sailing, a mutiny was discovered on the Alliance. John Kessler, mate of the frigate, who wrote a narrative of her voyages, says that " on March 30th an Indian, one of the forecastle men, gave Captain Barry information of a combination among the crew for the purpose of taking the ship, and pointing out three who had strove to prevail on him to be concerned therein. The three men were immediately put in irons and all the officers, with such of the crew as could be confided in, were armed and required to remain all night on deck. On the next morning all hands were called and placed on the forecastle, booms, and gangways, excepting the officers and such part of the crew in whom Captain Barry confided, who, armed, strongly guarded the quarter deck, the steerage, and the main deck, to keep the remainder of the crew together on the forecastle and boom. The three designated men were

---

[1] *Barry*, ch. xii; *Wharton*, iv, 249, 250, 252, 279, 826; *Mass. Court Rec.*, January 29, 1781; *Mass. Acts and Resolves*, February 6, 1781; *Boston Gazette*, January 1, 1781.

brought out of their irons on the quarter and, being stripped and hoisted by the thumbs to the mizzen stay, underwent a very severe whipping before either would make any confession. The names of 25 of their accomplices were obtained from them before the whipping was discontinued. As their accomplices were disclosed, they were called to the quarter deck, stripped and tied to the ridge-rope of the netting and the whipping continued until it was thought all were disclosed that could possibly be obtained, which proved to be. That it was intended to take the ship on her passage out by killing all the officers in the middle watch of the night, except the second Lieutenant, P. Fletcher, who was to navigate her to some port in Ireland, or on failure, to be destroyed. A quartermaster, one of the mutineers, was to have command. They had all been bound by an oath on the Bible administered by the Captain's assistant cabin steward, and had also signed their names in a round robin so-called, but that they found no good opportunity on the outward passage and intended to accomplish the taking of the ship as aforesaid immediately on leaving France. But on coming out of L'Orient we lost a man overboard who was one of the chief ringleaders and they considering that as a bad omen, threw the round robin overboard and relinquished their designs. The three principles were placed securely in irons and the remainder, after being admonished by Captain Barry and on their solemn declaration to conduct themselves well, were permitted to return to ship's duty."[1] The three principals were afterwards tried and sentenced to death, but this penalty was not exacted.

Kessler further relates that "on April 2nd, 1781, two brigs gave us chase and were permitted to come up. One ran close on board of us and without any hail fired the whole broadside at us and immediately every one run off her deck. We had commenced firing, but on discovering their retreat the firing ceased and we boarded them. She proved to be a brig with flush deck and 20 twelve pounders, two six pounders and 14 [four-pound coehorns], with 112 men, called the Mars and belonging to the Guernsey. The crew were taken aboard the Alliance and all put in irons without distinction, Captain Barry considering them as not meriting other treatment in consequence of their firing on us with no intention of bravely fighting. The other brig was a Jersey called the Minerva, of 10 guns and 55 men. She was taken possession of and manned by the Marquis de Lafayette, our consort. Soon after, in a gale of wind, we parted with our consort and the prizes."[2] A month later two other prizes were taken. May 16, the Alliance was struck by lightning, which shattered her main topmast and burned several men.

An action was fought, May 29, with the British ship Atalanta and brig Trepassey in about north

[1] *Barry*, 133.   [2] *Ibid.*, 134.

latitude 40° and west longitude 63°, which is described by Kessler. "Towards evening [of the 28th]
discovered two sail on the weather bow standing
for us and which after coming near enough to be
kept in sight, hauled to wind and stood on our course.
Towards day it became quite calm. After it became
light it appeared that they were an armed ship and
brig, about a league distant. At sunrise they hoisted
the English colors and beat drums. At the same
time the American colors were displayed by the
Alliance. By little puffs of wind we were enabled
to get within short hailing distance." At eleven
o'clock the ships hailed each other. "The firing
then began, but unfortunately there was not wind
enough for our steerage way and they being lighter
vessels, by using sweeps got and kept athwart our
stern and on our quarters, so that we could not
bring one-half our guns, nay, oft time only one gun
out astern to bear on them, and thus laying like a
log the greatest part of the time. About two o'clock
Captain Barry received a wound by a grape shot
in the shoulder. He remained, however, on the
quarter deck until by the much loss of blood he was
obliged to be helped to the cock-pit. Some time
after, our colors were shot away and it so happened
that at the same time such guns as would bear on
them had been fired and were then loading, and
which led the enemy to think we had struck the
colors, and manned their shrouds and gave three
cheers; by that time the colors were hoisted by a

mizen brail and our firing again began. A quarter-master went to the wheel in place of one just killed there. At the moment a small breeze of wind happening, a broadside was brought to bear and fired on the ship and then one on the brig, when they struck their colors at three o'clock." [1]

Captain Edwards of the Atalanta, testifying at his court martial, said of the Alliance that when "about two cables lengths to leeward she hoisted Rebel colours and fir'd a Shot across us. I immediately hoisted our colours, when she fired her broadside, wore, and as soon as on the other tack and her Guns woud bear, kept a constant Fire on us; our Firing began on her, but being at too great a distance, I ceast our Fire and endeavour'd to get nearer to her, which having effected she haild us, said she was the Alliance continental Frigate and desired we would strike." Edwards tried to keep up a conversation until the Trepassey could get up, but the Alliance began the action again. The Trepassey was so anxious to get up that she passed under the stern of the Alliance "with too much way and in hauling under her Quarter, shot abreast of her; in this situation she received two broadsides." The Atalanta was then brought under the frigate's stern and got between her and the Trepassey. The Atalanta continued the action an hour and a half longer, nearly three hours in all; she was then so greatly disabled in masts, yards, sails, and rigging as to be

[1] *Barry*, 135, 136.

unmanageable. It was accordingly necessary to strike and the Trepassey, unable to get away, struck also. The Atalanta's mainmast soon went over the side.[1] The master of the Trepassey, describing the battle, says that the Alliance, at a distance of half a mile to leeward, " hoisted rebel colours and gave the Atalanta and us a broadside, we being then very nigh to each other; we then bore up close alongside of her, the Atalanta on the starboard and the Trepassey on the larboard quarter, and began to engage. About an hour after the action began Capt. Smith of the Trepassey was killed." [2]

The Atalanta, which carried sixteen guns and a hundred and twenty-five men, lost six killed and eighteen wounded; the Trepassey, with fourteen guns and eighty men, lost six killed, including the captain, and eleven wounded. The Alliance mounted twenty-eight twelve-pounders and eight nines; her crew was reduced by manning prizes and weakened by disaffection and sickness. Her loss was five killed, including the lieutenant of marines, and twenty-two wounded, three of them mortally. Captain Edwards and a few other officers were sent on board the Alliance; also some of the wounded. Captain Barry agreed with the British to send the Trepassey as a cartel to Halifax with all his other prisoners, about two hundred and fifty in number, to be exchanged for Americans; before entering

[1] *Brit. Adm. Rec., Courts Martial*, No. 5319 (October 15, 1781).
[2] *Almon*, xii, 160.

upon this service the Trepassey's guns were thrown overboard. She arrived in due time at Halifax. The Atalanta, which had been dismasted in the engagement, was fitted with jury masts and put in charge of Hezekiah Welch, second lieutenant of the Alliance as prize master. Some weeks later, in the Vice-Admiralty Court at Halifax, Welch testified that he was ordered by Captain Barry "to take possession of the Atalanta and proceed with her to Boston, New England ; that on their passage thither the 7th June last, being near Cape Cod, they fell in with His Majesty's ships of War the Assurance, Charlestown, Amphitrite and Vulture, which retook the said sloop Atalanta, put a British officer & Seamen on board her & sent her safe into this Port of Halifax."[1] The Marquis de Lafayette, letter of marque, which parted from the Alliance in April, was also unlucky. She fell in with the enemy's Jamaica fleet under a strong convoy and after a hard fight of three hours was captured by a greatly superior force. The Alliance arrived at Boston, June 6. During the summer she was sheathed with copper on Barry's recommendation.[2]

The presence in Massachusetts Bay of the British squadron which recaptured the Atalanta, and which the Alliance had the good fortune not to meet with, is explained in a letter of Admiral Ar-

[1] *Essex Inst. Coll.*, January, 1909.

[2] *Barry*, chs. xiii, xiv ; *Almon*, xii, 158–160 ; *Boston Gazette*, June 11, July 9, 1781; *London Chronicle*, August 7, 1781; *Lee MSS.*, July 15, 1782, report on loss of the Lafayette.

buthnot to the Admiralty, dated off Sandy Hook, July 4, 1781 : " The rumours that had been abroad for a considerable time past, that a reinforcement of troops was daily expected from France, induced me to send a squadron into Boston Bay of superior force, as the enemy's guard was reported to be only two frigates; the Assurance, Charles-Town, Amphitrite, Vulture, and Savage are employed on this service, and the Royal Oak, on her way to Halifax, was directed to take that route. I have since, by the channel of the Rebels, received intelligence that a few recruits and some storeships have notwithstanding got into Boston, with a French fifty gun ship and two frigates; but Captain Duncan of the Medea, which arrived from Halifax on the 30th ult., informs me that his Majesty's sloop the Atalanta, which had been taken after a very gallant action by the rebel Frigate Alliance, of 40 guns, was retaken by that detachment in Boston Bay, and that he spoke a store-ship of near 800 tons, also a prize, on her entrance into the port of Halifax as he came out. It is believed that they have been much more successful, but I have no authentic advices of their operations. . . . The Medea on her return captured two privateers from Salem, the ship Rover, of 18 six pounders and 140 men, and the sloop Revenge of 10 guns." [1]

The frigate Trumbull, Captain James Nicholson, spent the first half of the year 1781 fitting out at

[1] *Almon*, xii, 158, 159.

Philadelphia for a cruise, under the accustomed difficulties imposed by lack of money and scarcity of seamen. The Deane, Captain Samuel Nicholson, the Confederacy, Captain Harding, and the Saratoga, Captain Young, cruised in the West Indies during the winter and early spring. They sailed, March 20, from Cape François bound north in company with a French frigate and a large convoy of American and French merchantmen. The Deane arrived at Boston about the middle of April. The Confederacy, on April 15, fell in with the British ships Roebuck, 44, and Orpheus, 32. In the face of so superior a force, and with the working of his ship hindered by a large cargo of military supplies, Captain Harding considered resistance useless and promptly struck his flag. Thus ended the brief and unlucky career in the Continental service of this fine frigate. She was taken into the British navy under the name of Confederate. Several of the convoy were also taken. It would appear that the Saratoga, after parting from her consorts, was lost at sea, for she was never heard of again.[1]

The Trumbull got to sea at last and took her departure from the Delaware capes August 8; among her lieutenants were Richard Dale and

[1] *Pap. Cont. Congr.*, **37**, 355, 411, 471, 475, 505 (February 7, April 28, May 5, June 6, 1781) ; *Boston Gazette*, January 29, March 19, April 16, 30, May 14, 1781; *Continental Journal*, March 22, April 19, 26, 1781 ; *Independent Chronicle*, May 4, 10, 1781 ; *Papers New London Hist. Soc.*, IV, i, 62; *Navy Rec. Soc.*, vi, 109; *Barney*, 86.

Alexander Murray, a volunteer. She sailed in company with a twenty-four-gun privateer, a fourteen-gun letter of marque and a convoy of twenty-eight merchantmen. The same day three sail were discovered to the eastward, two of which gave chase to the convoy. Night came on rainy and squally and the Trumbull carried away her fore-topmast and main-topgallantmast. She was obliged to run before the wind and the rest of the fleet left her. Captain Nicholson reported: "The wreck of the topmast with the yard and rigging laying aback of the foresail and over the bows, the topsail yard arm came through the foresail and on the forecastle, so that with our utmost exertion we could not clear ourselves of the wreck until one of the ships came alongside and the other in sight. Immediately all hands were called to quarters; instead of coming, three quarters of them ran below, put out the lights, matches, &c. With the remainder and a few brave officers we commenced an action with the Iris for one hour and thirty-five minutes, at the end of which the other ship came up and fired into us. Seeing no prospect of escaping in this unequal contest, I struck, having my first and third lieuts. and Capt. Murray, a volunteer, with eight others wounded and 5 killed. My crew consisted of 180 men, 45 of whom were taken out of the new goal — prisoners of war; they through treachery and others from cowardice betrayed me, or at least prevented my making the resistance I would have done. At no time of the engagement had I more than 40 men upon deck."[1] The British thirty-two-gun frigate Iris had formerly been the American frigate Hancock, captured by the Rainbow in 1777. Her consort was the eighteen-gun ship General Monk, also a prize, having been originally an American privateer called the General Washington. The Trumbull was almost a wreck and was towed into New York by the Iris. She was not taken into the British service. A few weeks after this the Iris and another British frigate were captured by the French.[2]

In the summer of 1781 the Board of Admiralty ceased to exist and the management of naval affairs passed under the control of Robert Morris as Agent of Marine.[3] He issued orders for a cruise together of the Alliance and Deane, which were now the only Continental vessels in commission. He wrote to Captain Barry, September 21: " When these ships are ready you will proceed to sea. The Ships are both under your command, the Captain of the Deane being instructed to obey your orders, wherefore you had best to furnish him a copy of these instructions, giving such in addition as you shall judge necessary for Keeping Company, respecting Signals, Places of Rendevous in case of Separation

[1] *Continental Journal*, September 13, 1781.

[2] *Port Folio*, May, 1814; *Clark*, i, 124; *Almon*, xii, 259, 260; *Independent Ledger*, October 8, 1781; *Papers New London Hist. Soc.*, IV, i, 57, 58.

[3] See above, p. 37.

and all other things that tend to promote Success and Glory or secure Safety against superior force. It is my intention that you should go upon a cruize and therefore you will be ready to sail from the Harbour of Boston and use your best Efforts to disturb the Enemy. Such prizes as you may make you will send into the Port which you will find endorsed, a list of Persons in several Ports to whom to apply in Case you go yourselves or send your Prizes thither. . . . I do not fix your cruizing ground nor limit the length of your cruize, because I expect you will know the most likely course and will be anxious to meet such events as will do honor to the American flag and promote the general interest. When you want provisions, I think it will be best that you should enter the Delaware and send up as far as New Castle, to which place they can best be sent in shallops. The latitude I have given precludes both the necessity and propriety of more particular instructions. Let me hear from you by every convenient opportunity and don't fail to transmit to His Excellency the Commander-in-Chief of our Army, as well as to me, any intelligence that you may obtain which you think may in any wise affect his operations." [1] October 17, the Deane not being ready, Morris sent orders to Barry to cruise alone in the Alliance, but the fall of Yorktown soon after this caused a change of plans and both ships remained in port.[2]

[1] *Barry*, 151.   [2] *Ibid.*, 150–154; *Publ. R. I. Hist. Soc.*, viii, 273.

The quarrels of Jones and Landais in France in 1780, the failure of the Alliance to bring over the clothing and stores so much needed by the army, and other circumstances led to much dissatisfaction in and out of Congress, and in March, 1781, soon after his return to America in the Ariel, Jones was called upon to explain his conduct. The Board of Admiralty propounded a list of forty-seven questions covering all his movements since taking command of the Ranger in 1777. Jones answered these questions promptly and fully, and his replies cleared up all doubts as to his various transactions in Europe, naval, political, and financial. Influenced by the good impression he made in this matter and by the honors paid him in Europe, Congress resolved, April 14, 1781, "That the thanks of the United States in Congress assembled be given to Captain John Paul Jones, for the zeal, prudence and intrepidity with which he has supported the honor of the American flag, for his bold and successful enterprises to redeem from captivity the citizens of these States who had fallen under the power of the enemy, and in general for the good conduct and eminent services by which he has added lustre to his character and to the American arms; that the thanks of the United States in Congress assembled be also given to the officers and men who have faithfully served under him from time to time for their steady affection to the cause of their country and the bravery and perseverance they have mani-

fested therein." [1] A few weeks after this a special
committee of Congress recommended Jones's promotion to the rank of rear-admiral, but, owing to
the jealousy and opposition of other officers, no
action was taken. The Ariel was sent back to
France in the summer or early fall of 1781. [2]

The Massachusetts ship Mars remained in the
river Loire [3] about three months and then returned
to Boston, arriving February 28, 1781, with a
prize. The frigate Protector, during the early part
of the year, cruised in the West Indies, part of
the time in company with the Continental frigate
Deane, and with some success. In the Massachusetts House of Representatives, March 3, the following action was taken: "Whereas by recent
Advices received by express from the Eastward it
appears that the Enemy with a Number of Armed
Vessels are daily committing the most horrid Depredations and Cruelties on the Inhabitants who
reside on or near the Sea Coasts in the County of
Lincoln," it was resolved to request the French
admiral at Newport to send one or two frigates, to
fit out the ship Mars immediately, and to grant
bounties to privateers which should capture the
enemy's vessels. [4] May 19, it was resolved to send
an armed vessel with provisions for the relief of

[1] *Sherburne*, 225.

[2] *Ibid.*, 214–226; *Sands*, 321–328; *Wharton*, iv, 288–297; *Logs
of Serapis, Alliance, Ariel*, 125; *Barry*, 149; *Pap. Cont. Congr.*,
37, 401, 405; *Royal Gazette*, July 10, 1782.

[3] See above, p. 540.   [4] *Mass. Court Rec.*

the garrison at Machias, and to reinforce the garrison. Conditions along the Maine coast continued to be a source of chronic irritation at the seat of the state government in Boston and strongly worded resolves were from time to time adopted in the General Court. Notwithstanding the Penobscot disaster of two years before, the possibility of driving out the British remained, with the more sanguine, a practical question. The Mars, under the command of Captain Nevins, and apparently unaccompanied by the French frigates asked for, cruised during the spring and took two prizes. The new ship Tartar seems to have met with great delay in building and it was proposed to sell her, but this was not done at the time; she was not ready for service until the following year. The sale of the Mars was also considered. In the summer a sloop called the Defence was added to the Massachusetts navy and made one cruise, after the return to port of the Mars and under the same captain, James Nevins. Another severe blow came to the Massachusetts navy in 1781, in the loss of its most powerful vessel, the Protector, which was captured, May 5, by the British ship Roebuck and frigate Medea.[1]

The frigate Indien, which had been built at

[1] *Boston Gazette*, March 5, 19, April 30, May 14, July 2, 1781; *Independent Chronicle*, May 4, 1781; *Massachusetts Mag.*, July, October, 1910, January, 1911, January, 1912; *Mass. Court Rec.*, February 14, March 3, 6, 7, May 19, 1781; *Mass. Rev. Rolls*, xxxix, 45; *Mass. Archives*, clviii, 212; *Fox*, 79-88.

Amsterdam for the Continental navy and then sold
to the King of France,[1] later became the property
of the Chevalier Luxembourg, who leased her in
1779 or 1780 to Commodore Alexander Gillon of
the South Carolina navy. Gillon had been in Europe
since 1778, employed in furthering the naval and
commercial interests of his state. He made enemies
and his reputation has suffered from statements
concerning his financial transactions. He changed
the name of the Indien to South Carolina, manned
her largely with American sailors from English
prisons, and armed her with twenty-eight thirty-
six-pounders[2] and twelve twelves. He moved her
from Amsterdam to the Texel during the summer
and fall of 1780, the passage being much obstructed
by shoal water. While on the way the South Carolina was joined by Lieutenant Matthewman, who
had been engaged as master. This officer gives an
account in his " Narrative " of conditions on board
the frigate during his stay. " In Rotterdam," he
says, " I saw Commodore Gillon, the commander of
the ship, who gave me his directions. On my arrival
on board the ship, then laying about half way between Amsterdam and the Texel, everything was
in confusion, three of the Lieutenants were under
arrest, and the ship like a mere wreck, her crew
then about 250 men mostly Americans, who had

[1] See above, p. 285.
[2] Thirty-nine-pounders, according to the British account, *Brit.
Adm. Rec., A. D. 490,* January 18, 1783. See below, p. 586.

made their escape and had got on board under pretence of giving them a passage to America; where
they were near a twelve month . . . and were
never allowed the liberty of slipping over the ship's
side. I myself was seven months on board, though
master of the ship. On some disagreement I quit
the ship and returned to Amsterdam." [1] The South
Carolina remained at the Texel until August, 1781,
when she was finally ready for sea. She had a crew
of five hundred and fifty, including three hundred
French marines. She cruised first in the North Sea,
and on August 25, captured and burned a prize.
September 1, she was off the Shetland Islands and
on the 3d her log records: " Hove the Corps of a
French Mareen over Aboard at 8 P.M." On the 7th,
she captured a sixteen-gun Liverpool privateer; the
same day, " Put 2 French Mereens in Irons for Insulting Lieut. White." By the middle of the month
the South Carolina was making a southerly course,
and on the 24th, " Mored att Carone in Spain."
October 17, she sailed from Coruna, and on the
21st, in latitude 37° 52', " Brought Tew A Brigg;
She Pruved to Be A Brigg from Newfound Land
Called the Venus." On the 31st, the South Carolina was off Teneriffe. She made a short cruise in
the West Indies, then sailed north, and, December
31, was off Charleston. The next day, however, she
" Bore Away for the Havannah." [2]

[1] *Mag. Amer. Hist.*, March, 1878.
[2] *Log of the South Carolina; Paullin*, 436–438 ; *Wharton*, iv, 546,

In a letter, dated September 23, 1781, Captain Stirling reported the capture of his ship, a sixteen-gun sloop of war of the British navy, by an American privateer. "It is," he says, "with the most poignant grief I acquaint your Excellency of the capture of his Majesty's sloop Savage, late under my command. . . . Early in the morning of the 6th instant, 10 leagues East of Charles-town, we espied a ship bearing down on us, who when about four miles distant, hauled her wind to the East-ward, shewing by her appearance she was an American cruizer; her force could not be so easily distinguished. I therefore gave way to the pleasing idea that she was a privateer carrying 20 nine-pounders, whom I had intelligence was cruizing off here, and instantly resolved either to bring her to action or oblige her to quit the coast, for which purpose we gave chase, but were prevented continuing it long by her edging down, seemingly determined to engage us. Conscious of her superiority in sailing and force, this manœuvre coinciding with my wishes, I caused the Savage to lay by till we perceived on her nearer approach she was far superior to what we imagined and that it was necessary to attempt making our escape, without some fortunate shot, in the course of a running fight we

547; *So. Carolina Hist. and Gen. Mag.*, January, April, 1900; *Boston Gazette*, November 19, 1781; *Independent Chronicle*, November 22, 1781; *Royal Gazette*, July 10, 1782; *Lee MSS.*, July 5, 1779, June, 1780; *Adams MSS.*, March 8, September 26, October 26, 1781.

saw inevitable, admitted our taking advantages and bring on a more equal conflict. At half past ten she began firing bow chacers and at eleven, being close on our quarter, the action commenced with musquetry, which after a good deal of execution was followed by a heavy cannonade on both sides. In an hour's time I had the mortification to see our braces and bow-lines shot away and not a rope left to trim the sail with, notwithstanding every precaution had been taken; however, our fire was so constant and well-directed that the enemy did not see our situation, but kept alongside of us till accident obliged him to drop astern. The Savage was now almost a wreck, her sails, rigging and yard so much cut that it was with the utmost difficulty we could alter our position time enough to avoid being raked, the enemy lying directly athwart our stern for some minutes. This was the only intermission of great guns, but musquetry and pistols still did execution and continued till they opened again, which was not till both ships were almost on board each other, when the battle became more furious than before. Our quarter-deck and forecastle were soon now nearly cleared, scarce a man belonging to either not being killed or wounded, with three guns on our main-deck rendered useless. In this situation we fought near an hour with only five six-pounders, the fire from each ship's guns scorching the men who opposed them, shot and other implements of war thrown by hand doing execution,

when our mizen-mast being shot away by the board,
our main-mast tottering with only three shrouds
standing, the ship on fire dangerously, only 40 men
on duty to oppose the foe who was attempting to
board us in three places, no succour in sight or
possibility of making further resistance, I was necessitated at a quarter before three P.M. to surrender to the Congress, a private ship of war belonging to Philadelphia, who carried 215 men and
mounted 20 twelve pounders on her main-deck and 4
sixes above, fourteen of which were fought on one
side. She lost during the action eleven men and
had near thirty wounded, several of them mortally;
her masts, her sails and rigging were so much damaged that she was obliged to return to port, which
partly answered my wishes prior to the action, as
a great part of the Carolina trade was daily expected on the coast and this privateer we saw sailed
remarkably fast. Three days were employed putting
her in a condition to make sail and five for the Savage, who was exceedingly shattered. Indeed it is as-
tonishing more damage was not done, as the weather
was fine, the water remarkably smooth, and the ships
never 30 yards asunder." [1] Stirling reported a loss
of eight killed and twenty-six wounded. The Congress was commanded by Captain Geddes and her
loss was eight killed and thirty wounded. The Savage was recaptured by the British frigate Solebay.[2]

[1] *Almon*, xiii, 48, 49; *Ann. Reg.* (1781), 251.
[2] *Clark*, i, 125; *Penn. Gazette*, September 19, November 28,

In addition to privateering upon the sea, active maritime warfare was carried on during the Revolution by means of boats alongshore and in harbors, inlets, and bays. Whaleboats, barges, and other small open craft were employed, with eight or more oars, sometimes as many as twenty-four, and also carrying sail, and with a swivel or heavier gun mounted in the bow. Their crews numbered from less than a dozen to thirty or more. A flotilla of four or five such boats made a formidable armament. Sometimes by surprise at night and sometimes by direct attack, they captured merchantmen, transports, and supply ships, and occasionally armed vessels of considerable force. Nantucket and Vineyard Sounds, Long Island Sound, Chesapeake Bay, and, most of all, the New Jersey shore and lower New York Bay were the waters chiefly frequented by these whaleboat privateersmen. The British and loyalists employed the same sort of boats in their predatory warfare along the shores of Chesapeake Bay and Long Island Sound; and boat expeditions were sent out from British men-of-war for the same kind of work. The most famous of the American flotillamen was Adam Hyler of New Jersey, who

1781; *Brit. Adm. Rec., Instance and Prize Records*, **44**, 401. See further on privateering in 1781, *Clark*, i, 120, 127; *Tucker*, ch. viii; *A. Sherburne*, 37–49; *Mil. and Nav. Mag. U. S.*, July, 1833; *Papers New London Hist. Soc.*, IV, i, 20; *Massachusetts Mag.*, January, 1908; *Boston Gazette.* February 19, April 9, 16, 30, May 7, June 4, 25, July 2, August 6, September 10, 1781; *Continental Journal*, February 1, May 24, 1781; *Conn. Courant*, August 7, 1781; *Freeman's Journal*, May 16, 1781; *London Chronicle*, May 10, 1781.

bore a commission from his state. He and others began their operations after the occupation of New York by the British in 1776. They cruised between Egg Harbor and Staten Island. Sometimes their boats were destroyed by parties sent from the British fleet, but new ones were soon built to replace them. Hyler was most active in 1781 and 1782.[1]

Several marauding expeditions in Chesapeake Bay were conducted by the British during the Revolution. That of Collier and Mathew in 1779 has been noticed.[2] In the fall of 1780, General Leslie, with about three thousand men and a naval force consisting of the Romulus of forty-four guns, the frigate Blonde, and some smaller vessels, including one of John Goodrich's, seized Portsmouth, Virginia. December 30, the expedition of Benedict Arnold with sixteen hundred men, which had sailed from New York on the 12th with several frigates, arrived in Chesapeake Bay. During the early part of January, 1781, Arnold raided up the James River as far as Richmond and destroyed much property. Governor Jefferson of Virginia

---

[1] *Naval Mag.*, November, 1836 ; *Mag. Amer. Hist.*, March, 1878, March, 1882 ; *N. Y. Gen. and Biogr. Rec.*, April, 1891 ; *Clark*, i, 113, 120 ; *Boston Post*, October 17, 1778, January 23, February 6, 1779, May 11, 1782 ; *Penn. Packet*, May 2, 1780, May 29, 1781 ; *Independent Chronicle*, May 17, 1781, January 9, 1783 ; *Freeman's Journal*, April 25, December 26, 1781, June 26, 1882 ; *Salem Gazette*, August 15, 1782 ; *Boston Gazette*, March 31, 1783 ; *Pickering MSS.*, xliv, 162 ; *Almon*, xiv, 35 ; *N. Y. Eve. Post*, July 18, 1883, quoted in *Proc. Mass. Hist. Soc.*, January, 1884.

[2] See above, p. 395.

made strenuous efforts in the defense of his State. Arnold soon retired to Portsmouth where he remained until spring. Meanwhile, in February, a French sixty-four-gun ship and two frigates captured the Romulus and several small vessels of Arnold's fleet. Another raid was made in April and May by twenty-five hundred men under Generals Phillips and Arnold. The expedition left Portsmouth April 18, fell down to Hampton Roads, and thence proceeded up the James and Chickahominy Rivers. April 27, the British met with firm resistance on the part of the Virginia navy on the James River; the most important of these vessels were the ships Tempest and Renown of sixteen guns each and the fourteen-gun brigantine Jefferson. This force, however, the invaders finally overcame, capturing a number of vessels that the Americans had not time to destroy. This nearly put an end to the Virginia navy. Phillips died May 13, leaving Arnold in command. Soon after this, upon the arrival of Cornwallis in Virginia, Arnold returned to New York.[1]

When the American and French armies marched south in August, 1781, General Clinton sought to divert them from their purpose by sending Arnold on another marauding expedition, this time to Con-

[1] *Almon*, xi, 157, 322, xii, 60; *Jefferson*, ii, 391–410; *Boston Gazette*, March 5, 1781; *Navy Rec. Soc.*, vi, 93–102; *Dawson*, ch. lxxx; *Narr. and Crit. Hist.*, vi, 546; *Virginia Hist. Reg.*, July, 1848, July, 1849, October, 1851; *So. Lit. Messenger*, June, 1839, March, 1857.

necticut. Having collected a force on the Long
Island shore at a point about thirty miles from
New London, Arnold weighed anchor early in the
evening of September 5. He had about seventeen
hundred men on board twenty-four vessels. Captain Bazeley was in command of the fleet. They
appeared off New London early the next morning.
The force was landed in two divisions, nine hundred men on the west side of the Thames River and
eight hundred on the east. Arnold led the western
division and had little difficulty in taking New
London; the town was burned. Fort Griswold, at
Groton, on the east side of the river, made a strong
resistance, but it was finally captured by the British and loyalists and a massacre of the garrison
followed. A very large amount of property on shore
was destroyed; also all the shipping, except a few
vessels that escaped up the river. The expedition
then returned to New York.[1]

The most important naval event of 1781 was the
culmination of the struggle for naval supremacy in
American waters on the part of the French and
British, which decided the outcome of the war. In
December, 1780, war between Holland and England
was declared, and in February, 1781, Admiral
Rodney, the British naval commander-in-chief in
the West Indies, seized the Dutch island of St.
Eustatius, with a vast amount of property both

[1] *Almon*, xiii, 53, 58; *Dawson*, ch. xcviii; *Narr. and Crit. Hist.*,
vi, 562.

public and private, thereby breaking up a depot for the supply and transshipment of goods and military stores, which had been during the war of great importance to the Americans and an invaluable aid to their cause. After the capture, through the very questionable expedient of leaving Dutch colors flying, Rodney was able greatly to increase the amount of booty by decoying into the roadstead many unsuspecting vessels. He wrote to Germain, March 26 : " I may speak within bounds when I say that since taking this island upwards of two hundred thousand pounds in value of tobacco has fell into our hands." The spoils were sent home to England in thirty-four ships, most of which were fortunately captured by the French in the English Channel. Before the end of the year, St. Eustatius also was captured by the French.[1]

The French fleet in Newport, now commanded by Commodore Destouches, sailed for Chesapeake Bay early in March, closely followed by Arbuthnot from Gardiner's Bay, who by superior sailing arrived off the capes in time to head off the French. A battle followed in which Destouches had the advantage and yet he ran out to sea, allowing Ar-

[1] *Mahan*, 382 ; *Channing*, iii, 323–327 ; *Almon*, xi, 260, xiii, 119 ; *Amer. Hist. Rev.*, viii (July, 1903), 699–708 ; *London Chronicle*, March 15, 1781 ; *Boston Gazette*, April 2, 1781 ; *Navy Rec. Soc.*, xxxviii, 123–126 ; *Stopford-Sackville MSS.*, 202, 207 (Rodney to Germain, March 4, 26, 1781) ; *Letters of Lord Rodney*. Rodney's letters disclose the vindictiveness which marked his conduct at St. Eustatius.

buthnot to enter the bay undisturbed and form a
junction with Arnold. Reinforcements under Phillips were then sent from New York to the army in
Virginia. The operations of these officers on the
James River, already mentioned, then took place.
Late in March the Comte de Grasse with a powerful fleet sailed from Brest for the West Indies. Rodney being still occupied at St. Eustatius, the French
on their arrival late in April had to deal only with
Rear-Admiral Hood, whose force was inferior. If
Rodney had been less intent on prize money he
could, perhaps, have given De Grasse a reception
that might possibly have upset French and American plans. He would neither go out himself to meet
the French nor allow Hood to do so. De Grasse
did not make full use of his advantage, however,
and beyond releasing four blockaded French ships
at Martinique he accomplished little. He anchored
at Cape François late in July.[1]

Meanwhile Washington and Rochambeau, having
united their forces near New York, were prepared
to move on that place or against Cornwallis in
Virginia, according to whether the one or the other
movement could most advantageously be supported
by the French fleet. Having been apprised of this
situation upon his arrival at Cape François, De
Grasse decided on the Chesapeake and promptly

---

[1] *Mahan,* 382–387; *Almon,* xi, 310–315; *Stopford-Sackville
MSS.,* 207 (March 28, 1781); *Navy Rec. Soc.,* iii (*Hood's Letters*),
15–18; *Rodney's Letters,* 58–62.

dispatched a frigate to notify the generals. They at once moved the allied army to the head of Chesapeake Bay and thence by transports to the York Peninsula, where Cornwallis in his camp at Yorktown was soon invested. De Grasse sailed north, August 5, and anchored in Lynnhaven Bay, just inside the capes of the Chesapeake, on the 30th. There was no English naval force in the bay at this time. Arbuthnot had departed long before, returning to England on leave, and a few days before, Hood, sent north from the West Indies by Rodney, had passed the capes, and seeing no French had kept on to New York, where he joined Admiral Graves, now in command of the North American station. August 31, Graves sailed with the whole force for the Chesapeake, and upon arriving off the capes, September 5, saw De Grasse inside. The English had nineteen ships of the line, the French twenty-four. De Grasse got under way and ran out to sea to meet his adversary, and five days were spent in manœuvring and desultory fighting. This gave an opportunity for another French fleet to get into the bay. This was the Newport fleet, now commanded by Commodore De Barras with a convoy of transports carrying siege artillery for the use of the army before Yorktown, which it was most important to conduct in safety. Graves, overmatched, was obliged to return to New York. De Grasse again entered the bay, where he found De Barras safely anchored. The action of September 5 was a

DE GRASSE

subject of controversy among British officers. Graves fought the battle under a new system of instructions, and believed that his want of success was due to the failure of his captains, bound by tradition to the old system, to interpret his signals intelligently. Hood sharply criticized the management of the fleet and has been charged with purposely failing to get into action and with a willingness to see Graves blunder.[1]

The naval supremacy of France at the seat of war was now complete, the sea power so much desired by Washington had been won for the allies. The situation of Cornwallis seemed hopeless, although if he had held out a few weeks longer, it is possible that Clinton's efforts to relieve him might have been successful. He considered his position untenable, however, and surrendered to the allies, October 19.

Before the end of 1781, the Continental navy was reduced to the lowest point it reached during the war. Three vessels had been lost within the year: the frigates Confederacy and Trumbull and the sloop of war Saratoga. The Trumbull was the last of the original thirteen frigates of 1775. The frig-

[1] *Mahan*, 387–400; *Almon*, xii, 283, xiii, 33–48, xiv, 36; *Boston Gazette*, October 1, 1781; *Stopford-Sackville MSS.*, 212–215; *Navy Rec. Soc.*, iii, 24, 28–36, 40, 44, vi, 111–127, xxix, 213, xxxii, 120, 121, 124, 125, 129, xxxv, 53–55, 260, 261; *Clowes*, iii, 488–502; *Channing*, iii, 334–339, 345; *Doniol*, iv, chs. xiii, xiv; *Chevalier*, ch. viii. See article on Rochambeau, by J. J. Jusserand in *Harvard Graduates' Mag.*, December, 1912.

ates Alliance and Deane now constituted the whole strength of the navy in commission. The America of seventy-four guns and the frigate Bourbon were still on the stocks, with no likelihood of their being finished for a long time to come. On the list of officers were twenty-two captains and thirty-nine lieutenants, and of marine officers twelve captains and twelve lieutenants.[1] The great majority of these officers were either unemployed or serving on board privateers; several were prisoners of war. The administration of naval affairs continued to be in charge of Robert Morris as Agent of Marine until after the end of the war.

Five hundred and fifty letters of marque were issued to private armed vessels by the Continental Congress in 1781, a much larger number than in any other year and an increase over the figures for 1780 of two hundred and forty-nine.[2] This indicates a decided activity and enterprise on the part of American privateers. A correspondent of John Adams wrote to him early in the following year: "It is true that a large number of our private armed ships to the Eastward have been taken in the course of the last season, but in every other respect we have been successful. And indeed we have captured a number of valuable ships belonging to the enemy."[3]

[1] *Pap. Cont. Congr.*, **37**, 473. This list is dated September, 1781, and is doubtless inaccurate.

[2] *Naval Records* (calendar), 217–495.

[3] *Adams MSS.*, January 18, 1782.

During the year 1781 the number of vessels of all classes in the British navy increased from five hundred and thirty-eight to five hundred and fifty-one, a much smaller growth than in the previous years of the war. The number in commission reached three hundred and ninety-eight at the end of the year, an increase of only two over the figures for the first of January. The number on the North American station seems to have varied considerably and to have been largest in October, when Graves had forty-five in his fleet; there were about forty in the West Indies. The total number of seamen and marines in the navy was ninety thousand.[1]

According to the table of losses and captures before referred to, the British lost six hundred and twenty-five vessels, of which thirty-eight were privateers and the others merchantmen; of these, two hundred and seventeen were recaptured or ransomed. England took from her enemies three hundred and seventeen, including forty privateers, and ten of them were recaptured.[2] Another correspondent of John Adams, writing from Boston, says: " The British frigates have done more damage to Our trade the last Season than any time since the Warr; that confounded Penobscot is a handy resort." [3]

John Paul Jones wrote to Washington, May 7, 1781: " Our Navy has been badly conducted; it has

[1] *Hannay*, ii, 211; *Schomberg*, ii, 36, iv, 376–384.
[2] *Clowes*, iii, 396.   [3] *Adams MSS.*, January 23, 1782.

ever been without a head and is now almost entirely lost. . . . I have pointed out many desirable operations that promised success and would have taught the barbarous Britains humanity, but my voice has been as a cry in the desert. The importance and necessity of a marine establishment does not appear sufficiently impressed on the minds of our Legislature." [1]

[1] *Sparks MSS.*, xii, 247.

ALTHOUGH the surrender of Cornwallis virtually put a stop to military operations on land, hostilities on the sea continued until the conclusion of peace. Notwithstanding the fact that the naval resources of the country were nearly exhausted, cruising was actively carried on by the few Continental and State ships still remaining, while privateersmen, lured by the hope of prize money, did not cease fitting out their craft and sending them to sea as long as there were enemies to pursue.

After the victory at Yorktown it was deemed necessary to send the Alliance again to France with Lafayette, and the cruise which had been planned for her by the Agent of Marine was accordingly abandoned. Washington wrote to Lafayette, November 15, 1781, once more strongly urging the importance of sea power. If De Grasse had remained a few weeks longer on the American coast, the English forces in the Southern States, in Washington's opinion, would have suffered " total extirpation." He says: " As you expressed a desire to know my Sentiments respecting the operations of the next Campaign, before your departure for France, I will without a tedious display of reasoning declare in one word, that the advantages of it to America and the honor and glory of it to the allied arms in these States must depend absolutely upon the naval force which is employed in these Seas and the time of its appearance next year. No land force can act decisively unless it is accompanied by a maritime superiority ; nor can more than negative advantages be expected without it. . . . It follows then, as certain as that night succeeds day, that without a decisive naval force we can do nothing definitive, and with it everything honorable and glorious. A constant naval superiority would terminate the war speedily; without it I do not know that it will ever be terminated honorably." [1] The magnitude of the advantage gained at Yorktown and the temper of the enemy were evidently not appreciated in America at this time. As it turned out, the British were in no need of a further exhibition of force to dispose them to thoughts of peace. In fact they were so in fear of another great disaster that orders, dated April 4, 1782, were issued to General Carleton, who was sent to relieve General Clinton, to evacuate New York at once, or even to capitulate, if beset by a force so formidable as to render evacuation without heavy loss impracticable. For lack of transports, however, evacuation was impossible, and the tide soon turned somewhat in England's favor. The defeat of De Grasse by Rodney in the West Indies, in April, 1782,

[1] *Washington*, ix, 406, 407.

revived the spirits and restored the confidence of
the British. Nevertheless, efforts to procure transports for removing the troops from New York
continued, but as a sufficient number could not be
collected to embark the whole army at once, the
matter rested until at length the cessation of hostilities removed the supposed hazard of the situation.
The British state of mind after Yorktown was of
course unknown in America.[1]

Lafayette proceeded to Boston and on board the
Alliance. Several other passengers accompanied him.
Morris issued minute instructions, dated November
27, 1781, in which Captain Barry was directed to
give special attention to the comfort of his passengers. " Let it be done with discretion ; remember
that we are not rich enough to be extravagant, nor
so poor as to act meanly." The importance of landing these distinguished persons safely was such that
it would be necessary to avoid all vessels, it being
the sole object " to make a quiet and safe passage
to some port in France." The Alliance was to remain
in Europe until about the 1st of March, cruising
" where you can promise yourself of the best chance
of Success " ; she was then to set sail from L'Orient
on her return voyage, making as many prizes on the
way as possible and finally putting into the most
convenient American port, preferably Philadelphia,
there to await further instructions. The frigate's

[1] *Sparks MSS.*, lviii, 145–149; *Navy Rec. Soc.*, xxxviii, 73, 77–
80.

crew was finally made up. A number of French sailors were obtained through the efforts of the French minister and some of the Deane's crew were transferred to the Alliance. She sailed December 23, 1781, and in spite of her orders to avoid all vessels, she made a prize of a large ship from Jamaica which was sent into Boston. The frigate arrived at L'Orient, January 18, 1782.[1]

The Alliance made a short and unsuccessful cruise in February, and on March 16 set sail on her homeward voyage. She was again unfortunate in the matter of taking prizes and fell in with no vessel of the enemy until off the Delaware capes, May 10, when a British sixty-four-gun ship appeared and gave chase. The Alliance succeeded in eluding her and ran for New London, where she arrived, May 13, and remained until August.[2]

The General Court of Massachusetts, on February 25, 1782, resolved to allow Captain Nicholson, who had unwillingly given up some of his crew to the Alliance, to enlist not more than twelve men from the garrison of the Castle in Boston Harbor, for the frigate Deane. This ship sailed from Boston in March on a two months' cruise in the West Indies. She captured two ships, a brig, and a schooner, three of them armed vessels. She returned to Boston in May with many prisoners on board, also

---

[1] *Barry*, 153–161; *Independent Chronicle*, January 24, 1782.

[2] *Barry*, ch. xv; *Boston Post*, May 11, 1782; *Independent Chronicle*, May 23, 1782; *Independent Ledger*, June 10, 1782.

several cases of fever. She remained in Boston Harbor four or five months.[1]

The frigate South Carolina, Commodore Gillon, arrived at Havana, January 12, 1782. Here it was learned that the Spaniards were making plans for an expedition against New Providence, under General Cagigal, the governor of Cuba. Gillon joined forces with them, taking command of the fleet consisting of fifty-nine vessels, presumably mostly Spanish. The next three months were spent in fitting out this armada. April 22, the expedition sailed, and, May 5, the whole fleet lay before New Providence. Several outlets at the north side of the island were blocked by some of the American vessels, while others were stationed in the offing. The South Carolina stood off and on until five o'clock, then took a position as near the bar of the harbor as possible, within gunshot of Fort Nassau, in order to draw attention that way while the transports prepared to land the troops. General Cagigal sent a flag to the governor asking on what terms he would surrender the Bahama Islands to Spain. Meanwhile Gillon directed the transports to follow a leading vessel, which repeated his signals for anchoring before the town, that the general might debark when he saw fit. The next day at nine o'clock the British governor sent proposals on board the South Carolina which were not accepted. All

[1] *Mass. Court Rec.*, February 25, 1782; *Boston Gazette*, May 13, July 29, 1782, *Independent Chronicle*, May 23, 1782.

the American vessels continued as near their stations as wind, shoals, and circumstances allowed. The Spanish transports, with armed vessels and galleys, kept anchoring as ordered, and at three o'clock Cagigal with the Spanish officers on the South Carolina departed in order to make preparations for debarking the troops. At five o'clock another flag was sent to the governor and returned the next day, having agreed on a capitulation. On the following day, May 8, Cagigal landed the army and took possession of the forts and town. This made the third capture of New Providence during the Revolution. Gillon thought that the success of the expedition was due to the captains of the American armed vessels, who led the fleet against head winds through difficult passages among the islands and reefs, a route so unfrequented and unexpected by the enemy that they had made no preparations to obstruct or defend it.[1]

The South Carolina then sailed north and arrived at Philadelphia, May 28. Here she remained nearly six months. Gillon was displaced from the command of the ship by an agent of the owner, Chevalier Luxembourg, the exact reason for which does not appear. The command was given to Captain John Joyner of the South Carolina navy. In November the frigate sailed from Philadelphia hav-

[1] *Royal Gazette*, June 19, 1782, Gillon's report to the governor of South Carolina (May 15, 1782); *Penn. Packet*, March 5, June 4, October 19, 1782; *Log of the South Carolina; Almon*, xiv, 148–151.

ing three vessels under convoy, bound to Europe. Apparently she did not clear the capes for about a month, as she had not gone far when, on the night of December 19, she fell in with three British men-of-war, the forty-four-gun ship Diomede and the frigates Quebec and Astrea of thirty-two guns each. A chase of eighteen hours ensued, during which two of the convoy were captured by the British and found to be a ship and brig from Philadelphia; the third, a schooner, got away. "Prisoners inform'd us," says the Astrea's log "the large Ship was the South Carolina Frigate, 40 Guns. ... At 3 [P.M., December 21] the Carolina fir'd several stern chace Guns at the Diomede & Quebec. ... At $\frac{1}{2}$ past 3, the Quebec hauld up for the South Carolina's Weather Quarter. The Diomede continued stand-ing on & Fir'd her Bow Chace Guns at the South Carolina; she ret'd her stern Chace Guns. At 45 Min. past, the Diomede bore up and fir'd her Starbd Guns at the Chace. At 50 Min. past 4 the Chace struck her Colours & hove too." The prize was sent into New York. Soon afterwards a survey of the South Carolina was made which furnishes a description of this interesting ship, which might have done so much and really did so little for the American cause. Her length on the upper deck was one hundred and seventy feet, on the keel one hundred and forty-four feet and one inch; extreme breadth, forty-three feet and three inches. She measured fourteen hundred and thirty tons burden.

" She appears to be about Five Years Old, Built in Holland ; had on board when taken, 28 No. (about) Thirty-Nine Pounders on the Upper Deck, 10 No. Twelve Pounders on the Quarter Deck, and 2 No. Nine Pounders on the Fore Castle." [1]

Two new vessels were added to the Massachusetts navy early in 1782, the Tartar and the sloop Winthrop. The Tartar had been under construction nearly two years and was only just ready for service; she was a ship of four hundred tons and carried eighteen nine-pounders and two sixes. These vessels seem to have cruised together in June for a short time. In a letter, dated July 1, William Vernon says : " The State Ship Tartar and Sloop of 12 Guns went out the last Week, in quest of the Bermuda Brigt., but they were soon drove in by the appearance of a Ship wch they supposed to be of 50 Guns and proved to be only a Sloop of War of 18, much to the discredit of Capt. Cathcart, I think." [2] Cathcart, however, apparently retrieved his good name and later in the season the Tartar took several prizes. She was sold before the end of the year 1782 and was fitted out as a privateer, still under Cathcart's command. After cruising a short time in 1783, she was captured by

[1] *Brit. Adm. Rec., A. D. 490*, January 18, 1783 ; *Captains' Logs*, Nos. 23 and 749 (logs of the Astrea and Quebec) ; *Boston Gazette*, September 16, 1782 ; *Independent Chronicle*, November 29, 1782, January 9, 1783 ; *Penn. Packet*, December 31, 1782 ; *Almon*, xv, 227 ; *Clowes*, iv, 91.

[2] *Publ. R. I. Hist. Soc.*, viii, 274.

the British frigate Bellisarius and taken into New York. The Winthrop, Captain George Little with Edward Preble as lieutenant, was employed on the Maine coast. She came into Boston, September 16, 1782, after a short cruise in which she took five prizes, including two privateers and a brig which was cut out of her anchorage under the fort in Penobscot Bay. "Much Praise is due to the Bravery and good Conduct of Capt. Little and his Crew for this spirited Enterprise and for the great Service they have rendered this Commonwealth in captivating the above Privateers, that have for a long Time infested this Coast and taken many valuable Vessels from us."[1] In February, 1783, the governor, in a message relating to the employment of Little and the Winthrop, said: "I considered that he had most essentially prevented the Depredations on that coast by Capturing & sending into this Port near the whole of the Arm'd force they possess'd at Penobscot."[2] The Winthrop made two cruises in 1783, the last one ending in June. She was the last ship of the Massachusetts navy in commission and was sold soon after her return to port.[3]

In the winter and early spring of 1782, Dela-

[1] *Boston Gazette*, September 23, 1782.

[2] *Mass. Archives*, clviii, 274.

[3] *Mass. Acts and Resolves*, May 2, November 12, 1782, March 26, June 4, 1783; *Mass. Archives*, clviii, 238, 274; *Boston Post*, August 10, October 12, November 23, 1782; *Boston Gazette*, September 23, October 14, November 11, 1782, March 17, 1783; *Continental Journal*, October 3, 1782; *Independent Chronicle*, November 7, 1782; *Massachusetts Mag.*, January, April, 1911.

ware Bay was infested with privateer barges and other small craft, fitted out by loyalists, which preyed upon the commerce of Philadelphia and ravaged the shores of the bay. The merchants of the city applied to the state government for protection and as a result, provision was made for fitting out a number of armed vessels for the defense of the bay. This action was taken April 9. On the 29th, the Philadelphia merchants appealed to the Continental Congress, more especially, however, in behalf of American shipping in general. Robert Morris reported on this memorial that the Continental navy was unable to give sufficient protection to commerce and recommended calling upon the navies of France and Spain for assistance. Meanwhile conditions in Delaware Bay were too acute to admit of waiting for the slow progress of legislation and in March the merchants of Philadelphia had purchased on their own responsibility and fitted out as a privateer under a Continental commission a ship called the Hyder Ally. She was armed with four nine-pounders and twelve sixes and manned by a crew of a hundred and twenty. The command was given to Joshua Barney, a lieutenant in the Continental navy, who had recently returned from a long imprisonment in England.[1]

On April 7, the Hyder Ally with a convoy of

[1] *Barney*, 303; *Pap. Cont. Congr.*, **41**, 6, 283 (April 29, 1782), **28**, 241, 243 a (May 2, 4, 1782), **137**, 1, 435 (May 4, 1782).

JOSHUA BARNEY

merchantmen dropped down the bay to Cape May Road. Here they were seen towards evening by the British frigate Quebec and the sloop of war General Monk, formerly the American privateer General Washington, which anchored outside the capes. At daylight the next morning the General Monk entered the Cape May Channel in pursuit of the Americans, while the Quebec stood up the Henlopen Channel to cut off their retreat to Philadelphia. The General Monk was joined by a New York sixteen-gun privateer called the Fair American. At noon these two vessels came into Cape May Road. The American fleet got under way, stood up the bay, and dispersed. One of them ran ashore and another struck to the General Monk. The Fair American then got aground, and the Monk continued the chase alone. An English account says : " We soon came up with the Hyder Ally, notwithstanding she cut her boat adrift and did everything else to get away. We meant to have run upon her quarter and board her at once, but after firing two of our bow chaces when at 100 yards distance, she put her helm a-port and stood right athwart us, therefore we did the same, to prevent being raked, when the action began and we edged towards her till within close pistol-shot. We with great concern soon found our short guns (carronades) to become totally unmanageable and that two-thirds of the shot we fired did not strike the hull of our antagonist. After having sustained the action for ten

minutes with musketry only, the decks full of killed
and wounded (among the former the Lieutenant
and Master, two brave Officers), our rigging so
much shot as to render it impossible to haul off,
and lastly, seeing no prospect of assistance from
the Fair American, Captain Rogers was under the
mortifying necessity of striking his Majesty's colours to the Hyder Ally, of 18 long nine and six
pounders and between 130 and 140 men, belonging
to the state of Philadelphia." [1] The General Monk,
according to the same authority, was armed with
eighteen nine-pounder carronades and two sixes;
her crew numbered a hundred and ten. Her loss
was eight killed and thirty-two wounded, four of
them mortally; the Hyder Ally lost four killed
and eleven wounded. The time of the action was
about half an hour. It is very doubtful if, as the
English asserted, Barney tried to escape at the outset of the engagement. This impression may have
arisen from the fact that he shouted his orders in
a manner intended to deceive the enemy. The
capture of the Monk produced great satisfaction
in Philadelphia. A dispatch from that place says:
"Capt. Barney with the officers and men of the
State ship Hyder Ally have received the thanks of
the honorable House of Assembly of Pennsylvania
as a mark of the high sense which they entertain
of their bravery and intrepid conduct in the above
action; and have also ordered that an elegant

[1] *London Chronicle*, September 10, 1782.

THE HYDER ALLY AND THE GENERAL MONK

sword be presented to Capt. Barney." [1] Some time
after her capture, the General Monk was purchased
by the national government and taken into the Continental navy under her original name of General
Washington. Barney was given command of her
and she was used as a packet. [2]

The brig Holker of Philadelphia was one of the
most famous privateers of the Revolution. She began her career in 1779, and cruised three years or
more under different commanders. In the winter
of 1782, a squadron of American privateers made
their rendezvous at Martinique and planned an attack on Tortola, one of the Virgin Islands. Besides
the Holker there were four ships and a sloop, with
about five hundred men ; only four vessels, however, finally took part in the expedition. They left
Martinique about March 1, and were seen off Tortola on the 4th. They intended to anchor off the
forts and cover a landing party at night, but were
delayed and the movement was deferred. They were
seen standing into the harbor by moonlight and the
alarm was given, so the attack was postponed until
morning. Three brigantines attempting to escape
from the harbor were chased and one of them was
captured by the Holker. Several letters of marque
at St. John came out to meet the American squad-

[1] *Boston Gazette*, May 6, 1782.

[2] *Barney*, 112–117, 304–308; *Freeman's Journal*, April 10, 1782;
Penn. Gazette, April 17, 1782; *Boston Gazette*, April 22, May 6,
1782; *Mag. Amer. Hist.*, March, 1878, Matthewman's narrative;
Brit. Adm. Rec., A. D. 490, May 10, 1782.

ron and an action of half an hour's duration followed. A few days later the British sloop of war Experiment, coming in from a cruise, had an engagement with the Holker and the Junius Brutus, one of the other American vessels. The Experiment succeeded in beating them off and went into Antigua. The American squadron then cruised a few days and captured a rich prize. The attempt on Tortola was abandoned. The Holker returned to Philadelphia, May 11, having taken fourteen prizes.[1]

Captain Mowatt, the British commander at Penobscot, in March, 1782, sent a fourteen-gun brig to cruise off Cape Ann. She captured a fishing-boat, put twenty-five men on her and sent her into Gloucester. There it was found that a ship with a valuable cargo was about to go to sea. At half-past four the next morning, April 1, the boat ran in, boarded the ship and brought her out. The ship Polly, pierced for twenty guns, was on the ways at Gloucester, with her topmasts struck and otherwise unprepared. Work was begun on her at seven o'clock and at eleven she got to sea with a hundred volunteers on board. She chased the brig, fishing-boat, and prize ship on their way to Penobscot and at twelve o'clock recaptured the prize. She then chased Mowatt's brig, but night came on and she escaped.[2]

[1] *Boston Post*, September 11, October 2, 1779, May 25, 1782; *Penn. Packet*, August 21, 1779; *Boston Gazette*, January 14, 1782, March 10, 1783; *Independent Chronicle*, May 30, 1782; *Royal Gazette*, June 5, 1782; *Clark*, i, 112, 119, 120, 129.

[2] *Salem Gazette*, April 11, 1782.

One hundred and fifty-eight private armed vessels, with about two thousand guns and six thousand men, were sent out of Salem during the Revolution. They captured nearly four hundred and fifty vessels, nine tenths of which safely reached port. One of the most noted of these Salem privateers was the ship Grand Turk, of three hundred tons, built in 1781. She was armed with twenty-two guns and carried a crew of a hundred and ten men. She was actively and successfully employed as long as the war continued. She cruised off the coast of Europe and in the West Indies.[1]

The privateer Jack of Salem, a sloop of twelve guns and sixty men, fought a long and severe engagement off Halifax with the British sloop of war Observer, carrying twelve guns and a hundred and seventy-three men. At nine in the evening, May 28, 1782, the Observer came alongside the Jack. William Gray, the first lieutenant of the privateer, says : " It was our misfortune to have our worthy commander, Capt. Ropes, mortally wounded by the first broadside. I was slightly wounded at the same time in my right hand and head, but not so as to disable me from duty. The action was maintained on both sides, close, severe and without intermission, for upwards of two hours, in which time we had 7

[1] *Hunt's Mag.*, February, 1857; *Coll. Essex Inst.*, xliv (1908), 214–218; *Boston Gazette*, October 22, 1781, May 6, 1782; *Independent Chronicle*, January 24, 1782; *Boston Post*, April 5, 1783. A list of 196 Salem privateers is given in Paine's *Ships and Sailors of Old Salem*.

killed, several wounded, and many abandoned their quarters. Our rigging was so destroyed that not having command of our yards, the Jack fell with her larboard bow foul of the brig's starboard quarter, when the enemy made an attempt to board us, but they were repulsed by a very small number compared with them. We were engaged in this position about a quarter of an hour, in which time I received a wound by a bayonet fixed on a musket and which was hove with such force as, entering the fore part of my right thigh and passing through close to the bone, entered the carriage of a bow gun, where I was fastened, and it was out of my power to get clear till assisted by one of the prize masters. We then fell round and came with our broadsides to each other, when we renewed the action with powder and balls, but our match rope, excepting some which was unfit for use, being all expended and being to leeward, we bore away, making a running fight. The brig being far superior in her number of men, was able to get soon repaired and completely ready to renew the action, indeed had constantly kept up a chasing fire, for we had not been out of reach of her musketry. She was now close alongside of us again with 50 men picked out for boarding. I therefore called Mr. Glover and the rest together and found we had but 10 upon deck and two of them besides myself wounded. I had been repeatedly desired to strike, but I mentioned the sufferings of a prison ship and made use of every other argument in my power for continuing the engagement. All the foreigners however deserted their quarters every opportunity. At 2 o'clock P.M. on the 29th I had the inexpressible mortification to deliver up the vessel." [1]

Four Massachusetts privateers engaged in an enterprise on the Nova Scotia coast which is described in the newspapers of the time. "Captains Babcock of the Hero, Stoddard of the Scammel, Woodbury of the Hope, and Tibbets of the Swallow, having determined to surprize and possess themselves of Lunenburgh, an elegantly situated Town, ten Leagues West of Halifax, landed Ninety Men two Miles below it, under the Command of Lieut. Barteman, on Monday the first Day of July Instant at half after Seven o'Clock A.M. This gallant Corps with amazing Rapidity reached the Town, and amidst many heavy Discharges of Musquetry from the Enemy, burnt the commanding Officer's House, a Blockhouse in the North West Part of the Town, spik'd up two 24 pounders, and forc'd the Enemy into the South Blockhouse, from whence they kept up a brisk and animating Fire and declared their Intention to hold out to the last Extremity. But their Animation subsided upon the Receipt of a few 4-pound Shot from the Hero and they reluctantly surrendered themselves Prisoners of War. The victorious Party with a natural and

[1] *Salem Gazette*, July 11, 18, 1782; *Boston Post*, June 15, 1782; *Hunt's Mag.*, February, 1857.

pleasing Vivacity fell to plundering, and quickly emptied the Stores of a Variety and considerable Quantity of Dry Goods, twenty Puncheons of good West-India Rum and the King's Beef, Pork and Flour. Upon the near Approach of the Combined Fleet, two 18 pounders were spiked up and dismounted and the Royal Magazine was safely deposited in the Hold of the Scammel. The strictest Decorum was observed towards the Inhabitants and their Wearing Apparel and Household Furniture inviolably preserv'd for their Use. The Town was ransomed for a Thousand Pounds Sterling and Colonel Creighton with some of the principal Inhabitants were shipped on board the Scammel. On the Side of the brave Sons of Liberty, three were wounded slightly, one dangerously; on the Part of the Abettors of Oppression and Despotism, the Number of slain and wounded unknown, only one of their slain being found."[1]

Thomas Truxtun, who afterwards became a famous commodore of the reëstablished navy, was one of the successful privateersmen of the Revolution. He cruised throughout the whole war, most of the time in West Indian and European waters. In 1780, at L'Orient, he incurred the displeasure of Paul Jones by hoisting in his presence a broad pennant, contrary to a rule established by Congress.[2] In

[1] *Boston Gazette*, July 15, August 5, 1782; *Massachusetts Spy*, August 8, 1782.

[2] *Sands*, 298; *Hist. Mag.*, April, 1857; *Jones MSS.*, Jones to Truxtun (October 24, 1780).

1782, he was in command of the ship Commerce of Philadelphia, in the West Indies; she carried fourteen guns and fifty men. November 15, she fell in with a brig of sixteen six-pounders and seventy-five men and a schooner, fourteen sixes and eighty men. The Commerce engaged these vessels at a distance of thirty yards for twenty minutes. Her loss was one killed and two wounded; the brig lost five killed and thirteen wounded and the schooner ten killed and eleven wounded. The Commerce was then driven off by a British ship and brig which appeared in time to rescue the thoroughly beaten vessels.[1]

At the end of November, 1782, a desperate battle of barges took place in Chesapeake Bay off Tangier Islands, near the boundary between Maryland and Virginia on the eastern shore of the bay. Four Maryland barges and one from Virginia set out to attack six barges drawn up off the islands, manned by tories, refugees, and sailors from the British fleet. The Virginia barge got aground and the leading Maryland barge, the Protector, flagship of Commodore Whaley, being far in advance, engaged the British flotilla unsupported. An explosion took place on the Protector and in the confusion which ensued the other barges retreated. Whaley was killed, but the fight was kept up by the Protector alone under Colonel Cropper of Virginia, a volunteer, until he was forced to surrender. Out of a crew of sixty-five the Protector lost

[1] *Boston Gazette*, January 6, 1783; *Port Folio*, January, 1809.

twenty-five killed or drowned and twenty-nine wounded, some of them mortally.[1]

The letter of marque brig Iris, eight six-pounders and forty-two men, sailed from Havana for Virginia, January 23, 1783, and off the capes of the Chesapeake, February 7, was chased by a British frigate and a New York privateer called the Admiral Digby, with fifty-four men, fourteen four-pounders and four nines. The Iris struck on a sand-spit at Cape Charles, and shortly afterwards the Admiral Digby also grounded within pistol-shot. The two vessels lay parallel to each other and fought two hours and a half, the American loss being four wounded and the British four killed and twelve wounded. A high wind and heavy surf came up in the night and both vessels were lost. The crews got safely ashore.[2]

Privateers from the United States continued to cruise in European waters at a late period of the war, sending their prizes into France.[3] Furthermore, the services of American privateers commissioned and fitted out in France were important and some of them have already been mentioned. Most of them sailed under the French flag. Dunkirk seems to have been the home port of many if not of the greater part of these vessels. During the war seventy-eight Dunkirk privateers were commanded

---

[1] *So. Lit. Messenger*, March, 1857.

[2] *Salem Gazette*, April 17, 1783.

[3] *London Chronicle*, May 9, 1782; *Boston Gazette*, January 6, 1783.

by Americans, six of them under American commissions; of these six, it would appear that two only, the Black Prince and Black Princess, were owned by Frenchmen.[1] These French-American privateers fought many hard engagements; they greatly annoyed the enemy's shipping in the English Channel and visited the shores of the British Isles. One of them, a twenty-gun ketch called the Franklin, in 1781 captured two of the vessels sent to England by Admiral Rodney, loaded with plunder from St. Eustatius. Captain William Fall in the Sans Peur of nineteen guns bombarded the town of Arbroath, which had refused to pay ransom, and a few days later captured two British privateers of sixteen and eight guns after a sharp action within close range of batteries on the Scotch coast.[2]

The conduct of these privateers fitted out in France seems sometimes to have been much less orderly than that of American ships in general. The crews were recruited from the heterogeneous seafaring population of the French ports and their commanders were not always able to control them. Respect for private property and for neutral flags was occasionally lacking. The cutter Eclipse was commanded during the latter part of her career by Nathaniel Fanning, who had served as a midshipman

[1] See above, p. 539.
[2] *U. S. Nav. Inst. Proc.*, **xxxvii** (September, 1911), 935, 964-972.

on board the Bonhomme Richard. The Eclipse was manned by a crew of a hundred and ten, just half of whom were Americans; the other half was made up of French, English, Irish, Dutch, Flemish, Germans, Italians, Genoese, Maltese, Turks, Tunisians, and Algerines. She sailed from Dunkirk under the French flag and cruised in the English Channel and in British waters. She took many prizes, including several of decidedly superior force, which were sent into French ports. In the summer of 1782, the Eclipse boarded a Danish vessel in the English Channel and the personal property of some French passengers was plundered. Fanning had given special orders to the boarding officer to respect private property, and that the robbery occurred seems to show loss of control over his men, to say the least. As the result of an investigation and trial at the order of the French Minister of Marine, the judges of the admiralty sentenced Thomas Potter, the officer of the Eclipse who had boarded the Danish vessel, "to be hanged to a gallows erected for the purpose on the quay of this port and strangled by the executioner of high justice until he is dead," and two other men "to be whipped and flogged naked by said executioner of high justice and then branded on the right shoulder by a red-hot brand bearing the letters G A L and then conducted to the gallies of his Majesty, where they shall be made to serve during three years, their effects to be seized and confiscated"; they also declared "the aforesaid Nathaniel Fanning duly guilty and convicted of having failed to maintain subordination among his crew and of not having supervised that which was done during the search of neutral vessels, which gave rise to the aforesaid thefts, in punishment for which we declare him incapable during three years of any command as captain of vessels within the realm, and we enjoin him to be more circumspect for the future under penalty of the law." The three chief culprits being absent, "our present judgment will be executed in effigy by the attachment of figures to the aforesaid gallows and scaffold." [1] These three men had absconded before the trial, which was conducted without any defense on their part. In the fall of 1782, before the legal proceedings just narrated, Fanning cruised in a small cutter called the Ranger, in which he took one prize and was then himself captured by the British. He very soon escaped, however, and in a few days was again in Dunkirk.[2]

[1] *U. S. Nav. Inst. Proc.*, xxxvii, 982.

[2] *Ibid.*, 972–983; *Fanning*, 132–137, 141–144, 174–181, 197–229, 240–242. Privateering continued until the spring of 1783 was well advanced and prizes were still being tried as late as December. See *Clark*, i, ch. x; *A. Sherburne*, ch. v; *Boston Gazette*, January 28, February 11, 18, 25, March 11, April 8, 22, June 3, July 1, 8, August 5, September 2, 30, December 2, 16, 1782, May 5, August 4, December 22, 1783; *Independent Chronicle*, April 4, June 6, 1782, January 9, 1783; *Boston Post*, June 8, 29, July 6, 20, October 26, 1782, March 1, April 5, 1783; *Freeman's Journal*, January 23, February 6, 1782; *Penn. Packet*, May 11, 14, July 30, August 6, 1782. For privateering throughout the war, see Mac-

The prize ship General Washington, formerly the General Monk, was not purchased by the Continental government until September, 1782, but in May she was loaned by the owners to Robert Morris, who sent her to the West Indies in June under the command of Joshua Barney. She sailed down the bay with a convoy which returned upon seeing a British squadron outside. The General Washington managed to elude the enemy and got to sea. Upon approaching Cape François she fought an action with a British privateer and captured another vessel which she sent into port. At Cape François, Barney learned of Rodney's victory over de Grasse and found the remnant of the French fleet under the Marquis de Vaudreuil, who a little later took his ships to Boston. The letters of Robert Morris, which Barney had with him, procured for him the escort of a French sixty-four-gun ship, to insure the safety of his mission, which was the shipment of a large quantity of specie from Havana to the United States. All this was accomplished, and the Washington again ran by the British fleet off the Delaware capes, and, after destroying a number of the enemy's barges in the bay, returned to Philadelphia, July 17.[1] Under orders of Morris,

lay's *American Privateers;* Weeden's *New England,* ch. xx; *Coll. Essex Inst.,* xlii–xlv, letters of George Williams to Timothy Pickering.

[1] *Barney,* ch. x; *Freeman's Journal,* July 24, 1782; *Independent Chronicle,* August 8, 1782; *Mag. Amer. Hist.,* March, 1878, Matthewman's narrative.

dated October 7, 1782, the General Washington sailed for France with dispatches for Franklin; after a short passage she arrived at L'Orient before the end of the month. In January, 1783, she sailed on the return voyage and arrived at Philadelphia, March 12.[1]

The Alliance sailed from New London, August 4, 1782, on a cruise. Soon after leaving port she recaptured a prize brig. Barry sent home a narrative of this cruise, dated L'Orient, October 18, saying that he "proceeded as fast as possible off Bermudas; in my way I took a schooner from that place for Halifax. After cruizing off there for twelve or fifteen days, I retook a sloop from New London and sent her for Cape Francois. Finding the prizes I had taken of little value either to myself or country and in all likelihood should be obliged to return into port soon for want of men, was determined to alter my cruizing ground. I therefore thought it best to run off the banks of Newfoundland. In my way there I fell in with a whaling brigantine with a pass from admiral Digby; I mann'd her and sent her for Boston. A few days after, off the banks of Newfoundland, I took a brigantine from Jamaica bound to London, loaded with sugar and rum, and sent her for Boston; by this vessel I found the Jamaica fleet were to the eastward of us. I then carried a press of sail for four days; the fifth day

[1] *Barney*, ch. xi; *Barry*, 184; *Boston Gazette*, March 24, 1783; *Adams MSS.*, December 18, 1782, Barney to Adams.

I took two ships that had parted from the fleet. After manning them and having a fresh gale westwardly, I thought best to order them for France; a day or two after, I took a snow and a ship belonging to the same fleet. Being short of water and a number of prisoners on board, the westwardly winds still blowing fresh, and in expectation of falling in with some more of them, I thought it best to proceed to France, with a determined view to get those I had already taken in safe, and after landing the prisoners, to put out immediately; but meeting with blowing weather and a high sea, I lost the rails of the head and was in great danger of losing the head, which accident obliged me to put in here where I arrived yesterday with the above four prizes. After repairing the damages and getting what the ship may want, I shall put to sea on a cruize. I have likewise to inform you that the Ramilies, admiral Graves' ship, foundered, but all the crew were saved, several of which were on the prizes I took."[1] Some days later the Continental packet General Washington, Captain Barney, came into L'Orient. Captain Henry Johnson of the Continental navy, who had been in command of a privateer, was in Bordeaux at the same time. Several officers of the Alliance, being dissatisfied at not having received their pay, refused obedience to the captain and Barry ordered them under arrest. He was unable to obtain others to take their places

[1] *Freeman's Journal*, December 18, 1782.

and was obliged to sail with inexperienced lieutenants promoted from the lower grades.[1]

The Alliance sailed from L'Orient, December 8,
on a cruise. January 8, 1783, she arrived at Martinique, where Barry found orders to proceed to
Havana. On the way thither he was chased by a
British fleet and again by a seventy-four and a
frigate. At Havana he found the twenty-gun ship
Duc de Lauzun, which had been purchased by
Morris for the Continental navy. Barry's orders
were to sail at once for the United States with
this vessel in company and with a quantity of specie
for the use of Congress. After a delay of about
three weeks, owing to the fact of the port of Havana being closed by an embargo, the Alliance and
the Duc de Lauzun, Captain Green, sailed March
6. On the 10th, they saw three sail, which gave
chase. The strangers turned out to be the British
frigates Alarm and Sybil, and the sloop Tobago.
The headmost, which seems to have been the Alarm,
got within gunshot of the Alliance and they exchanged fire, while the other two were fast coming
up with the Lauzun. She was a dull sailer and
Barry feared that if he stood by her, both American ships would be captured. He advised Green to
heave his guns overboard and run off before the
wind, and all but two or three of them were accordingly thrown over. Another sail soon appeared

[1] *Barry*, chs. xvi, xvii; *Boston Gazette*, August 12, 1782; *Mass.
Spy*, January 2, 1783.

which was recognized as a French ship of fifty guns that had been seen at Havana. Barry was thereupon encouraged and looked for help from this ship. At this time the Alliance had dropped astern, nearer the Lauzun, and the Alarm shortened sail and held off from them. The Sybil got within gunshot of the Lauzun and opened fire with her bow chasers, which was returned by the Lauzun with stern chasers. Barry ran between them in order to give Green a chance to get away. The other two British ships kept at a distance to windward; the French ship also lay to. Kessler, the mate of the Alliance, says: " Captain Barry went from gun to gun on the main deck, cautioning against too much haste and not to fire until the enemy was right abreast. He ordered the main topsail hove to the mast, that the enemy (who had already fired a Bow gun, the shot of which struck into the cabin of the Alliance) might come up as soon as he was abrest, when the action began and before an half hour her guns were silenced and nothing but Musketry was fired from her. She appeared very much injured in her hull. She was of 32 guns and appeared very full of men, and after an action of 45 minutes She sheered off." [1] The Alliance lost ten wounded, one of them mortally; the Sybil, two killed and six wounded.

The log of the Sybil records that the American vessels were sighted at half-past five in the morn-

[1] *Barry*, 223.

ing and the British then gave chase; at eleven the Alliance showed Continental colors. At half-past eleven "the Comr[1] fired two or three broadsides at the large ship, who returned it; we were at this time about 3 miles astern of the Comre. The Tobago was abreast of us carrying a press of sail to get up." Twenty minutes later the Sybil got into action with the Alliance and received considerable injury to sails and rigging. At half-past twelve "a large ship bore down to the ship we Engaged, wch obliged us to sheer off."[2] Kessler's story continues: "As soon as the ship which we had engaged hove from us, her consorts joined her and all made sail, after which the French ship came down to us and Captain Barry asked them why they did not come down during the action. They answered that they thought we might have been taken and the signal known and the action only a sham to decoy him. His foolish idea thus perhaps lost us the three frigates."[3] They then chased the British, but the French ship was slow and the pursuit was abandoned. The voyage was then continued. The Alliance and Duc de Lauzun became separated off Cape Hatteras. Finding two British cruisers off the Delaware capes, the Alliance bore away for Newport, arriving there March 20. The Lauzun got into Philadelphia on the 21st. The Alliance a

---

[1] Commodore, evidently meaning the Alarm.
[2] *Brit. Adm. Rec., Ships' Logs*, No. 875.
[3] *Barry*, 224.

few days later went up to Providence, where in due time the crew were paid off and discharged.[1]

After the return of the frigate Deane from her cruise in the spring of 1782, Captain Nicholson was relieved of his command, for what reason is not clear; he was tried by a court martial in September, 1783, and honorably acquitted. Meanwhile, in September, 1782, the name of the ship was changed to Hague and "on Monday 11th instant John Manly, Esq., Captain in the American navy was appointed to the command of the Continental frigate Hague in this harbour, agreeable to an order from the Hon. Robert Morris, Esq., principal Agent of Marine, investing said command in the senior officer resident in the department. Capt. Manly, at 2 P.M. of the same day, repaired on board, attended by his principal officers, and was welcomed with united acclamations; 13 guns were fired in honor of the appointment, the ship beautifully decorated with colours and every possible demonstration of joy expressed a general satisfaction."[2] Manley had recently returned from a long imprisonment in England. The Hague made a cruise in the West Indies and took several prizes. In January, 1783, she was chased by a British ship and ran aground near Guadaloupe. Manley wrote, January 26: "I have already acquainted you that I have been drove on

---

[1] *Barry,* ch. xviii; *Independent Chronicle,* February 27, 1783; *Continental Journal,* February 27, 1783.

[2] *Independent Chronicle,* September 26, 1782.

shore, after a 36 hours chace, by a 50 gun ship, and lay at the mercy of her incessant fire for two days, who with the assistance of a 74 and two other sail of the line to back her, were not very sparing of a heavy and brisk cannonade. However, without a man killed and only one slightly wounded and my damages repaired in hull, masts, &c. &c., it is with pleasure I look to the prospect of getting out to-morrow for Martinico, Fort Royal, for heaving down."[1] The Hague returned to Boston not long after and was soon put out cf commission.[2]

After his return to America in the Ariel, in February, 1781, Captain Jones spent another long period on shore, waiting for an important command and again doomed to disappointment. Before he left France, Jones received an intimation that the America, seventy-four, would be reserved for him,[3] and June 26, 1781, he was appointed to command her by a unanimous vote of Congress. In August, he went to Portsmouth to superintend the completion of the ship. This work had previously been conducted by Captain Barry. Instead of being nearly ready to launch, as Jones had been led to expect, he found her only partly built. He calls her the largest seventy-four in the world, one hundred and eighty-two feet, six inches long on the upper gun-

[1] *Independent Chronicle*, February 27, 1783.

[2] *Boston Post*, December 14, 1782, November 8, 1783; *Boston Gazette*, December 16, 1782, January 27, February 3, March 3, 1783; *Essex Inst. Coll.*, January, 1909.

[3] *Jones MSS.*, November 8, 1780.

deck, a hundred and fifty feet on the keel, and with an extreme breadth of fifty feet, six inches; she measured nineteen hundred and eighty-two tons. She was to mount thirty eighteen-pounders on the lower gun-deck, thirty-two twelves on the upper deck, and fourteen nines on the quarter-deck and forecastle, all long guns. Her full complement would have been six hundred and twenty-six officers and men. Jones remained in Portsmouth more than a year, scarcity of money causing the accustomed delay in the construction of the ship. Delay and other difficulties, however, also resulted from lack of experience, among those employed on the work, in building so large a ship. In constant fear of parties landing from the enemy's squadron, for the purpose of destroying the ship, it was necessary to keep a guard of workmen and citizens at night for her protection. Several times the enemy's boats appeared in the river at night, and twice, coming close, were fired upon. August 13, 1782, the Magnifique, a ship of the line belonging to the French fleet of the Marquis de Vaudreuil, at that time entering Boston Harbor, ran aground on Lovell's Island and was lost. September 3, the Continental Congress, being "desirous of testifying on this occasion to his Majesty the sense they entertain of his generous exertions in behalf of the United States: Resolved, That the agent of marine be and he is hereby instructed to present the America, a 74 gun ship, in the name of the United States, to the Chevalier de la Luzerne

for the service of His Most Christian Majesty." So
Jones again lost a fine ship. He remained at Portsmouth, however, until after the launch of the America, which took place November 5, 1782. The ship
remained less than four years in the French service, being condemned as unseaworthy in 1786, and
broken up. Immediately after the launching, Jones
returned to Philadelphia. With the consent of Congress he made a cruise to the West Indies in Vaudreuil's fleet. Upon news of the conclusion of peace
he again returned to Philadelphia, and later was
sent by Congress to France in order to prosecute
claims for prize money, still unpaid and due for the
capture of the Serapis and other vessels.[1]

One of the latest naval exploits of the war was the
capture of a British privateer in Long Island Sound
by a detachment of forty men from the army. Colonel
Tallmadge, in a report to General Washington, dated
Greenfield, Connecticut, February 21, 1783, says:
"Yesterday the Enemy's Vessel was discovered near
Stratford Point, when at 2 o'Clock P.M. the troops
were embarked in a fast sailing Vessel prepared
for that purpose, which was commanded by Capt.
Hubbel, and at 4 P.M. they came up with her, when

[1] *Sherburne*, 227-238; *Sands*, 328-352; *Almon*, xv, 24; *U. S.
Nav. Inst. Proc.*, xxxiv (June, 1908), 573-580; *Amer. Cath. Hist.
Res.*, April, 1904; *Boston Gazette*, August 19, November 11, 1782;
Independent Chronicle, November 14, 1782; *Mar. Com. Letter Book*,
244, 245 (November 6, 1779); *Archives de la Marine*, B⁴ **185**, 304-
307, 310-316, 318, 319. For the prosecution of the prize claims, see
Paullin's *Diplomatic Negotiations of American Naval Officers*, ch. i.

she gave a discharge of her Cannon followed by her Swivels and Musketry (our troops being concealed) till both Vessels met, when the troops rose, gave the Enemy one discharge of Musketry and boarded them with fixed Bayonets. The Captain of the Privateer was killed and only three or four of his Men were wounded, two of them supposed mortally wounded. Tho' Captain Hubbel's Vessel was much damaged in her Hull, Spars & Rigging, Yet not a man on board was killed or wounded. Captain Brewster, who commanded the Troops, as well as the other Officers and Soldiers on board, deserve Commendation for the Spirit and Zeal with which this Service has been performed. The Privateer is called the Three Brothers, was commanded by Captain Johnstone, mounting eleven Carriage Guns, four Swivels and twenty-five Stand of small Arms, and navigated by twenty-one men."[1]

The battle between the Alliance and the Sybil was doubtless the last naval action of the Revolution, with the possible exception of some privateering exploit. Provisional articles of peace had been signed at Paris, November 30, 1782, and January 20, 1783, an armistice had been arranged. In compliance with this, dispatches were sent to belligerents on land and sea proclaiming the cessation of hostilities. In the newspapers appeared the following order signed by Robert Morris: "To all Captains, Commanders, Masters and other officers of

[1] *Pap. Cont. Congr.*, **152**, 11, 87.

armed vessels, commissioned by the United States in Congress assembled, and to all others whom it shall or may in any wise concern: According to the orders of the United States in Congress unto me given on the 24th day of this present month of March, I do hereby recall all armed vessels cruising under commissions from the United States of America, whereof you will please to take notice. Done in the Marine Office of the United States of America, this twenty-fifth day of March, in the Year of our Lord, one thousand seven hundred and eighty-three."[1] The signing of the definitive treaty, September 3, 1783, and its ratification by Congress, January 14, 1784, were the remaining steps necessary for the establishment of peace.

In the spring of 1783, there were five vessels remaining of the Continental navy: the frigates Alliance, Hague, and Bourbon, the first two only in commission, and the ships General Washington and Duc de Lauzun. In 1782, three hundred and eighty-three letters of marque were granted by the Continental Congress to private armed vessels; in 1783, the number dropped to twenty-two.[2]

The British navy increased during 1782 from five hundred and fifty-one vessels of all classes to six hundred and eight; vessels in commission from three hundred and ninety-eight to four hundred and

---

[1] *Mass. Spy*, April 17, 1783.
[2] *Naval Records* (calendar), 217–495.

thirty. In 1782, there were seventy vessels on the North American station, and in January, 1783, there were sixty-two, besides more than twice as many in the West Indies. The total number of seamen and marines was one hundred thousand in 1782 and in the following year there were ten thousand more.[1]

In the last two years of the war England lost five hundred and fifteen vessels, taken by her enemies, and recaptured or ransomed a hundred and thirteen of them; she captured one hundred and eighty-six, of which only three were retaken. According to the same authority the total number of merchantmen and privateers captured from the British during the whole war was thirty-one hundred and seventy-six, eighty-nine of them belonging to the latter class; of this total eight hundred and ninety-three were retaken or ransomed. From her enemies England took during the war thirteen hundred and fifty-one, including two hundred and sixteen privateers; of all these only twenty-eight were recaptured.[2] Of the regular navy of England there were taken, destroyed, burnt, foundered or wrecked during the war, two hundred and three vessels; of those captured, eighteen were retaken.[3]

[1] *Hannay*, ii, 211; *Schomberg*, ii, 68, 124, iv, 418, 420; *Clowes*, iii, 327, 328.

[2] *Ibid.*, 396. Unfortunately, in these tables Americans cannot be distinguished from other enemies, after 1777.

[3] *Ibid.*, iv, 109–113. For other estimates, see *Almon*, xvi, 190, 191; *Schomberg*, v, 41–43.

The ships of the Continental navy were gradually disposed of, their crews disbanded, and this interesting organization passed into history. The Duc de Lauzun was loaned to the French minister, converted into a transport, and sent to France, where she was sold. The Bourbon was launched at Middletown, Connecticut, July 31, 1783, and in September was advertised for sale. Meanwhile the Hague had been advertised in August; she was described as being of five hundred and seventeen tons burden, ninety-six feet long on the keel and thirty-two feet wide. These two vessels soon passed into private hands. The General Washington was employed as a packet until the summer of 1784, when she also was sold. The Alliance was retained a year longer. There was a strong sentiment in favor of keeping this ship permanently in the national service, and on January 15, 1784, a committee of Congress reported that the honor of the flag and the protection of the coast required her repair. Many felt, however, that all naval expenditure should cease. The question was deliberated from time to time until May 23, 1785, when considerations of economy prevailed and a committee of Congress recommended the sale of the frigate. She was accordingly sold in August, 1785.[1]

[1] *Barney*, 148; *Barry*, 258; *Independent Chronicle*, August 7, 1783; *Boston Post*, August 30, September 13, 1783; *Pap. Cont. Congr.*, **26**, 441, 443 (April 11, 18, 1783), **28**, 213, 221, 225 (January 15, March 30, 1784, May 23, 1785), **137**, 2, 677 (July 22, 1783); *Jour. Cont. Congr.*, April 21, 1783, June 3, 1785.

Adequate naval protection was needed at the close of the Revolution and has been ever since, and will be, until international arbitration has taken the place of war. Even before the sale of the Alliance, the Algerines began their aggressions upon American commerce. With this frigate as the flagship of a small squadron, with John Paul Jones in command, the insolence of the Barbary pirates might have been checked at the outset, saving much blood and money and avoiding humiliation. It may be affirmed with confidence that with a suitable naval force our troubles with France and England during the wars of the French Revolution and Empire might have been prevented. In the summer of 1782 there was published a newspaper letter "On the Subject of an American Navy"; it was signed "Leonidas." It pointed out the importance of commerce and naval protection and recommended a fleet of five ships of the line and ten frigates.[1] In a report on the condition of the navy, July 31, 1783, Robert Morris urged the need of a fleet, but advised against taking any steps until funds should be obtained. Lack of money was necessarily the determining factor.[2]

Captain Jones was a close student of naval science and his opinions, freely expressed, are of interest

[1] *Independent Chronicle*, September 5, 1782, from the *Penn. Gazette.*

[2] *Pap. Cont. Congr.*, 137, 2, 725. For John Adams's views of sea power in general and of American needs, see *Wharton*, iii, 542, 543, 833, 834.

and value. In 1777, he prepared " A Plan for the Regulation and Equipment of the Navy, drawn up at the request of the Honorable the President of Congress." He proposed to establish a dockyard for building and fitting out ships in each of three sections of the country, the eastern, middle, and southern, and to divide the navy into three squadrons, one to rendezvous at each dockyard. The qualifications and duties of the officers at these yards were set forth in detail. The chief officers, or Commissioners, one from each yard, were to hold yearly conferences at Philadelphia with the Board of Admiralty, to whom they were to report on conditions at the yards. " The Authority of the Commissioners must by no means extend to the destination of Ships or their internal Government, it being their Province only to keep the Navy in fit Order for Sea service and it being the Province of Commanders in the Navy to govern their Ships according to the Rules and Regulations established by the supreme Power of Congress and to follow the Instructions which they may Receive from the board of Admiralty or their deputies, or from Senior or Flag Officers. Consequently Commanders of Squadrons or of single Ships have a right to call on the Commissioners or Agents for supplies whenever they are in want of them, being always accountable to Senior Officers in their division for their Conduct, but more especially so to the Board of Admiralty. As the extent of the Continent is so great that the most advantageous Enterprize may be lost before Orders can arrive within the eastern and Southern districts from the board of Admiralty, it will perhaps be expedient to appoint deputies for executing the Office of High Admiral within these extreme districts, to continue in Office only during the Pleasure and at all times accountable to the Board of Admiralty. Perhaps one deputy to the Eastward and another to the Southward may be found equal to the Business, but the number in each department ought not to exceed three. They ought to be Men of inviolable Secrecy, who inherit much discernment and Segacity and are endowed with consummate Knowledge in Marine Affairs. Besides pointing out proper Services for single Ships and for Squadrons, it may be the duty of the deputies, with the assistance of three or more of the most Judicious commanders of the Fleet who may be named by the board of Admiralty, to examine the abilities of Men who apply for Commissions, and make report to the Board, also to examine divers Persons who now bear Commissions in the Service and whoe's Abilities and accomplishments are very suspicious and uncertain; the board may do the same within the middle district. . . . It may also be expedient to establish an Academy at each Dockyard under proper masters, whoe's duty it should be to Instruct the Officers of the Fleet when in Port in the Principles and Application of the Mathematicks, Drawing, Fencing and

other manly Arts and Accomplishments. It will
be requisite that young Men serve a certain time
in Quality of Midshipmen or Master's mate, before
they are examined for Promotion. And the necessity of Establishing an Hospital near each Dockyard, under the care of Skilful Physicians, is self
evident." [1]

Writing to Robert Morris, September 22, 1782,
Jones says: " I have many things to offer respecting the formation of our navy, but shall here limit
myself to one, which I think a preliminary to the
formation and establishment of a naval constitution
suitable to the local situation, resources and preju-
dices of the Continent. The constitution adopted
for the navy in the year 1775 and by which it has
been governed ever since, and crumbled away I may
say to nothing, is so very defective that I am of
opinion it would be difficult to spoil it. Much wis-
dom and more knowledge than we possess is, in my
humble opinion, necessary to the formation of such
a naval constitution as is absolutely wanting. . . .
We are a young people and need not be ashamed
to ask advice from nations older and more experienced in marine affairs than ourselves. . . . My
plan for forming a proper corps of sea officers is by
teaching them the naval tactics in a fleet of evolu-
tion. . . . When in port the young officers should
be obliged to attend at the academies established at
each dock-yard, where they should be taught the

[1] *Jones MSS.*, April 7, 1777.

principles of every art and science that is necessary to form the character of a great sea officer; and every commission officer of the navy should have free access and be entitled to receive instruction gratis at those academies. All this would be attended with no very great expense and the public advantage resulting from it would be immense. I am sensible it cannot be immediately adopted and that we must first look about for ways and means, but the sooner it is adopted the better. . . . In time of peace it is necessary to prepare and be always prepared for war by sea." [1]

[1] *Sherburne*, 232, 233.

CHAPTER XVIII

THE lot of the prisoner of war has always been an unhappy one at best; in early times put to the sword, at a later day enslaved, and even in modern wars sometimes unavoidably subjected to most unfavorable conditions in the exigencies of a campaign. Civilized countries have at times permitted a treatment of prisoners unnecessarily harsh and even cruel. At the outset of a civil war the question arises whether or not the rebel shall be dealt with as a traitor and criminal, but fear of reprisals soon forces the virtual if not explicit recognition of belligerent rights. Lord George Germain, writing to General Howe, February 1, 1776, in regard to some American officers captured on a privateer by the British, says: "It is hoped that the possession of these prisoners will enable you to procure the release of such of his majesty's officers and loyal subjects as are in the disgraceful situation of being prisoners to the rebels; for although it cannot be that you should enter into any treaty or agreement with rebels for a regular cartel for exchange of prisoners, yet I doubt not but your own discretion will suggest to you the means of effecting such exchange without the king's dignity and honor being com-

mitted or His Majesty's name used in any negotia-
tion for that purpose." [1] Here may be noted an intimation of the bitterness commonly exhibited in
civil strife, which is sometimes conveniently visited
upon the helpless prisoner. This should impose
upon governments and officers of rank an increased
sense of responsibility for the acts of subordinates.
The accounts of the treatment of prisoners in New
York, unquestionably authentic though perhaps
colored by privation, are difficult to reconcile with
the undoubted humane character of some of the
British officers in command. The situation of the
British at that place and their resources could hardly
have been such as to prevent the proper care of
prisoners.

At New York many buildings were converted
into prisons and several prison-ships were moored
in the harbor, especially in Wallabout Bay, where
the Navy Yard at Brooklyn now is. Most of the
prisoners taken at sea were confined in these hulks.
There were probably prison-ships in most British
harbors frequented by cruising vessels, and other
ships were at times temporarily used for the purpose. The best known places in England where
Americans were confined were Mill Prison at Plymouth and Forton Prison at Portsmouth.

The treatment of American prisoners by the British gave rise to much discussion in Congress and to
a voluminous correspondence between commanding

[1] *Hist. Mag.*, March, 1862.

officers and commissaries of prisoners. January 13, 1777, General Washington wrote to Admiral Howe " on the subject of the cruel treatment which our officers and men in the naval department, who are unhappy enough to fall into your hands, receive on board the prisonships in the harbour of New York." To General Howe on the same day he wrote: " Those who have been lately sent out give the most shocking account of their barbarous usage, which their miserable, emaciated countenances confirm. . . . Most of the prisoners who have returned home [by exchange] have informed me that they were offered better treatment provided they would enlist into your service. This I believe is unprecedented; and what, if true, makes it still more unnecessary for me to apologize for the freedom of expression which I have used throughout this letter." [1] Washington threatened retaliation. Admiral Howe replied, January 17, that the reports of illtreatment were exaggerated, that some prisoners having escaped, less liberty was allowed than formerly and crowding made necessary, that the prisoners had the same ration and medical attendance as British sailors. May 28, Washington wrote to the President of Congress that many of the prisoners released by the British were unfit for exchange by reason of the severity of their treatment and that a deduction should be made on their account. This was before the Jersey, a dismantled sixty-four-gun

[1] *Washington*, v, 166, 169, 170.

ship, was brought to New York and moored in Wallabout Bay, and became the most notorious of all the prison-ships. In 1779, there was an improvement on board these ships at New York, acknowledged by Washington and confirmed by a letter from one of the prisoners.[1] This was only temporary, however, and a year or two later conditions were at their worst, although an attempt at reform seems to have been made by Admiral Graves in 1781.[2]

In addition to the practice, alluded to by Washington, of tempting prisoners to enlist in the British service by promises of better treatment, they were sometimes impressed, and on board cruising ships also, at times, they were forced to bear arms against their countrymen. In 1776, William Barry, a prisoner on the Roebuck in Delaware Bay, and Elisha Cole, an American shipmaster on the frigate Milford, were compelled to do this, and both afterwards made depositions to the fact. In retaliation Congress authorized Captain Biddle to take British prisoners from jail to fill his complement. There are several accounts, however, of humane treatment on board British cruising ships and on prison-ships

[1] See below, p. 628.

[2] *Jour. Cont. Congr.*, resolves: December 7, 1776, June 10, 1777, April 21, 1780, September 4, 18, 1781; committee reports: December 7, 1776, January 7, 9, 1777; *Pap. Cont. Congr.*, 152, 3, 505, 4, 113 (Howe to Washington, January 23, April 21, 1777), 5, 221 (Washington to Howe, November 23, 1777), 10, 233 (Affleck to Washington, August 30, 1781); *Washington*, v, 170, 394, 423, vi, 193, viii, 121, 338, ix, 119; *Boston Gazette*, September 17, 1781.

at Halifax and elsewhere. Captain Daniel Lunt of
Newburyport was well treated on board the British
cruiser Lively, which captured him off Cape Ann
in 1776, although afterwards, when transferred to
the Renown, he and other shipmasters were robbed
of their money and put at hard labor. Joshua Barney
was treated with marked kindness on three different cruising ships and with an equal degree of severity on two others. Nathaniel Fanning, who was
several times a prisoner, was robbed and maltreated
on two British vessels, but on other occasions fared
very well. In 1777, Captain Stephen Hills was well
treated on a prison-ship at Halifax, and in 1782
eighty-one Americans at the same place, and others
in a hospital there, had the best of care. In 1781,
Captain Tucker of the privateer Thorn escaped
from the Island of St. John's (Prince Edward Island) and reported that he had been very kindly
treated there. The same year some prisoners who
arrived in Salem from Newfoundland acknowledged
" the very humane and benevolent treatment which
they received from Admiral Edwards." The next
year nearly three hundred Americans were brought
home from there in a cartel.[1]

[1] *Am. Arch.* IV, v, 759, vi, 809, V, ii, 538; *Pap. Cont. Congr.*,
19, 3, 581 (December 7, 1776); *Barney*, 51, 66, 70, 86; *Fanning*,
14–18, 144–148, 229–238; *A. Sherburne*, 49–76; *Tucker*, 163; *Boston Gazette*, September 30, 1776, July 28, 1777; *Mass. Spy*, September 11, 1776; *Independent Chronicle*, February 5, 1778; *Continental Journal*, August 23, 1781; *Salem Gazette*, November 15,
1781, July 18, October 17, 1782; *Boston Post*, July 20, 1782;
Hunt's Mag., February, 1857. See above, pp. 141, 152, 250.

Many years after the war Nathaniel Bowditch told the following Revolutionary anecdote, which had been related to him by his father: " Capt. Tuck of Manchester in a small privateer was taken by a British vessel of war, & his crew was carried on board & detained as prisoners. Cruising afterwards on the eastern shore, the vessel struck on a sunken ledge at some distance from a small island then in sight and soon bilged. Their situation soon became extremely dangerous, the greatest confusion prevailed on board, and the British seamen finding that none of the stores on board the ship could possibly be saved, procured from the store room considerable quantities of rum & drank so freely that they soon became incapable of doing their duty, and in getting out the boats bilged & lost them. Their situation now became desperate, they seemed to have no chance of saving their lives, as the crew were so disorderly and incompetent of doing their duty. Capt. Tuck then proposed to the British commander to make a raft out of the spars, yards, &c. of the ship and offered his services in doing it, provided he could have it under his own direction, with none to assist except the American prisoners, most of whom were free from intoxication. This offer was cheerfully accepted & he made out to get the crew safely ashore without losing a man, but before anything else could be got from the ship, she went to pieces. The British Commander on the Halifax Station liberated Capt. T. and his crew without parole or exchange, on account of his services." [1]

In June, 1778, Robert Sheffield, a shipmaster of Stonington, Connecticut, made his escape from one of the New York prison-ships after a confinement of only six days. There were three hundred and fifty men on board confined below, although it is to be presumed that they were allowed on deck in the daytime, as was the custom. Sheffield says the heat was "so intense that they were all naked. . . . Their sickly countenances and ghastly looks were truly horrible, some swearing and blaspheming, some crying, praying and wringing their hands and stalking about like ghosts, others delirious, raving and storming; some groaning and dying, all panting for breath; some dead and corrupting, air so foul at times that a lamp could not be kept burning, by reason of which the boys were not missed till they had been dead ten days." There were five or six deaths a day. [2] Captain John Chester wrote to General Webb, January 17, 1777 : " The inhuman treatment our prisoners met with while in New York is beyond all description. Humanity cannot but drop a tear at sight of the poor, miserable, starved objects. They are mere skeletons, unable to creep or speak in many instances. One vessel lost 27 in her passage from New York to Milford [Con-

[1] *Pickering MSS.;* **xxx**, 415.

[2] *Conn. Gazette,* July 10, 1778, quoted in Onderdonk's *Revolutionary Incidents,* 227, 228.

necticut], and 7 died the night they were put ashore; and they are dying all along the road."[1] According to a report from Boston, February 4, 1779, "a cartel lately brought 136 prisoners from prison-ships in N. Y. to N. London. Such was the condition in which these poor creatures were put aboard the cartel, that in this short run 16 died on board and 60, when they landed, were scarcely able to move, and the remainder greatly emaciated."[2] The most favorable account comes from Daniel Stanton, who writes from Stonington, August 28, 1779: "I was taken with a number of others on or about the 5th of June last in the ship Oliver Cromwell, carried into New York and put on the Prison Ship Jersey. There was nothing plundered from us, we were kindly used by the Captain and others that belonged to the ship. Our Sick were attended by Physicians who appeared very Officious to recover them to health. Our Allowance for Subsistance was wholesome and in reasonable Plenty, including the Allowance by the Continental Congress sent on Board. About three or four weeks past we were removed on board the Prison Ship Good Hope, where we found many sick; there is now a hospital ship provided, to which they are removed and good Attention paid, and doubt not the same Hospitality is used towards those of the Enemy, where the Fortune of War has cast into

[1] *Correspondence of General Webb*, i, 184.
[2] *Onderdonk*, 229.

our hands. On the whole we were as humanely treated as our Condition and the Enemy's Safety would admit." [1] Another good account is given by Captain Thomas Dring and others who escaped from the Good Hope.[2] According to Joshua Barney, a prisoner in 1778, Admiral Byron during his short stay on the station took great pains to improve as far as possible the conditions on New York prison-ships.[3] These conditions probably varied from time to time according to the characters of different officers and subordinates in charge, and according to the weather and other circumstances, especially the number of prisoners on board. The Continental Congress provided the means for supplying the prisoners at New York with extra food and appointed a merchant named Pintard as agent to look after them.[4]

Philip Freneau, the poet, was a passenger on the armed ship Aurora of Philadelphia, which was captured after an hour's engagement by the British frigate Iris, May 26, 1780, and taken to New York. Freneau was sent on board the prison-ship Scorpion in the North River, where he was " almost suffocated with the heat and stench." He relates that on the night of June 4 " about thirty-five of our people formed a design of making their escape, in which

---

[1] *Conn. Gazette*, September 1, 1779, quoted in *Papers New London Hist. Soc.*, IV, i, 44.

[2] *N. J. Gazette*, October 12, 1779, quoted in *Onderdonk*, 230.

[3] *Barney*, 74.

[4] *Pap. Cont. Congr.*, 37, 322 (October 6, 1780).

they were favored by a large schooner accidentally alongside of us. . . . We were then suffered to continue upon deck, if we chose, till nine o'clock. We were all below by that time except the insurgents, who rushed upon the sentries and disarmed them in a moment," and drove them into the cabin. " When the sentries were all silent they manned the ship's boat and boarded the schooner, though the people on board attempted to keep them off with hand-spikes. The wind blowing fresh at south and the flood of tide being made, they hoisted sail and were out of sight in a few minutes. . . . As soon as the sentries got possession of the vessel again, which they had no difficulty in doing, as there was no resistance made, they posted themselves at each hatchway and most basely and cowardly fired fore and aft among us, pistols and marquets, for a full quarter of an hour without intermission. By the mercy of God they touched but four, one mortally." The next morning " all that were found wounded were put in irons and ordered to lie upon deck, exposed to the burning sun. About four o'clock P. M., one of the poor fellows who had been wounded the night before died. They then took him out of irons, sent him on shore, and buried him. After this no usage seemed to them severe enough for us. We had water given us to drink that a dog could scarcely relish; it was thick and clammy and had a dismal smell. They withdrew our allowance of rum and drove us down every night strictly at sunset,

where we suffered inexpressibly till seven o'clock
in the morning, the gratings being rarely opened
before that time. Thus did I live with my miserable companions till the 22d of June. When finding myself taken with a fever, I procured myself to
be put on the sick list, and the same day was sent
with a number of others to the Hunter hospital-
ship, lying in the East River. Here was a new
scene opened. The Hunter had been very newly put
to the use of a hospital-ship. She was miserably dirty
and cluttered. Her decks leaked to such a degree
that the sick were deluged with every shower of
rain. Between decks they lay along, struggling in
the agonies of death, dying with putrid and bilious
fevers, lamenting their hard fate to die at such a
fatal distance from their friends; others totally in-
sensible and yielding their last breath in all the
horrors of light-headed frenzy." [1]

In the fall of 1780, Captain Silas Talbot was
confined on the Jersey. There were then about
eleven hundred prisoners on board, with no berths
to lie in nor benches to sit on; many were almost
without clothes. Dysentery and fever prevailed.
The scantiness and bad quality of the provisions,
the brutality of the guards, and the sick pining for
comforts they could not obtain, altogether furnished
one of the greatest scenes of human distress ever
beheld. The weather was cool and dry, with frosty
nights, so that the number of deaths was reduced

[1] Freneau's *Capture of the Aurora*, 15–41.

to an average of ten a day, which was small compared with the mortality for three months before. The human bones and skulls still bleaching on the shore of Long Island as late as 1803, and daily exposed by the falling of the high bank on which the prisoners were buried, was a shocking sight.[1] A few years after that these bones were collected and buried and a monument erected over them.

Ebenezer Fox, describing the Jersey as she was in 1781, says: " Her external appearance was forbidding and gloomy. She was dismantled; her only spars were the bowsprit, a derrick that looked like a gallows, for hoisting supplies on board, and a flagstaff at the stern. The port-holes were closed and secured. Two tiers of holes were cut through her sides, about two feet square and about ten feet apart, strongly guarded by a grating of iron bars." [2] Fox and his shipmates upon their arrival " were ordered to ascend to the upper deck of the prison ship. Here our names were registered. . . . Each of us was permitted to retain whatever clothing and bedding we had brought, after having been examined " for weapons and money; " and then we were directed to pass through a strong door on the starboard side, down a ladder leading to the main hatchway. I now found myself in a loathsome prison, among a collection of the most wretched and disgusting looking objects that I ever beheld in human form. Here was a motley crew, covered

[1] *Historical Sketch of Silas Talbot,* 106–109.   [2] *Fox,* 96.

with rags and filth, visages pallid with disease,
emaciated with hunger and anxiety, and retaining
hardly a trace of their original appearance." [1] " The
various messes of the prisoners [of six men each]
were numbered, and nine in the morning was the
hour when the steward would deliver from the window in his room, at the after part of the ship, the
allowance granted. . . . Each mess received daily
what was equivalent in weight or measure, but not
in quality, to the rations of four men at full allowance ; that is, each prisoner received two thirds as
much as was allowed to a seaman in the British
navy. Our bill of fare was as follows : on Sunday,
one pound of biscuit, one pound of pork and half a
pint of peas ; Monday, one pound of biscuit, one
pint of oatmeal and two ounces of butter ; Tuesday,
one pound of biscuit and two pounds of salt beef ;
Wednesday, one and a half pounds of flour and
two ounces of suet. Thursday was a repetition of
Sunday's fare, Friday of Monday's and Saturday
of Tuesday's. If this food had been of a good
quality and properly cooked, as we had no labor to
perform, it would have kept us comfortable, at least
from suffering. But this was not the case. All our
food appeared to be damaged." [2] " The cooking for
the prisoners was done in a great copper vessel that
contained between two and three hogsheads of water,
set in brick work. The form of it was square and
it was divided into two compartments by a parti-

[1] Fox, 99.   [2] Ibid., 101, 102.

tion. In one of these the peas and oatmeal were boiled; this was done in fresh water. In the other the meat was boiled in salt water taken up from alongside the ship. The Jersey, from her size and lying near the shore, was imbedded in the mud. . . . All the filth that accumulated among upwards of a thousand men was daily thrown overboard and would remain there till carried away by the tide. The impurity of the water may be easily conceived; and in this water our meat was boiled." [1]

" In the morning the prisoners were permitted to ascend the upper deck, to spend the day till ordered below at sunset. A certain number, who were for the time called the 'working party,' performed in rotation the duty of bringing up hammocks and bedding for airing, likewise the sick and infirm and the bodies of those who had died during the night; of these there were generally a number every morning. After these services it was their duty to wash the decks. . . . About two hours before sunset, orders were given to the prisoners to carry all their things below, but we were permitted to remain above till we retired for the night. . . . At sunset our ears were saluted with the insulting and hateful sound from our keepers, of 'Down, rebels, down,' and we were hurried below, the hatchways fastened over us and we were left to pass the night amid the accumulated horrors of sighs and groans, of foul vapor, a nauseous and putrid atmosphere, in a

[1] *Fox*, 105, 106.

stifled and almost suffocating heat. The tiers of holes through the sides of the ship were strongly grated, but not provided with glass, and it was considered a privilege to sleep near one of these apertures in hot weather. . . . But little sleep, however, could be enjoyed even there, for the vermin were so horribly abundant that all the personal cleanliness we could practise would not protect us from their attacks." When the dead, sewn in blankets, were taken ashore, some of the prisoners went with them, "under a guard, to perform the labor of interment. . . . Here in a bank near the Wallabout a hole was excavated in the sand, in which the body was put and then slightly covered, the guard not giving time sufficient to perform this melancholy service in a faithful manner. Many bodies would, in a few days after this mockery of a burial, be exposed nearly bare by the action of the elements." [1]

Thomas Andros was also on the Jersey in 1781, and says : " When I first became an inmate of this abode of suffering, despair and death, there were about four hundred prisoners on board, but in a short time they amounted to twelve hundred. And in proportion to our numbers the mortality increased." [2] Dysentery, smallpox, and yellow fever were prevalent. " Now and then an American physician was brought in as a captive, but if he could obtain his parole he left the ship, nor could we much blame him for this. For his own death was

[1] *Fox*, 109–111.   [2] Andros, *Old Jersey Captive*, 12.

next to certain and his success in saving others by medicine in our situation was small. I remember only two American physicians who tarried on board a few days. No English physician or any one from the city ever to my knowledge came near us." [1] "Our water was good, could we have had enough of it; our bread was bad in the superlative degree. I do not recollect seeing any which was not full of living vermin; but eat it, worms and all, we must or starve." [2] Andros eventually escaped. Attempts to escape from the prison-ships were frequent and not uncommonly successful. The crew of the Jersey consisted of a captain, two mates, a steward, a cook, and about a dozen sailors, besides a guard of ten or twelve invalid marines and about thirty soldiers. By eluding the vigilance of these guards, or perhaps bribing a sentry, it was sometimes possible to get away from the ship in a boat or by swimming. Upon reaching shore, however, fugitives had many difficulties to encounter, especially the unfriendliness of the tory population of Long Island. [3]

The method of exchange for the relief of the prisoners' sufferings was not as generally applicable as could have been wished, partly because the supply of British in the hands of the Americans was

---

[1] *Andros*, 15.   [2] *Ibid.*, 17.

[3] *Ibid.*, 24 *et seq.*; *Fox*, ch. viii. For other experiences of prisoners, see Dring's *Recollections of Jersey Prison Ship*; Taylor's *Martyrs in the Prison-Ships*; A. Sherburne, ch. v; *Hist. Mag.*, July, 1866 (*Suppl.*); *Mag. Amer. Hist.*, March, 1878, Matthewman's narrative.

inadequate. British prisoners were released in large numbers by their American captors, especially privateersmen, because they had no means of supporting them, often, apparently, neglecting to take their paroles. Washington stated his views on the subject in a letter to the President of Congress, February 18, 1782, saying: " Mr. Sproat's proposition of the exchange of British soldiers for American seamen, if acceded to, will immediately give the enemy a very considerable reinforcement and will be a constant draft hereafter upon the prisoners of war in our hands. It ought also to be considered that few or none of the naval prisoners in New York and elsewhere belong to the Continental service. I however feel for the situation of these unfortunate people and wish to see them released by any mode which will not materially affect the public good. In some former letters upon this subject I have mentioned a plan by which I am certain they might be liberated nearly as fast as captured. It is by obliging the captains of all armed vessels, both public and private, to throw their prisoners into common stock, under the direction of the commissary-general of prisoners. By these means they would be taken care of and regularly applied to the exchange of those in the hands of the enemy. Now the greater part are dissipated and the few that remain are applied partially."[1] Washington cor-

[1] *Washington*, ix, 444. See negotiations for a general cartel for the exchange of prisoners, in *Webb*, ii, 19–85.

responded with various British naval commanders during the last two years of the war and received replies from Admiral Arbuthnot, Captain Affleck, and Admiral Digby, expressing concern at the prisoners' plight and a purpose to apply remedies. General Carleton also made plans in 1782 to correct abuses. The American and British commissaries of prisoners, Abraham Skinner and David Sproat, also corresponded freely on the subjects of treatment and exchange of prisoners. Whether or not as a result of these efforts, conditions seem to have improved in June, 1782, according to the report of six American shipmasters on parole, "that they had been on board the prison and hospital ships to inspect the state of the American naval prisoners and found them in as comfortable situation as it is possible for prisoners to be on board ships and much better than they had an idea of." This report was published about two weeks after a letter from Washington to Digby on the subject.[1]

The Americans captured in European waters and many also from this side of the ocean were sent to prisons in England. The American Commissioners in Paris began early to interest themselves in the welfare of these prisoners, and Franklin especially, until the end of the war, was untiring in his efforts to mitigate their hardships. February 23, 1777,

[1] *Almon,* xiv, 262, 263; *Onderdonk,* 233-235, 240-244; *Mar. Com. Letter Book,* 261, 262; *Mass. Spy,* August 8, 1782.

began a correspondence of the commissioners with Stormont, the British ambassador, in regard to the exchange of prisoners, which defined the positions of the two nations on the subject at that time. They wrote: "Captain Wickes of the Reprisal frigate, belonging to the United States of America, has now in his hands near one hundred British seamen, prisoners. He desires to know whether an exchange may be made for an equal number of American seamen now prisoners in England? We take the liberty of proposing this matter to your Lordship and of requesting your opinion (if there be no impropriety in your giving it) whether such an exchange will probably be agreed to by your Court. If your people cannot be soon exchanged here, they will be sent to America." [1]

No reply was received to this and on April 2 they wrote again: "We did ourselves the Honour of writing some time since to your Lordship on the Subject of Exchanging Prisoners. You did not condescend to give us any Answer and therefore we expect none to this. We however take the Liberty of sending you Copies of certain Depositions, which we shall transmit to Congress, whereby it will be known to your Court that the United States are not unacquainted with the barbarous Treatment their People receive, when they have the Misfortune of being your Prisoners here in Europe. And that if your Conduct towards us is not altered, it is not

[1] Sparks's *Franklin*, ix, 166.

unlikely that severe Reprisals may be thought justifiable, from the Necessity of putting some Check to such abominable Practices. For the sake of Humanity it is to be wish'd that Men would endeavour to alleviate as much as possible the unavoidable Misseries attending a State of War. It has been said that among the civilized Nations of Europe the ancient Horrors of that State are much diminished, but the Compelling Men by Chains, Stripes & Famine, to fight against their Friends and Relations, is a new Mode of Barbarity which your Nation alone has the Honour of inventing. And the sending American Prisoners of War to Africa and Asia, remote from all Probability of Exchange and where they can scarce hope ever to hear from their Families, even if the Unwholesomeness of the Climate does not put a speedy End to their Lives, is a manner of treating Captives that you can justify by no Precedent or Custom, except that of the black Savages of Guinea." [1] The following message, unsigned and undated, was received in reply: " The King's Ambassador receives no applications from rebels but when they come to implore His Majesty's Mercy." The commissioners then closed the correspondence: " In answer to a letter which concerns some of the most material interests of humanity and of the two nations, Great Britain and the United States of America, now at war, we received the inclosed indecent paper as com-

[1] Smyth's *Franklin*, vii, 36.

ing from your Lordship, which we return for your Lordship's more mature consideration." [1]

Stormont sent copies of the letter of April 2 and his unsigned reply to Lord Weymouth and with them the following: "I send your Lordship a Copy of a very Extraordinary and Insolent Letter, that has just been left at my House by a Person who called himself an English Gentleman; I thought it by no means Proper to appear to have received and kept such a Letter, and therefore, My Lord, instantly sent it Back by a Savoyard, seemingly unopened, under Cover to Mr. Carmichel, who I discovered to be the Person that had brought the Letter." [2] Weymouth wrote to Stormont April 11: "I entirely approve of the note Your Excellency sent to Mr. Carmichael with the Letter you returned to him. The Style and Subject deserved no other treatment." [3]

The brig Dalton of Newburyport was taken in December, 1776, by the sixty-four-gun ship Raisonable. The crew were sent to Plymouth, England, where after a while they were transferred to the Burford of seventy guns, Captain George Bowyer. Here their fortunes, which had been hard, made a great change for the better. Each man was given an outfit of clothes and bedding, provided by the captain at his own expense. They were well fed

[1] *Sparks*, ix, 167.　　　[2] *Stevens*, 1507; *Smyth*, vii, 36.
[3] *Stevens*, 1503, 1507, 1515; *Almon*, v, 371, 372, 511; *Hale*, i, 194–198.

and kindly treated. This was also the case in the hospital on shore, where the sick had the best care. After several weeks on the Burford they were transferred to another ship and early in June, 1777, to Mill Prison, near Plymouth, which had been prepared for them. They were committed on the charge of high treason, to await trial, and could only be released on receiving the King's pardon. Two members of the Dalton's crew, Charles Herbert and Samuel Cutler, kept journals in prison. Cutler says the ration " is ¾ lb. beef, 1 lb. bread, 1 qt. very ordinary beer, and a few greens per man for 24 hours. The beef when boiled weighs about 6 oz. This is our allowance daily, except Saturday, when we have 6 oz. cheese instead of the beef. To sleep upon, we have a hammock, straw bed and one very thin rug. . . . We are allowed every day to walk in the airing ground from 10 to 12, then locked in till 3 o'clock, then we are let out again till 7 o'clock, then in and locked up for the night." [1]

Herbert wrote, August 31 : " Many are strongly tempted to pick up the grass in the yard and eat it and some pick up old bones in the yard that have been laying in the dirt a week or ten days and pound them to pieces and suck them. Some will pick up snails out of the holes in the wall and from among the grass and weeds in the yard, boil them and eat them and drink the broth. . . . Our meat is very poor in general; we scarcely see a

[1] *N. E. Hist. and Gen. Reg.*, April, 1878.

good piece once in a month. Many are driven to
such necessity by want of provisions that they have
sold most of the clothes off their backs for the sake
of getting a little money to buy them some bread." [1]
Some of the prisoners were able occasionally to
earn a few shillings with which to buy extra food
and other necessities. Andrew Sherburne, who was
in Mill Prison in 1782, says there were between
eight hundred and a thousand men confined there
at that time.[2]

In September, 1777, an improvement began and
continued for more than a year. This was due to
outside causes and did not indicate any relaxation
of severity on the part of the government or prison
authorities. The sympathies of charitable people in
London and elsewhere had been aroused and a fund
was subscribed which furnished extra food and
clothing.[3] Jonathan Archer wrote to his parents
from Mill Prison, September 25, 1778: "The
time seems long and teagous to me; I shall embrace every opportunity of writing. We have plenty
of provisions ; the gentlemen have raised a large
sum of money for the relief of the Americans." [4]
Letters of Franklin to correspondents in England
also did much to excite interest in the prisoners.[5]
When the money that had been raised for their

[1] Livesey's *Prisoners of 1776*, 65, 66.

[2] *A. Sherburne*, 85. For an English account, see *Annual Register*, xxi (1778), 78.

[3] *Livesey*, 68, 70, 91, 92, 96.   [4] *Essex Inst. Coll.*, June, 1864.

[5] *Wharton*, ii, 409, 410, 448, 492.

benefit had become exhausted, about the end of 1778, the old conditions returned. The prisoners hunted for rats, and if a dog strayed in, he was immediately killed and eaten. To be put upon half allowance, as many frequently were for punishment, was to be reduced nearly to the last extremity. Nevertheless, the health of the prisoners as a rule was good, and the death rate, at least for the first two years, compared with that of the New York prison-ships, was very low. Early in 1782, however, there was much sickness.[1]

After France, Spain, and Holland had become involved in the war, the prisoners from those countries were better treated than the Americans, whose allowance of bread was a third less than theirs. In the House of Lords, July 2, 1781, an effort was made to place the Americans on an equality in this respect with the French, Spanish, and Dutch, but the proposal was defeated by a vote of forty-seven to fourteen. In the course of the debate on the question it was argued " that the diet of prisoners, as persons in a state of inactivity, ought to be sparing, and that just enough to sustain life ought to be the measure of it ; for that if more than enough was allowed, it would render the prisoners unhealthy by producing gross humours if they eat it, or if they sold what was superabundant, it was probable they would buy spirits with it and thereby render them-

[1] *Livesey,* 109, 123, 166, 175, 186, 196, 201, 203, 207, 216, 218; *A. Sherburne,* 91.

selves unhealthy and unhappy." [1] Very touching was this solicitude of the Lords for the health of the American prisoners. Their old enemies, the French and Spanish, might be encouraged to ruin their digestions by overeating, but in the case of their kinsmen from across the sea, it was not to be thought of.

Captain Conyngham's experiences in captivity have been alluded to.[2] After his escape he wrote to Franklin from the Texel, December 1, 1779 : "I shall acquaint you of the many favours I received since I became a captive. 1st, in New York, that Sir George Collier ordered irons on my legs, with a centry on board the ship. Mr. Collier going on an expedition ordered me to jaole, there put me into the condemned room. The first night a cold plank my bed a stone for a pillow. 2d night allowed a something to lay on ; in this horrid room was kept for eight days without the least morsel of bread, or anything but water, from the keeper of the prison. . . . After expostulating of the impropriety of such treatment, [the jailer] told me he had such orders, but would take it upon himself to release me on my giving him my strongest assurances I would not make my escape. I readily consented, it not being in the power of man to get out of the condemned room. . . . In the prison of New York I continued till that tyrant Collier returned. . . .

[1] *Almon*, xii, 222, 223 ; *Mag. Amer. Hist.*, June, 1882.
[2] See above, pp. 376, 377.

Then I was told to get ready to go on board the prison-ship. . . . Then a pair of criminal irons put on my legs, weight 50 pounds; at the door, put into the hangman's cart, all in form as if bound to the gallows. I was then put into a boat and took alongside the Raisonable, . . . to be sent to England in the packet. In those Irons I was brought to Pendennis Castle. Then not contented, they manacled my hands with a new fashioned pair of ruffels fitted very tite. In this condition I was kept there 15 or 16 days, then brought to Plymouth and lodged in the black hole for eight days, before they would do me the honour of committing me on suspicion of high treason on his majesties high seas; then put into Mill prison, where we committed treason through his earth and made our escape. This, Sir, is an account of their favors, insults excepted. I must acquaint your excellency that the poor unfortunate prisoners in Plymouth are in a most distressed situation." [1]

Attempts to escape from Mill Prison were numerous, sometimes by climbing over the walls, sometimes by burrowing under them, and sometimes by bribing sentries, the last generally by officers who had money. Among the officers confined at this place were Captains Manley, Talbot, Johnson, and O'Brien, and Lieutenants Dale and Barney. Of these the last four escaped, besides Conyngham; Manley and Talbot made several attempts. Most

[1] *Hale*, i, 349; *Almon*, viii, 340.

AUGUSTATUS KUNINGAM

GUSTAVUS CONYNGHAM

prisoners' efforts in this direction failed, but in the aggregate a large number got off and made their way to Holland and France. At Paris they found a good friend in Franklin, who gave them money and assistance to the extent of his ability. Those who were caught after escaping were brought back, confined forty days in a dungeon called the "black hole," and put upon half allowance of food.[1] Some escaped by entering the British service, yielding to inducements constantly held out to them. Those doing so were comparatively few in number, and most of them were foreigners who had served on American ships. In December, 1778, over a hundred men in Mill Prison signed an agreement to remain loyal to their country and under no circumstances to enter the British service.[2] In June, 1778, rumors of exchange began to be heard, which for many months seemed only to hold out false hopes. In September, the American Commissioners in Paris wrote to their countrymen in English prisons that they had at last "obtained assurances from England that an exchange shall take place." They added : " We have now obtained permission of this government to put all British prisoners — whether taken by continental frigates or by privateers — into the king's prisons, and we are determined to

[1] *Livesey*, 56–60, *passim*, 209–213; *Barney*, 87–102; *O'Brien*, 180–183; *Port Folio*, June, 1814; *N. E. Hist. and Gen. Reg.*, October, 1878; *Essex Inst. Coll.*, January, 1909; *Lee MSS.*, February 28, 1778; *Adams MSS.*, July 16, 1780, June 5, 1781.

[2] *Livesey*, 161, 163, 177, 183, 208, 221.

treat such prisoners precisely as our countrymen are treated in England, to give them the same allow-ance of provisions and accommodations and no other. We therefore request you to inform us with exactness what your allowance is from the government, that we may govern ourselves accordingly." [1] It was not until March 15, 1779, that hopes of release were realized and ninety-seven of the inmates of Mill Prison embarked on a cartel bound for France. [2]

The brigantine Rising States sailed from Boston, January 26, 1777, and on April 15 was captured in the English Channel by the Terrible, 74, though only after a spirited resistance. Two weeks later the Terrible arrived at Spithead and the prisoners remained on board until June 14, harshly treated and on three quarters allowance. They were then removed to Forton Prison, near Portsmouth, being the first Americans to occupy it. Their experiences are told in the journal of Timothy Connor, one of the crew of the Rising States. The prison ration was three quarters of a pound of beef, a pound of bread, and a quart of small beer for twenty-four hours, and some cabbage every other day. Prisoners in the black hole, for trying to escape or other misdemeanor, had six ounces of beef, half a pound of

[1] *Wharton*, ii, 729, 730.

[2] *Livesey*, 139, 141, 179, 182, 199, 200, 219, 223, 224, 233; *Wharton*, iii, 188. For another account of conditions on board a receiving-ship in Plymouth Harbor and in Mill Prison, see *A Sherburne*, 76–100; see also journal of William Russell in *Ships and Sailors of Old Salem*, chs. vii, viii.

bread, and a pint of beer. Five days after entrance
the prisoners "made a large hole through the wall
of the prison and eleven made their escape," two
of whom were caught and brought back. During
the first six months more than sixty escaped, about
half of whom were retaken. December 25, Connor
says: "Now the people begin to use humanity
throughout England. . . . They begin to use us
better. There are subscription books opened in many
parts of England for our relief." [1] The officers were
given five shillings a week each and the men two
shillings. The Reverend Thomas Wren of Portsmouth took a great interest in the prisoners and
visited them daily. David Hartley, M.P., one of
Franklin's English correspondents and an old friend
of his, also visited the prison. Besides the fund
raised in England, Franklin sent over what money
he could spare, to be used for the benefit of the prisoners. Much of this was entrusted to an American
merchant in London named Digges, who a few
years later turned out to be a British spy and a
defaulter and who embezzled nearly all the money
he had received for the use of the prisoners.[2] May
12, 1778, Connor wrote in his journal: "Nothing
to eat these two days but stinking beef. All the
men in the prison, or at least best part of them,
carried their beef back and threw it into the cook's

[1] *N. E. Hist. and Gen. Reg.*, July, 1876.
[2] *Wharton*, ii, 492, iii, 523, iv, 623, 645; *Hale*, i, ch. xi; *Adams
MSS.*, July 10, 1778.

window, and left and went without any." The next day the bad meat was served again, "but by the Agent's orders it was sent back again and we got a little cheese in the room of it."[1]   Captain Hinman of the Alfred and his officers were brought to Forton Prison in July, 1778, and in less than a week he and several other officers escaped. September 8, fifty-eight prisoners escaped. In March, 1779, there were two hundred and fifty-one Americans at Forton. July 2, one hundred and twenty of them were released by exchange.[2]

John Howard, the English prison reformer, wrote of Forton: "At my visit, Nov. 6, 1782, I found there was no separation of the Americans from other prisoners of war, and they had the same allowance of bread, viz: one pound and a half each. There were 154 French, 33 Dutch and 133 Americans. Of these, 12 French, 25 Dutch and 9 Americans were in the hospital. The wards were not clean. No regulations hung up. I weighed several of the 6 lb. loaves and they all wanted some ounces in weight."[3]

In the West Indies the unhealthfulness of the climate doubtless added to the tribulations of pris-

---

[1] *N. E. Hist. and Gen. Reg.*, July, 1876.

[2] *Ibid.*, April, 1876, to July, 1878; *Essex Inst. Coll.*, April, 1889; *Mag. Amer. Hist.*, March, 1878, Matthewman's narrative; *Wharton*, iii, 363. For another account of Forton Prison, see *Fanning*, 20–28.

[3] *Essex Inst. Coll.*, April, 1889, quoting from Howard's *History of Prisons*.

oners and increased the death rate. In 1782, the
privateer brig New Broom of New London was
captured by a British sloop of war and taken into
Antigua. One of the brig's crew, in a narrative of
the cruise, says : " We were all put on board of a
prison-ship, which lay in a cove on one side of the
harbor, where the heat was so severe as to be almost insupportable. We were allowed here but
barely enough to sustain nature, and the water they
gave us was taken out of a pond a little back of
the town, in which the cattle and negroes com-
mingled every sort of impurity, and which was
rendered, on this account and from the effect of
the heat upon it, so nauseous that it was impossible
to drink it without holding the nostrils. I soon
found that life was to be supported but for a short
time here and set myself therefore about contriving
some way to effect my escape from this floating
place of misery and torment. The doctor came on
board every morning to examine the sick, and three
negro sextons every night, to bury the dead. Early
one morning I swallowed tobacco juice and was so
sick by the time the doctor came, that I obtained
without difficulty a permit from him to go on shore
to the hospital. I was soon ready to disembark, for
I had been previously robbed of everything except
what I had on. After arriving at the hospital, I
was conducted into a long room where lay more
than two hundred of the most miserable objects
imaginable, covered with rags and vermin. I threw

myself down on a bunk and after suffering extremely for some time from the effects of the tobacco, went to sleep, but was soon waked by a man-nurse, who told me that there was physic for me and immediately went off to another. I contrived unperceived to throw my dose out of the window and was not again disturbed, except during the following night, when I was waked several times by the carrying out of the dead. The sickness occasioned by the tobacco having now ceased, it was still necessary to keep up the deception, and accordingly the next morning I feigned lameness." A few days later this prisoner escaped with two others; getting possession of a boat they found their way to Guadeloupe.[1] In 1779, the Marine Committee had called attention to the harsh treatment of prisoners at Antigua and urged efforts for their exchange.[2]

There appears to be less available material for a study of the treatment of British prisoners by the Americans. Before France became involved in the war the disposal of prisoners taken by American cruisers in European waters was attended with difficulties, because the French government would not allow them to be brought into the ports of that country, regarding it as a violation of neutrality to receive them. It was, therefore, often necessary to release them. Franklin and Deane advised the commanders of American ships to take from their

[1] *Hist. Mag.*, November, 1860.
[2] *Mar. Com. Letter Book*, 243 (October 26, 1779).

prisoners, before letting them go, a signed acknowledgment of the fact that they had been captured.[1] They hoped to secure in return the release of an equal number of American prisoners, but the British government would not admit any obligation in such cases, and indeed refused to honor formal paroles, except under certain circumstances. After France had begun hostilities, American vessels could bring their prisoners into port, but there was no provision for their reception until, after long delay, they were admitted into French prisons. Meanwhile it was necessary to keep them on shipboard under conditions of great discomfort, if not of actual suffering. The prisoners brought into Brest by the Ranger in May, 1778, were confined many months on one of her prizes and made bitter complaints of their situation. Captain Jones exerted himself as far as possible for their welfare, but was very unwilling to release them without exchange. Franklin supplied as well as he could the wants of the British prisoners in France. In February, 1780, he wrote to one of his English correspondents, enclosing the account of his agent at L'Orient, " for clothing one hundred and thirteen English prisoners last April," and adding : " Not that I expect anything from your government on that account towards clothing such of our people with you as may be in want of it. The refusal of compliance with the paroles of prisoners set at liberty have

[1] See above, p. 300.

taught me to flatter myself no more with expectations that a thing may be done because it is humane
or equitable, and reasonable that it should be done.
I only desire it may be considered as a small but
grateful acknowledgment, all hitherto in my power,
for the kindness shown by your charitable subscrip-
tions to our poor people. It may perhaps be some
satisfaction to those subscribers to know that, while
they thought only of relieving Americans, they were
at the same time occasioning some relief to distressed Englishmen." [1] When the exchange of
prisoners had become an established procedure, the
number of English in France must have been comparatively small and their stay short, for the British policy was to keep many American prisoners in
England, bringing them from New York.[2]

The Continental vessels Reprisal, Lexington,
and Dolphin made a cruise in the English Channel and Irish Sea in 1777 and took several prizes.[3]
According to a dispatch from Whitehaven, June
26, 1777, "the people in general speak in the
warmest terms of the humane treatment they met
with from the commanders of the Reprisal and
Lexington, both of whom endeavored to make the
situation of their prisoners as easy as their circumstances would admit." [4]

[1] *Wharton*, iii, 522.
[2] *Ibid.*, ii, 428, 581, 724, iii, 73, 488, 491, 535, 536, iv, 410; *Hale*,
i, 351–362; *Sands*, 104, 105, 148; *Mass. Spy*, January 4, 1781.
[3] See above, pp. 269, 270.
[4] *Boston Gazette*, October 6, 1777.

Quite different from this was the treatment of Captain Richard Cassedy of the British ship Priscilla by a prize crew put on board his vessel from the American privateer General Mifflin, which captured the Priscilla off the Irish coast in July, 1777. All his men having been transferred to the Mifflin, he was left alone at the mercy of a brutal prize crew. " These sons of freedom seized all the captain's clothes that were worth anything and £88 in cash." He was " bound hand and foot and put into confinement. In this miserable situation he remained until the 19th of July, when his vessel was retook by the Union, letter of marque, of London. . . . Captain Cassedy was in a very poor state of health . . . and not able to stand, through the cruel treatment he received. His remaining so long bound occasioned his flesh to swell to a shocking degree. All his prayers and intreaties were in vain; the inhuman tyrants had no compassion." [1]

The treatment of British prisoners in America varied according to place and circumstances. There were prison-ships at Boston, New London, and doubtless other towns, and jails on shore were used.[2] Captain Henry Barnes and his crew, captured with his vessel on the passage from Barbadoes to England by the American privateer Montgomery in 1776 and taken to Rhode Island, were

[1] Liverpool paper quoted in *Williams*, 210.
[2] *Boston Post*, June 15, 1782; *Mass. Court Rec.*, January 20, 1778; *Mass. Rev. Rolls*, viii, ix, xliv.

" treated with the greatest kindness and civility." [1] A letter from Boston, in 1777, says: " Hard as my case may appear to be, I bear it with patience. From the 3d day of my captivity I have, with near ninety others, been confined a close prisoner in a jail at this place lately erected, called the New-prison. The Americans treat us very cavalierly. The provisions we are allowed is barely sufficient to subsist on. My effects, to the amount of up-wards of 300*l.* have been taken from me and the bed I lie on is a bundle of straw." [2] A letter from New London, a few months later, says: " They behave very well to us." [3] A better reputation is given to Boston by an English shipmaster who had been exchanged. He writes: " The treatment of the English prisoners there is exceedingly humane and kind." [4]

The situation of British marine prisoners at Phila-delphia was possibly not always what it should have been, though as a rule not bad; their treatment was perhaps at times, but only in special instances, governed by a spirit of retaliation for the distress of Americans on the New York prison-ships. Ad-miral Arbuthnot wrote to John Jay, President of Congress, August 30, 1779, complaining that two British officers were " in close and cruel confine-ment at Philadelphia. I request that you will

---

[1] *Almon,* iv, 159, 160.

[2] *London Chronicle,* September 2, 1777.

[3] *Ibid.,* January 6, 1778.   [4] *Ibid.,* January 8, 1778.

assign satisfactory reasons for this treatment, that no improper retaliation may take place here on our part." [1] Congress investigated the case of these two officers and found the reports of their ill-treatment untrue. Just at this time, on account of the barbarous persecution of Conyngham in New York, the Marine Committee ordered against another British officer retaliatory measures which had recently been voted in Congress, after a vain appeal to Commodore Collier.[2] Arbuthnot wrote to Washington, April 21, 1781, again complaining of the treatment of British naval prisoners, saying : " Permit me now, Sir, to request that you will take the proper steps to cause Mr. Bradford, your commissary, and the jailor at Philadelphia, to abate that inhumanity which they exercise indiscriminately upon all people, who are so unfortunate as to be carried into that place. I will not trouble you, Sir, with a catalogue of grievances further than to request that the unfortunate may feel as little of the severities of war as the circumstances of the time will permit ; that in future they may not be fed in winter with salted clams and that they may be afforded a sufficiency of fuel." [3]

At last, in the spring of 1782, Franklin was able to inform Jay that the British Parliament had

[1] *Pap. Cont. Congr.*, **78**, 1, 313 (August 30, 1779).

[2] *Mar. Com. Letter Book*, 230 (August 31, 1779); *Almon*, viii, 340, 341; *Jour. Cont. Congr.*, July 17, 29, September 17, 1779.

[3] *Washington*, ix, 120, 121. No further information relating to the treatment of British prisoners has been discovered.

passed "an act for exchanging American prisoners. They have near eleven hundred in the jails of England and Ireland, all committed as charged with high treason. The act is to empower the king, notwithstanding such commitments, to consider them as prisoners of war, according to the law of nations, and exchange them as such. This seems to be giving up their pretensions of considering us as rebellious subjects and is a kind of acknowledgment of our independence. Transports are now taking up to carry back to their country the poor, brave fellows who have borne for years their cruel captivity, rather than serve our enemies, and an equal number of English are to be delivered up in return."[1] The British ministry now ordered the exchange of all American prisoners. A year later, April, 1783, came proclamations of the Continental Congress and the British commanders in New York, the latter a day or two in the lead, for the suspension of hostilities and the release of all prisoners of war.[2]

[1] *Wharton*, v, 326.
[2] *Ibid.*, 439, 512, 548, 556, vi, 369, 375, 377.

CHAPTER XIX

In the study of so closely contested a struggle as the American Revolution, where even a comparatively trivial circumstance might have turned the scale, it is interesting to examine the factors which may have affected the result. In the events that took place on the sea perhaps many such factors will be found. Such conclusions regarding them as may be drawn from the preceding chapters, will be more clearly brought out if presented in the condensed form of a summary.

Both the Americans and the British, while favored in some ways, were burdened with encumbrances of various sorts. The preponderance of the British naval forces in American waters during the early years of the war was so great that for the colonists in rebellion to overcome it was out of the question; annoyance only was possible. Their control of the sea was complete until challenged by the French in 1778. The British had much larger ships than the Americans, which meant that they not only carried more guns, but far heavier ones; the thirty-two-gun frigate was the largest we had in commission. Ship for ship also we were overmatched by the British with their ships more fully manned and their officers and men thoroughly trained. The raw material for their crews was certainly no better and probably not as good as that furnished by the fishermen and seafaring population of New England and other colonies, but the immense advantage of organization, of centuries of military discipline, of naval tradition and *esprit de corps*, was theirs.

The British, however, were embarrassed with difficulties which in large degree offset their superiority in force. Operating in a hostile country, their naval stations, even those most securely and permanently held, as New York, were unable to furnish sufficient stores and supplies; and these necessities had to be brought from England, subject to capture by American cruisers and privateers and requiring the diversion of a considerable part of their armed force for convoy. Owing to the incompetency or indolence of some of the British fleet commanders, their available offensive force was used with less effect than might have been the case. Jealousy and quarrels among the admirals also contributed to this result. Official corruption in British dockyards and naval stations, defective organization, and the waste of money and supplies interfered seriously with efficient naval administration. The navy lost large numbers of men through desertion and death from disease. It will thus be seen that the circumstances surrounding the British navy during that period were sufficiently complicated. The entry of other powers into the conflict naturally increased very much the perplexities of England's situation.[1]

Turning to our own side, there was little to help out the slender resources of the Americans beyond the advantage of operating in home waters and along shores inhabited by a friendly people and of a general aptitude for the sea, no greater, however, than that of their adversaries. The poverty of the Continental government, if not of the country, precluded anything like a strong naval organization, and the weakness of Congress, together with lack of experience, made efficient administration practically impossible. For want of money and of available workmen the construction and repair of ships was painfully slow. On this account they were frequently kept idle in port months at a time, nearly a whole season, perhaps, while cruises planned for them were prevented, postponed, or only partially carried out. The obstacles encountered in manning the Continental ships were equal to those which hindered their fitting out. The needs of the army and the attractions of privateering, especially the latter, drew so heavily on the seafaring population that capable men for the regular naval service were scarce. The result was that after almost interminable delay a ship would be obliged to go to sea with a crew deficient both in numbers and in quality, made up of material in large part not only inferior, but

[1] See Channing, iii, 279–283, 340–342; and above, pp. 52–58, 519.

sometimes dangerous, if, as was often the case, it included British prisoners who were willing to enlist. In such ships' companies a mutinous spirit prevailed, with occasional serious effects. Furthermore the officers of the navy, while generally good seamen and not lacking in courage, were without military training, and thus apt to be deficient in martial qualities and incapable of rising to the occasion at critical moments. The responsibility of an independent command, even of a single vessel on an important service, was often too much for such men. It is hardly necessary to add, however, that there were some notable exceptions.

As a consequence of these impediments the Americans never possessed a regular naval force capable of acting offensively against the enemy in any effective way. The Continental navy, therefore, naturally resorted to the readiest means of injuring the enemy, that is, by preying upon his commerce. The state navies and privateers were of course engaged in the same pursuit; and this, with convoy duty upon occasion, formed the chief occupation of the entire sea force, public and private, of the country. Engagements with regular British men-of-war were exceptional and commonly accidental.

The futility of commerce destroying as a military measure of first importance has been pointed out by naval authorities. " It is doubtless a most important secondary operation of naval war, and is not likely to be abandoned till war itself shall cease;

but regarded as a primary and fundamental measure, sufficient in itself to crush an enemy, it is probably a delusion." [1] The injury inflicted upon England, though large in the aggregate, was not disabling. Part of this predatory warfare consisted in the interception of the enemy's transports, conveying troops and warlike supplies, which were a godsend to our army and the loss of which was severely felt by the British; this perhaps was of too nearly a military nature to be classed as ordinary commerce destroying. During the early years of the war especially, such captures were of the utmost value to the American cause.

There were probably more than two thousand American vessels employed in privateering during the Revolution.[2] Privateers accomplished much independently in scouring the sea, but were ill adapted for cruising in squadrons and failed in nearly all attempts at coöperation with regular ships or with each other. One half the men, money, and energy absorbed in privateering, if it could have been put into a strong, well-organized Continental navy, would have provided a force able to act offensively against the British navy to some purpose. The other half, devoted to privateering, would have been able to accomplish more in destroying commerce than all the privateers actually did, and would have

[1] *Mahan*, 539. See also *Proc. U. S. Naval Inst.*, xxiii (1897), 472.

[2] See above, pp. 46, 47.

suffered fewer losses, because of the protection afforded by a strong, regular navy against British cruisers. Speculating as to what might have been has a practical interest and value when a choice of alternatives depends upon an accident or train of circumstances which might have happened otherwise. In the case under discussion, however, the fundamental conditions were such as to put any such rearrangement of naval power as that suggested so entirely out of the question that there remains no room for regret on the score of mistakes which could have been rectified. It is necessary to look at the events of the past from the point of view of the time and the persons concerned. In this case the temperament of the people, private interests, the sentiment of local independence and fear of centralized military power, the lack of authority on the part of Congress, the hopelessness of raising the necessary money, are at once evident to the student of this period of our history. Privateering, moreover, was thoroughly believed in as a means of striking at the enemy's vitals. Under the circumstances, therefore, it is obvious that a small, weak navy was one of the necessary conditions of the war and that a vigorous offense upon the sea was not in the nature of things.

When it is once admitted that an aggressive policy, aimed at the British fleets in American waters with any reasonable chance of gaining naval supremacy, was not to be expected, we are better

prepared to understand and to accept philosophic-
ally the gradual dwindling of the Continental navy,
always in the presence of a superior force, the loss
of ship after ship, the almost inevitable recurrence
of disaster; a dismal record, to be sure, but not dis-
creditable, and relieved by a few successes and
brilliant episodes. At the same time we can better
appreciate what was actually accomplished by the
American marine as a whole, how much it really
contributed to the cause of independence. The injury to British commerce was sufficiently serious to
aid materially in rendering the war unpopular in
England; insurance rates rose to an unprecedented
figure, and the available sources from which revenue might be derived by taxation were nearly
exhausted. The shores of the British Isles were
harassed as never before or since by the repeated
visits of American naval cruisers and privateers,
and the seacoast population alarmed. An active and
regular commerce was carried on between the United
States and continental Europe, providing the latter
with American products and furnishing the new
nation with much-needed money and supplies. Communication was kept open with France, diplomatic
correspondence maintained, and public men of
both countries crossed and recrossed the ocean repeatedly, Henry Laurens being the only one of
prominence to be captured. All this intercourse,
moreover, prevented the isolation of America, and
kept alive the interest and sympathy of Europe.

Continental ships aided this traffic by furnishing convoy through the danger zone off the American coast and also by taking an active part in it. Many a cargo of tobacco from America and of military stores from France, and many ministers and diplomatic agents, were conveyed in Continental frigates.

A rigorous blockade of the American coast from the beginning of the war, as was recommended by Lord Barrington, might have suppressed this commerce, and would probably have strangled the rebellion of the colonists in its infancy, without the help of the army.[1] If at any time during the early years the English had been alert, enterprising, and aggressive in the use of their great naval resources, they should have been able to crush or at least greatly to cripple this traffic. Presumably the main reason for its comparative immunity is to be sought in the supineness of British admirals and in administrative vices of the Admiralty.

Although the fortunes of our American marine chiefly concern us, a glance at the general naval war of 1778 is essential to the completeness of the subject. With her control of the sea threatened, the policy for England to adopt was a matter of vast importance. A foremost naval authority has said: "The key of the situation was in Europe, and in Europe in the hostile dockyards." England's " one hope was to find and strike down the enemy's

---

[1] See above, p. 18; also pp. 188, 189, 291, 334, for other projects of aggressive action.

navy. Nowhere was it so certainly to be found as in its home ports; nowhere so easily met as immediately after leaving them."[1] But the opportunity was lost, and it was necessary for England to pursue her enemy to distant seas, leaving an inadequate force in home waters. Luckily for England, the European allies failed to take advantage of her mistakes. Instead of using their superior force for a vigorous offense, they seemed ever bent on a defensive attitude; justified, perhaps, and certainly so from their point of view, by ulterior strategic considerations. However that may be, the French and Spanish, through lack of coöperation, through dilatory tactics, and for various reasons, either avoided their enemy or failed to seize opportunities as they occurred. Their plans for the invasion of England came to nothing, and their operations in America and the West Indies were generally disappointing and abortive, because of their failure to seek out and strike the enemy.[2] Their naval supremacy, therefore, was most of the time potential only, although by no means for that reason without effect. It finally became actual and decisive at one critical juncture, when a fortunate train of circumstances secured the control of Chesapeake Bay. Fortunate, indeed, was this event for the American cause, for

[1] *Mahan*, 525. For discussion of this subject, see *Ibid.*, 416–418, 527–535.

[2] *Ibid.*, 535–539; *Proc. U. S. Naval Inst.*, xxii (1896), 578; *Channing*, iii, 297.

whose success the temporary possession of sea power was indispensable.

To revert, in conclusion, to the maritime achievements of the Revolutionists, it would appear that keeping open the intercourse with Continental Europe, especially France, and the diversion of supplies from the British to the American army, were the most valuable services performed by the American armed forces afloat, public and private, during the war; the injury done to the British navy being almost negligible, and to British commerce far from disabling, to say the least, although not without effect in the general result. It is certain that the Revolution would have failed without its sailors. In spite of its shortcomings, the record of the American marine during this critical period was an honorable one. Many officers, through the experience of naval warfare acquired on board regular cruisers and privateers, were qualified to enter the national service a few years later, upon the reëstablishment of the Navy.

THE END

APPENDIX

APPENDIX

I

THIS list includes most of the authorities consulted. The abbreviations used in the footnotes are here indicated. Other works, cited only once or twice, are also referred to in footnotes.

Documents

Journals of the Continental Congress. Edited by Worthington C. Ford and Galliard Hunt. Washington, 1904–1912. [*Jour. Cont. Congr.*]
   Contain much naval information.

American Archives. Compiled by Peter Force. Series IV, vols. ii to vi, and V, vols. i to iii. Washington, 1837. [*Am. Arch.*, IV, ii, etc.]
   A very important source, containing a vast amount of material for the years 1775 and 1776. In transcribing documents, occasional errors have crept in.

The Revolutionary Diplomatic Correspondence of the United States. Edited by Francis Wharton. Washington, 1889. [*Wharton.*]
   Useful for operations in European waters.

B. F. Stevens's Facsimiles of Manuscripts in European Archives Relating to America, 1773–1783. London, 1889–1895. [*Stevens.*]
   Correspondence of French and British ministers and others relating to neutrality, American naval cruisers and privateers, etc.

Extracts Relating to the Origin of the American Navy. Compiled by Henry E. Waite. Boston, 1890.
  Documents and letters chiefly relating to Washington's fleet in Massachusetts Bay.

The Journals of Each Provincial Congress of Massachusetts in 1774 and 1775, and of the Committee of Safety. Boston, 1838.

Journals of the House of Representatives of Massachusetts, 1775–1783. Contemporary print.

The Acts and Resolves, Public and Private, of the Province of the Massachusetts Bay. Vol. v. Boston, 1886.

Acts and Resolves of Massachusetts, 1780–1783. Boston, 1890.

Records of the Colony of Rhode Island and Providence Plantations. Providence, 1856–1865.

Public Records of the Colony of Connecticut. Hartford, 1890.

Public Records of the State of Connecticut. Hartford, 1894.

Journals of the Provincial Congress, Provincial Convention, Committee of Safety and Council of Safety of the State of New York. Albany, 1842.

Pennsylvania Archives, Second Series. Vol. i. Harrisburg, 1874.

Pennsylvania Colonial Records. Philadelphia, 1852.

Maryland Archives. Baltimore, 1883–1901.

The Remembrancer, or Impartial Repository of Public Events. [Annual. Edited by J. Almon.] London, 1775–1783.   [*Almon.*]
  Contains many official reports and letters; a very useful source.

A History of All the Engagements by Sea and Land that happened in America and Europe and the East and West Indies during the American Revolution. Manchester, 1787.

Made up chiefly of reports of British officers.

Historical Manuscripts Commission. Fourteenth Report, Appendix I, Duke of Rutland. 1894. American Manuscripts in the Royal Institution. Vol. i. 1904. Various Collections. Vol. vi. 1909. Manuscripts of Mrs. Stopford-Sackville. Vol. ii. 1910.

[Hist. Man. Com.]

These British collections of manuscripts, printed in recent years, contain many references to American naval affairs.

A Calendar of John Paul Jones Manuscripts in the Library of Congress. Compiled by Charles Henry Lincoln. Washington, 1903.

Full outline of letters, with extracts.

Calendar of the Correspondence of George Washington. Prepared from the Original Manuscripts in the Library of Congress by John C. Fitzpatrick. Washington, 1906.

Naval Records of the American Revolution [Calendar], prepared from the Originals in the Library of Congress by Charles Henry Lincoln. Washington, 1906.

Contains a list of nearly 1700 letters of marque issued by Congress, giving the name of each vessel, with other information. These calendars, as an aid in consulting the manuscripts in the Library of Congress, are indispensable.

Histories

Narrative and Critical History of America. Edited by Justin Winsor. Vols. vi and vii. Boston, 1887, 1888.

[Narr. and Crit. Hist.]

Contains an extensive bibliography, with critical discussion of authorities.

The American Nation. Edited by Albert Bushnell Hart. Vol. ix. The American Revolution. By C. H. Van Tyne. New York, 1905.

A History of the United States. By Edward Channing. Vol. iii. The American Revolution. New York, 1912.   [*Channing.*]

Contains the results of the latest researches in the Revolutionary period.

Statistical History of the Navy of the United States. By Lieutenant George F. Emmons, U.S.N. Washington, 1853.

Lists of Continental navy, of captures, and of privateers.

A Contribution to the Bibliography of the History of the United States Navy. Compiled by Charles T. Harbeck. The Riverside Press, 1906.

Statistical and Chronological History of the United States Navy. 1775–1907. By Robert Wilden Neeser. New York, 1909.   [*Neeser.*]

Contains a most exhaustive bibliography and lists of captures.

Naval History of the United States. By Thomas Clark. Philadelphia, 1814.   [*Clark.*]

The author derived some of his information directly from actors in the scenes described.

United States Naval Chronicle. By Charles W. Goldsborough. Washington, 1824.

Gives lists of officers and other data.

Battles of the United States by Sea and Land. By Henry B. Dawson. New York, 1858.   [*Dawson.*]

Official reports and very copious references.

History of the Navy of the United States of America. By J. Fenimore Cooper. London, 1839.

Pictorial Field Book of the Revolution. By Benson J. Lossing. New York, 1850.

The Navy of [the American Revolution. By Charles Oscar Paullin. Chicago, 1906. [*Paullin.*]

Gives an exceedingly valuable account of the organization and administration of the Continental navy and of the state navies, with full references. It contains a vast amount of information hitherto practically inaccessible and is indispensable for the student of this subject.

Diplomatic Negotiations of American Naval Officers. By Charles Oscar Paullin. Baltimore, 1912.

The Influence of Sea Power upon History. By Captain A. T. Mahan, U.S.N. Boston, 1890. [*Mahan.*]

Naval Strategy. By Captain A. T. Mahan, U.S.N. Boston, 1911.

The Annual Register. London, 1775–1783.

The First American Civil War. By Henry Belcher. London, 1911. [*Belcher.*]

England under the Hanoverians. Ry G. Grant Robertson. New York, 1911.

Naval Chronology. By Isaac Schomberg, R.N. London, 1802. [*Schomberg.*]

Gives valuable statistics.

Naval and Military Memoirs of Great Britain. By Robert Beatson. London, 1804.

Naval Battles of Great Britain. By Charles Ekins, Rear Admiral. London, 1828.

Battles of the British Navy. By Joseph Allen, R.N. London, 1868.

The Royal Navy. By William Laird Clowes. Chapter

xxxi. By A. T. Mahan. Chapter xxxii. By H. W. Wilson. Boston and London, 1898. [*Clowes.*]

A Short History of the Royal Navy. By David Hannay. London, 1909. [*Hannay.*]

Gives much information respecting British naval administration and conditions in the navy.

Publications of the Navy Records Society. Vol. iii, Hood's Letters. Vol. vi, Journal of Rear-Admiral James. Vols. xxix and xxxv, Instructions and Signals. By J. S. Corbett. Vols. xxxii and xxxviii, Barham Papers. London, 1895–1911. [*Nav. Rec. Soc.*]

These volumes contain much original material of great value.

Histoire de la Marine Française pendant la Guerre de l'Indépendance Américaine. Par E. Chevalier. Paris, 1877. [*Chevalier.*]

Contains extracts from official letters and ships' journals.

Histoire de la participation de la France à l' établissement des États-Unis d'Amérique. Par Henri Doniol. Paris, 1886. [*Doniol.*]

Franklin in France. By Edward Everett Hale and E. E. Hale, Jr. Boston, 1887. [*Hale.*]

A History of American Privateers. By Edgar Stanton Maclay. New York, 1899.

Rhode Island Privateers and Privateersmen. By W. P. Sheffield. Newport, 1883.

History of the Liverpool Privateers. By Gomer Williams. Liverpool, 1897. [*Williams.*]

Contains letters and extracts from contemporary newspapers.

Economic and Social History of New England. By William B. Weeden. Boston, 1890.

Revolutionary Incidents of Suffolk and Kings Counties
with an Account of the British Prisons and Prison-
Ships at New York. By Henry Onderdonk, Jr. New
York, 1849.   [*Onderdonk.*]
Contains extracts from contemporary letters and
newspapers.

Martyrs to the Revolution in the British Prison-Ships in
the Wallabout Bay. [By George Taylor]. New York,
1855.

Some Account of the Capture of the Ship Aurora. By
Philip Freneau. New York, 1899.

History of Castine, Penobscot, etc. By George Augustus
Wheeler. Bangor, 1875.   [*Wheeler.*]
Documents relating to the Penobscot Expedition.

Detail of Some Particular Services performed in America, 1776–1779, compiled from journals kept aboard
the Ship Rainbow. By Ithiel Town. New York, 1835.
[*Town.*]

Biographies

Writings of George Washington. Collected and Edited
by Worthington Chauncey Ford. New York, 1889.
[*Washington.*]

The Works of John Adams. By Charles Francis Adams.
Boston, 1853.   [*Adams.*]

The Writings of Benjamin Franklin. Edited by Albert
Henry Smyth. New York, 1905.

Writings of Thomas Jefferson. Collected and Edited by
Paul Leicester Ford. New York, 1892.   [*Jefferson.*]

Life and Correspondence of John Paul Jones. [By
R. Sands.] New York, 1830.   [*Sands.*]

Life and Character of John Paul Jones. By John Henry
Sherburne. New York, 1851.   [*Sherburne.*]
These two books contain many of Jones's letters.

The Life of Paul Jones. By Alexander Slidell Mackenzie, U.S.N: New York, 1846.   [*Mackenzie.*]

Mémoire de Paul Jones, écrits par lui-même en anglais
et traduits sous ses yeux par le citoyen André. Paris,
1798.

Paul Jones, Founder of the American Navy. By Augustus C. Buell. New York, 1900.

    Mentioned only for the purpose of warning the
reader of naval history against it as a fabrication.
Made up largely of spurious documents ingeniously
concocted by the author, it has deceived many, although often exposed by various investigators.

Publications of the Naval History Society. Vol. i. The
Logs of the Serapis, Alliance, Ariel under the Com-
mand of John Paul Jones. Edited by John S. Barnes.
New York, 1911.

    Contains biographical matter. The Society's second
volume (1912), under the same editorship, is a reprint
of the life of Nathaniel Fanning, listed below. Vol.
iii, now in press (December, 1912), is The Despatches
of Molyneux Shuldham, Vice-Admiral of the Blue
and Commander-in-Chief of His Britannic Majesty's
Ships in North America, January–July, 1776. Edited
by Robert W. Neeser. New York, 1913.

Memoirs of the Life of Captain Nathaniel Fanning, an
American Naval Officer. New York, 1808.
                          [*Fanning.*]

Esek Hopkins, Commander-in-Chief of the Continental
Navy. By Edward Field. Providence, 1898.
                          [*Hopkins.*]

Commodore John Barry. By Martin I. J. Griffin. Philadelphia, 1903.   [*Barry.*]

The Life of Samuel Tucker, Commodore in the Ameri-

can Revolution. By John H. Sheppard. Boston,
1868. [*Tucker.*]

Life of Silas Talbot. By Henry T. Tuckerman. New
York, 1850. [*Talbot.*]

An Historical Sketch to the End of the Revolutionary
War of the Life of Silas Talbot. New York, 1803.
Published the same year in London under a differ-
ent title.

Life of Captain Jeremiah O'Brien. By Rev. Andrew M.
Sherman. [Morristown], 1902. [*O'Brien.*]

Biographical Memoir of the late Commodore Joshua
Barney. By Mary Barney. Boston, 1832. [*Barney.*]

Moses Brown, Captain, U.S.N. By Edgar Stanton Maclay. New York, 1904.

The Adventures of Ebenezer Fox in the Revolutionary
War. Boston, 1847. [*Fox.*]

Memoirs of Andrew Sherburne, a Pensioner of the Navy
of the Revolution. By Himself. Providence, 1831.
[*A. Sherburne.*]

The Old Jersey Captive, or a Narrative of the Captivity
of Thomas Andros. Boston, 1833. [*Andros.*]

The Prisoners of 1776. A Relic of the Revolution. By
Rev. R. Livesey. Compiled from the Journal of
Charles Herbert. Boston, 1854. [*Livesey.*]

Captain Thomas Dring. Recollections of Jersey Prison-
Ship. Morrisánia, 1865.

Narrative of Joshua Davis. Boston, 1811. [*Davis.*]

The Original Journal of General Solomon Lovell, kept
during the Penobscot Expedition, 1779. Published by
the Weymouth Historical Society, 1881.

Diary of Ezra Green, M.D., Surgeon on board the Continental Ship-of-War Ranger. Edited by Commodore
G. H. Preble, U.S.N. Boston, 1875.

Reprinted from the New England Historical and Genealogical Register.

Colonel William Bradford, the Patriot Printer of 1776. By John William Wallace. Philadelphia, 1884.

[*Bradford.*]

Correspondence and Journals of Samuel Blachley Webb. Edited by Worthington C. Ford. New York, 1893.

Letters from Sir George Brydges, now Lord Rodney, to His Majesty's Ministers. London, 1789.

Periodicals

(Some of the more notable articles are mentioned.)

Collections and Proceedings of the Maine Historical Society.

Proceedings of the Massachusetts Historical Society.

Publications of the Rhode Island Historical Society.

January, 1901. Papers of William Vernon and the Navy Board.

Rhode Island Historical Magazine.

July, 1885 — January, 1887. Journal of John Trevett, U.S.N.

Historical Collections of the Essex Institute.

January, 1909. The Naval Career of Captain John Manley of Marblehead. By Robert E. Peabody.

January–October, 1909. Records of the Vice-Admiralty Court at Halifax, N. S.

Records and Papers of the New London County Historical Society.

New England Historical and Genealogical Register.

New Hampshire Genealogical Record.

Collections of the New York Historical Society.

New York Genealogical and Biographical Record.

Pennsylvania Magazine of History and Biography.

Virginia Historical Register.
Virginia Magazine of History and Biography.
South Carolina Historical and Genealogical Magazine.
The American Historical Review.

July, 1903. St. Eustatius in the American Revolution. By J. Franklin Jameson.

October, 1904. Nova Scotia and New England during the Revolution. By Emily P. Weaver.

Historical Magazine.
American Historical Record.
Magazine of American History.
Magazine of History.
American Catholic Historical Researches.
Military and Naval Magazine of the United States, 1833–1836.
Naval Magazine, 1836.
United States Naval Institute Proceedings.

No. 79 (1896). Howe and D'Estaing. A Study in Coast Defense. By Commander C. F. Goodrich, U.S.N.

No. 83 (1897). The Sailor in the Revolution. By Commander C. F. Goodrich, U.S.N.

No. 99 (1901). The Coast in Warfare. By Lieutenant-Commander J. H. Sears, U.S.N.

No. 126 (1908). The True Story of the America. By Robert W. Neeser.

No. 139 (1911). American Privateers at Dunkerque. By Henri Malo. Translated by Stewart L. Mims.

The United Service.

July, 1895. Letters of Paul Jones.

October, 1905. Campaign of Vice-Admiral D'Estaing. By G. Lacour-Gayet. Translated by Chaplain T. G. Steward, U.S.A.

The earlier numbers of this magazine contain several biographical sketches of naval officers.

The Port Folio.

Biographical sketches of naval officers.

Southern Literary Messenger.

January — April, 1857. The Virginia Navy of the Revolution.

Hunt's Merchants' Magazine.

Atlantic Monthly.

September and October, 1861. Journal of a Privateersman, 1741. [Edited by Charles Eliot Norton.]

December, 1887. Paul Jones and the Armed Neutrality. By John Fiske.

The Century Magazine.

New England Magazine.

Scribner's Magazine.

February, July, and August, 1898. Articles by Captain Mahan on Lake Champlain and John Paul Jones.

Granite Monthly.

1881 and 1882. Log of the Ranger.

The Outlook.

January 3, 1903. James Barnes on Conyngham's Lost Commission.

Massachusetts Magazine.

1908–1912. The Massachusetts Navy. By F. A. Gardner.

Newspapers

The Boston Gazette and Country Journal (Watertown and Boston).

The New England Chronicle; name changed in September, 1776, to Independent Chronicle (Cambridge and Boston; had formerly been the Essex Gazette of Salem).

The Continental Journal and Weekly Advertiser (Boston).

The Independent Ledger and American Advertiser (Boston).

The Evening Post and General Advertiser (Boston).

The Massachusetts Spy, or American Oracle of Liberty (Worcester).

The Salem Gazette.

The Connecticut Courant and Hartford Weekly Intelligencer.

The Connecticut Gazette and Universal Intelligencer (New London).

The Royal Gazette (New York).

The Royal American Gazette (New York).

The New York Packet and American Advertiser (Fishkill).

The Pennsylvania Gazette.

Dunlap's Pennsylvania Packet, or the General Advertiser.

The Pennsylvania Evening Post.

The Freeman's Journal, or North American Intelligencer (Philadelphia).

The Maryland Journal and Baltimore Advertiser.

The London Chronicle.

Lloyd's Evening Post and British Chronicle (London).

Manuscript Sources

Navy Department. All the following are copies: Logbooks and journals of the Ranger, November 26, 1777, to May 18, 1778; of the Bonhomme Richard, May 8 to September 24, 1779; of the Serapis, September 26 to November 21, 1779; of the Alliance, November 22, 1779, to June 12, 1780; of the Ariel, June 16 to

October 14, 1780; of the South Carolina, August 4, 1781, to May 21, 1782; and of the letter of marque ship Queen of France, August 20 to September 9, 1782. Letter-book of John Paul Jones, March, 1778, to July, 1779. Miscellaneous material, including the court martial of Captain Pearson and letters of Admiral Rodney (1780) criticizing Admiral Arbuthnot.

Library of Congress. Papers of the Continental Congress, containing much correspondence relating to naval affairs, reports of officers, etc. Marine Committee Letter-Book, containing the instructions of the Marine Committee and Board of Admiralty to officers of the navy, letters to the navy boards, etc. Letters to Washington relating to naval affairs. John Paul Jones manuscripts in eleven volumes. Miscellaneous papers, including a list of officers in the Continental navy and marine corps. This material in the Library of Congress is of the utmost importance and is described more in detail in the bibliography of Paullin's *Navy of the American Revolution*. The Library has also acquired transcripts of the Admiralty Records in the British Archives.

Massachusetts State Library, Archives Division. Records of the Great and General Court, beginning July 26, 1775. Records of the Honorable the Council. Massachusetts Archives and Revolutionary Rolls Collection. In volumes v to ix, xxviii, xxxvii to xl, xliv, xlv, lii, liii, cxxxix, cxlv, cxlviii to cliii, clvii, clviii, clix, clxiv to clxxii a large amount of information will be found, including bonds and commissions of privateers, correspondence about prisoners, prize cases, letters, orders and minutes of the Board of War, reports of officers of the state navy, rolls, documents relating to the Penobscot Expedition, and miscellaneous papers.

Massachusetts Historical Society. Papers of Colonel
Timothy Pickering. Papers of Governor Trumbull of
Connecticut. Papers of Oliver Wolcott of Connecticut.

Essex Institute. Miscellaneous papers. Most letters of
interest have been printed in the society's collections.

Harvard College Library. Sparks Papers. Arthur Lee
Papers. Commodore Tucker Papers. Miscellaneous
papers, including Luther Little's narrative of the battle between tho Protector and the Admiral Duff.

Private Collections. Papers of John Adams, deposited
in the library of the Massachusetts Historical Society,
examined through the courtesy of Charles Francis
Adams, Esq. Copies of four letters kindly furnished
by Charles T. Harbeck, Esq., viz. : Hopkins's sailing
orders to his captains, dated February 14, 1776, two
letters of the Marine Committee, and a Jones letter
of November 1, 1776. James Barnes, Esq., kindly
sent a copy of a letter of William Bingham to Captain
Conyngham. The Log of the Ranger (August 24,
1778, to May 10, 1780) was sold by the estate of E.
P. Jewell, Esq., in April, 1910, and an opportunity to
copy extracts from it was obtained. This log, down
to March 2, 1779, was published in the Granite
Monthly.

Archives de la Marine aux Archives Nationales à Paris.
Campagnes ; Pays Étrangers, Commerce et Consulats ;
Travail du Roi et du Ministre ; Ordres et Dépêches ;
etc.

British Archives. Public Record Office. Admiralty Records : Admirals' Despatches, Captains' Letters, Con-
suls' Letters, Courts Martial, Captains' and Masters'
Logs. Transcripts of the British Admiralty Records
and of the French papers from the Archives de la

Marine, indispensable for a comprehensive study of Revolutionary naval history, were very kindly furnished by Robert W. Neeser, Esq. Customs House: Minutes of the Scottish Board of Customs; Irish Minute Books; Whitehaven Customs Letter-Book. Dr. Charles O. Paullin kindly allowed the use of his transcripts of these Custom House papers.

In quoting from documents, newspapers, manuscripts, etc., pains have been taken to avoid changes from the original except in punctuation, which has been amended when so doing has seemed essential to clearness.

II

RULES FOR THE REGULATION OF THE NAVY OF THE UNITED COLONIES

The Commanders of all ships and vessels belonging to the thirteen United Colonies are strictly required to shew in themselves a good example of honor and virtue to their officers and men, and to be very vigilant in inspecting the behaviour of all such as are under them, and to discountenance and suppress all dissolute, immoral, and disorderly practices, and also such as are contrary to the rules of discipline and obedience, and to correct those who are guilty of the same, according to the usage of the sea.

The Commanders of the ships of the thirteen United Colonies are to take care that divine service be performed twice a day on board, and a sermon preached on Sundays, unless bad weather or other extraordinary accidents prevent it.

If any shall be heard to swear, curse, or blaspheme

the name of God, the Commander is strictly enjoined to punish them for every offense by causing them to wear a wooden collar, or some other shameful badge of distinction, for so long time as he shall judge proper. If he be a commissioned officer, he shall forfeit one shilling for each offense, and a warrant or inferior officer six pence. He who is guilty of drunkenness, if a seaman, shall be put in irons until he is sober, but if an officer, he shall forfeit two days' pay.

No Commander shall inflict any punishment upon a seaman beyond twelve lashes upon his bare back with a cat of nine tails; if the fault shall deserve a greater punishment, he is to apply to the Commander in chief of the Navy, in order to the trying of him by a court-martial, and in the mean time he may put him under confinement.

The Commander is never by his own authority to discharge a commission or warrant officer, nor to punish or strike him, but he may suspend or confine them, and when he comes in the way of a Commander in chief, apply to him for holding a court-martial.

The Officer who commands by accident of the Captain's or commander's absence (unless he be absent for a time by leave) shall not order any correction but confinement, and upon the captain's return on board he shall then give an account of his reasons for so doing.

The Captain is to cause the articles of war to be hung up in some public places of the ship, and read to the ship's company once a month.

Whenever a Captain shall inlist a seaman, he shall take care to enter on his books the time and terms of his entering, in order to his being justly paid.

The Captain shall, before he sails, make return to,

and leave with the Congress, or such person or persons as the Congress shall appoint for that purpose, a compleat list of all his officers and men, with the time and terms of their entering; and during his cruize shall keep a true account of the desertion or death of any of them, and of the entering of others, and after his cruize and before any of them are paid off, he shall make return of a compleat list of the same, including those who shall remain on board his ship.

The men shall, at their request, be furnished with slops that are necessary by the Captain or purser, who shall keep an account of the same, and the Captain, in his return in the last mentioned article directed to be made, shall mention the amount delivered to each man, in order to its being stopped out of his pay.

As to the term "inferior Officer," the Captain is to take notice that the same does not include any commission or any warrant officer, except the second master, surgeon's mate, cook, armourer, gun-smith, master at arms and sail maker.

The Captain is to take care when any inferior officers or volunteer seamen are turned over into the ship under his command from any other ship, not to rate them on the ship's books in a worse quality, or lower degree or station, than they served in the ship they were removed from; and for his guidance he is to demand from the commander of the ship from which they are turned over, a list, under his hand, of their names and qualities.

Any officer, seaman, or others, intitled to wages or prize money, may have the same paid to his assignee, provided the assignment be attested by the Captain or Commander, the master or purser of the ship, or a chief magistrate of some county or corporation.

The Captain is to discourage the seamen of his ship from selling any part of their wages or shares, and never to attest the letter of attorney of any seaman, until he is fully satisfied that the same is not granted in consideration of money given for the purchase of his wages or shares.

When an inferior officer or seaman dies, the Captain is forthwith to make out a ticket for the time of his service, and to send the same by the first safe conveyance to the Congress, or agents by them for that purpose appointed, in order to the wages being forthwith paid to the executors or administrators of the deceased.

A convenient place shall be set apart for sick or hurt men, to which they are to be removed, with their hammocks and bedding, when the surgeon shall advise the same to be necessary, and some of the crew shall be appointed to attend and serve them, and to keep the place clean.

The cooper shall make buckets with covers and cradles if necessary, for their use.

All ships furnished with fishing tackle, being in such places where fish is to be had, the captain is to employ some of the company in fishing; the fish to be distributed daily to such persons as are sick or upon recovery, provided the surgeon recommend it, and the surplus by turns amongst the messes of the officers and seamen without favour or partiality and gratis, without any deduction of their allowance of provisions on that account.

It is left to the discretion of Commanders of squadrons to shorten the allowance of provisions according to the exigencies of the service, taking care that the men be punctually paid for the same.

The like power is given to Captains of single ships in cases of absolute necessity.

If there should be a want of pork, the Captain is to order three pounds of beef to be issued to the men, in lieu of two pounds of pork.

One day in every week shall be issued out a proportion of flour and suet, in lieu of beef, for the seamen, but this is not to extend beyond four months' victualling at one time, nor shall the purser receive any allowance for flour or suet kept longer on board than that time, and there shall be supplied, once a year, a proportion of canvas for pudding-bags, after the rate of one ell for every sixteen men.

If any ships of the thirteen United Colonies shall happen to come into port in want of provisions, the warrant of a Commander in chief shall be sufficient to the Agent or other instrument of the victualling, to supply the quantity wanted, and in urgent cases, where delay may be hurtful, the warrant of the Captain of the ship shall be of equal effect.

The Captain is frequently to order the proper officers to inspect into the condition of the provisions, and if the bread proves damp, to have it aired upon the quarter deck or poop, and also examine the flesh casks, and if any of the pickle be leaked out, to have new made and put in, and the casks made tight and secure.

The Captain or purser shall secure the cloaths, bedding, and other things of such persons as shall die or be killed, to be delivered to their executors or administrators.

All papers, charter parties, bills of lading, passports, and other writings whatsoever, found on board any ship or ships, which shall be taken, shall be carefully preserved, and the originals sent to the court of Justice for maritime affairs, appointed or to be appointed by the legislatures in the respective colonies, for judging concerning such prize or prizes; and if any person or persons shall wilfully or negligently destroy or suffer to be destroyed, any such paper or papers, he or they so offending shall forfeit their share of such prize or prizes, and suffer such other punishment as they shall be judged by a court-martial to deserve.

If any person or persons shall embezzle, steal or take away any cables, anchors, sails, or any of the ship's furniture, or any of the powder, arms, ammunition, or provisions of any ship belonging to the thirteen United Colonies, he or they shall suffer such punishment as a court-martial shall order.

When in sight of a ship or ships of the enemy, and at such other times as may appear to make it necessary to prepare for an engagement, the Captain shall order all things in his ship in a proper posture for fight, and shall, in his own person and according to his duty, heart on and encourage the inferior officers and men to fight courageously, and not to behave themselves faintly or cry for quarters, on pain of such punishment as the offence shall appear to deserve for his neglect.

Any Captain or other officer, mariner, or others, who shall basely desert their duty or station in the ship and run away while the enemy is in sight, or, in time of action, or shall entice others to do so, shall suffer death, or such other punishment as a court-martial shall inflict.

Any officer, seaman, or marine, who shall begin, excite, cause, or join.in any mutiny or sedition in the ship to which he belongs, on any pretence whatsoever, shall suffer death, or such other punishment as a court-martial shall direct. Any person in or belonging to the ship, who shall utter any words of sedition and mutiny, or endeavour to make any mutinous assemblies on any pretence whatsoever, shall suffer such punishment as a court-martial shall inflict.

None shall presume to quarrel with or strike his superior officer on pain of such punishment as a court-martial shall order to be inflicted.

If any person shall apprehend he has just cause of complaint, he shall quietly and decently make the same known to his superior officer, or to the captain, as the case may require, who shall take care that justice be done him.

There shall be no quarreling or fighting between shipmates on board any ship belonging to the thirteen United Colonies, nor shall there be used any reproachful or provoking speeches, tending to make quarrels and disturbance, on pain of imprisonment and such other punishment as a court-martial shall think proper to inflict.

If any person shall sleep upon his watch, or negligently perform the duty which shall be enjoined him to do, or forsake his station, he shall suffer such punishment as a court-martial shall judge proper to inflict, according to the nature of his offence.

All murder shall be punished with death.

All robbery and theft shall be punished at the discretion of a court-martial.

Any master at arms who shall refuse to receive such prisoner or prisoners as shall be committed to his charge, or having received them, shall suffer him or them to escape, or dismiss them without orders for so doing, shall suffer in his or their stead, as a court-martial shall order and direct.

The Captain, officers, and others shall use their utmost endeavours to detect, apprehend, and bring to punishment, all offenders, and shall at all times readily assist the officers appointed for that purpose in the discharge of their duty, on pain of being proceeded against and punished by a court-martial at discretion.

All other faults, disorders, and misdemeanours, which shall be committed on board any ship belonging to the thirteen United Colonies, and which are not herein mentioned, shall be punished according to the laws and customs in such cases at sea.

A court-martial shall consist of at least three Captains and three first lieutenants, with three Captains and three first lieutenants of Marines, if there shall be so many of the Marines then present, and the eldest Captain shall preside.

All sea officers of the same denomination shall take rank of the officers of the Marines.

.   .   .   .

The sentence of a court-martial for any capital offence, shall not be put in execution, until it be confirmed by the Commander in chief of the fleet; and it shall be the duty of the president of every court-martial to transmit to the Commander in chief of the fleet every sentence which shall be given, with a summary of the evidence and proceedings thereon, by the first opportunity.

The Commander in chief of the fleet for the time being, shall have power to pardon and remit any sentence of death, that shall be given in consequence of any of the aforementioned Articles.

There shall be allowed to each man serving on board

the ships in the service of the thirteen United Colonies, a daily proportion of provisions, according as is expressed in the following table, viz.

Sunday, 1 lb. bread, 1 lb. beef, 1 lb. potatoes or turnips.

Monday, 1 lb. bread, 1 lb. pork, $\frac{1}{2}$ pint peas and four oz. cheese.

Tuesday, 1 lb. bread, 1 lb. beef, 1 lb. potatoes or turnips, and pudding.

Wednesday, 1 lb. bread, two oz. butter, four oz. cheese and $\frac{1}{2}$ pint of rice.

Thursday, 1 lb. bread, 1 lb. pork, and $\frac{1}{2}$ pint of peas.

Friday, 1 lb. bread, 1 lb. beef, 1 lb. potatoes or turnips, and pudding.

Saturday, 1 lb. bread, 1 lb. pork, $\frac{1}{2}$ pint peas and four oz. cheese.

Half a pint of rum per man every day, and discretionary allowance on extra duty and in time of engagement.

A pint and half of vinegar for six men per week.

The pay of the officers and men [per calendar month] shall be as follows:

Captain or commander,	32	dollars
Lieutenants,	20	"
Master,	20	"
Mates,	15	"
Boatswain,	15	"
Boatswain's first mate,	$9\frac{1}{2}$	"
Boatswain's second mate,	8	"
Gunner,	15	"
Gunner's mate,	$10\frac{2}{3}$	"
Surgeon,	$21\frac{1}{3}$	"
Surgeon's mate,	$13\frac{1}{3}$	"
Carpenter,	15	"

Carpenter's mate,	$10\frac{2}{3}$	dollars.
Cooper,	15	"
Captain's or Commander's clerk,	15	"
Steward,	$13\frac{1}{3}$	"
Chaplain,	20	"
Able seamen,	$6\frac{2}{3}$	"
Captain of marines,	$26\frac{2}{3}$	"
Lieutenants,	18	"
Serjeants,	8	"
Corporals	$7\frac{1}{3}$	"
Fifer,	$7\frac{1}{3}$	"
Drummer,	$7\frac{1}{3}$	"
Privates [of] marines,	$6\frac{2}{3}$	"

III

INSTRUCTIONS TO COMMANDERS OF PRIVATEERS

Continental Congress, April 3, 1776:

I. You may, by force of arms, attack, subdue and take all ships and other vessels belonging to the inhabitants of Great Britain, on the high seas, or between high water and low water mark, except ships and vessels bringing persons who intend to settle and reside in the United Colonies; or bringing arms, ammunition, or war-like stores, to the said colonies, for the use of such inhabitants thereof as are friends to the American cause, which you shall suffer to pass unmolested, the commanders thereof permitting a peaceable search and giving satisfactory information of the contents of the ladings and destinations of voyages.

II. You may, by force of arms, attack, subdue and take all ships and other vessels whatsoever, carrying soldiers, arms, gunpowder, ammunition, provisions, or any other contraband goods, to any of the British armies or ships of war employed against these colonies.

III. You shall bring such ships and vessels, as you shall take, with their guns, rigging, tackle, apparel, furniture, and ladings to some convenient port or ports of the United Colonies, that proceedings may thereupon be had in due form, before the courts which are or shall be appointed to hear and determine causes civil and maritime.

IV. You, or one of your chief officers, shall bring or send the master and pilot and one or more principal person or persons of the company of every ship or vessel by you taken, as soon after the capture as may be, to the judge or judges of such court as aforesaid, to be examined upon oath, and make answer to the interrogatories which may be propounded, touching the interest or property of the ship or vessel and her lading; and, at the same time, you shall deliver, or cause to be delivered to the judge or judges, all passes, sea-briefs, charter-parties, bills of lading, cockets, letters and other documents and writings found on board, proving the said papers by the affidavit of yourself or of some other person present at the capture, to be produced as they were received, without fraud, addition, subduction or embezzlement.

V. You shall keep and preserve every ship or vessel and cargo by you taken, until they shall, by a sentence of a court properly authorized, be adjudged lawful prizes; not selling, spoiling, wasting, or diminishing the same, or breaking the bulk thereof, nor suffering any such thing to be done.

VI. If you, or any of your officers or crew, shall, in

cold blood, kill or maim, or by torture or otherwise, cruelly, inhumanly, and contrary to common usage and the practice of civilized nations in war, treat any person or persons surprized in the ship or vessel you shall take, the offender shall be severely punished.

VII. You shall, by all convenient opportunities, send to Congress written accounts of the captures you shall make, with the number and names of the captives, copies of your journal from time to time, and intelligence of what may occur or be discovered concerning the designs of the enemy and the destination, motions and operations of their fleets and armies.

VIII. One-third, at least, of your whole company shall be landsmen.

IX. You shall not ransom any prisoners or captives, but shall dispose of them in such manner as the Congress, or, if that be not sitting, in the colony whither they shall be brought, as the general assembly, convention, or council, or committee of safety, of such colony shall direct.

X. You shall observe all such further instructions as Congress shall hereafter give in the premises, when you shall have notice thereof.

XI. If you shall do anything contrary to these instructions, or to others hereafter to be given, or willingly suffer such thing to be done, you shall not only forfeit your commission and be liable to an action for breach of the condition of your bond, but be responsible to the party grieved for damages sustained by such malversation.

Additional articles, April 7, 1781:

1. You are to pay a sacred regard to the rights of neutral powers and the usage and customs of civilized

nations; and on no pretence whatever, presume to take or seize any ships or vessels belonging to the subjects of princes or powers in alliance with these United States [with certain exceptions], . . . under the pains and penalties expressed in a proclamation [See Appendix IV] issued by the Congress of the United States, the ninth day of May, in the year of our Lord one thousand seven hundred and seventy-eight.

2. You shall permit all neutral vessels freely to navigate on the high seas or coasts of America except such as are employed in carrying contraband goods or soldiers to the enemies of these United States.

3. You shall not seize or capture any effects belonging to the subjects of the belligerent powers on board neutral vessels, excepting contraband goods; and you are carefully to observe, that the term contraband is confined to those articles which are expressly declared to be such in the treaty of amity and commerce, of the sixth day of February, 1778, between these United States and his most Christian majesty, namely: arms, great guns, bombs, with their fusees and other things belonging to them, cannon-balls, gun-powder, matches, pikes, swords, lances, spears, halberts, mortars, petards, grenadoes, salt-petre, muskets, musket-ball, bucklers, helmets, breast-plates, coats of mail, and the like kind of arms proper for arming soldiers, musket-rests, belts, horses with their furniture, and all other warlike instruments whatever.

IV

A PROCLAMATION

Whereas Congress have received information and complaints, " that violences have been done by American armed vessels to neutral nations, in seizing ships belonging to their subjects and under their colours, and in making captures of those of the enemy whilst under the protection of neutral coasts, contrary to the usage and custom of nations " : to the end that such unjustifiable and piratical acts, which reflect dishonour upon the national character of these states, may be in future effectually prevented, the said Congress hath thought proper to direct, enjoin and command, and they do hereby direct, enjoin and command, all captains, commanders and other officers and seamen belonging to any American armed vessels, to govern themselves strictly in all things agreeably to the tenor of their commissions, and the instructions and resolutions of Congress ; particularly that they pay a sacred regard to the rights of neutral powers and the usage and custom of civilized nations, and on no pretence whatever presume to take or seize any ships or vessels belonging to the subjects of princes or powers in alliance with these United States, except they are employed in carrying contraband goods or soldiers to our enemies, and in such case that they conform to the stipulations contained in treaties subsisting between such princes or powers and these states ; and that they do not capture, seize or plunder any ships or vessels of our enemies, being under the protection of neutral coasts, nations or princes, under the penalty of

being condignly punished therefor, and also of being
bound to make satisfaction for all matters of damage
and the interest thereof by reparation, under the pain
and obligation of their persons and goods. And further,
the said Congress doth hereby resolve and declare, that
persons wilfully offending in any of the foregoing instances, if taken by any foreign powers in consequence
thereof, will not be considered as having a right to claim
protection from these states, but shall suffer such punishment as by the usage and custom of nations may be
inflicted upon such offenders.

Given in Congress at York, in the state of Pennsylvania, this ninth day of May, Anno Domini 1778.

V

VESSELS IN THE CONTINENTAL SERVICE

The dates indicate the period of active service, or,
where no service was performed during the war, the
date of launching is given. The Serapis is included for
the reason that she served temporarily as Commodore
Jones's flagship, replacing the Bonhomme Richard.

Continental Navy

Alfred, 24	ship	1775–1778
Columbus, 20	ship	1775–1778
Andrew Doria, 14	brig	1775–1777
Cabot, 14	brig	1775–1777
Providence, 12	sloop	1775–1779
Hornet, 10	sloop	1775–1777
Wasp, 8	schooner	1775–1777

Fly, 8	schooner	1775–1777
Lexington, 16	brig	1776–1777
Reprisal, 16	brig	1776–1777
Hampden, 14	brig	1776–1777
Independence, 10	sloop	1776–1778
Sachem, 10	sloop	1776–1777
Mosquito, 4	sloop	1776–1777
Raleigh, 32	frigate	1777–1778
Hancock, 32	frigate	1777
Warren, 32	frigate	1777–1779
Washington, 32	frigate	1777
Randolph, 32	frigate	1777–1778
Providence, 28	frigate	1777–1780
Trumbull, 28	frigate	1777–1781
Congress, 28	frigate	1777
Virginia, 28	frigate	1777–1778
Effingham, 28	frigate	1777
Boston, 24	frigate	1777–1780
Montgomery, 24	frigate	1777
Delaware, 24	frigate	1777
Ranger, 18	ship	1777–1780
Resistance, 10	brigantine	1777–1778
Surprise	sloop	1777
Racehorse, 10	sloop	1777
Repulse, 8	xebec	1777
Champion, 8	xebec	1777
Indien, 40	ship	1777
Deane (later Hague), 32	frigate	1777–1783
Queen of France, 28	frigate	1777–1780
Dolphin, 10	cutter	1777
Surprise, 10	lugger	1777
Revenge, 14	cutter	1777–1779
Alliance, 32	frigate	1778–1785

General Gates, 18	ship	1778–1779
Retaliation	brigantine	1778
Pigot, 8	schooner	1778
Confederacy, 32	frigate	1779–1781
Argo, 12	sloop	1779
Diligent, 12	brig	1779
Bonhomme Richard, 42	ship	1779
Pallas, 32	frigate	1779
Cerf, 18	cutter	1779
Vengeance, 12	brig	1779
Serapis, 44	ship	1779
Ariel, 20	ship	1780–1781
Saratoga, 18	ship	1780–1781
America, 74	ship of the line	1782
General Washington, 20	ship	1782–1784
Duc de Lauzun, 20	ship	1782–1783
Bourbon, 36	frigate	1783

Packets : —
   Active
   Baltimore
   Despatch
   Enterprise
   Fame
   Georgia Packet
   Horn Snake
   Mercury
   Phoenix

Washington's Fleet, 1775–1776

Hannah	schooner
Lynch	schooner
Franklin	schooner
Lee	schooner

Harrison	schooner
Warren	schooner
Washington	brigantine
Hancock	schooner
General Schuyler	sloop
General Mifflin	sloop
Lady Washington	galley

Lake Champlain, 1776

Enterprise, 12	sloop
Royal Savage, 12	schooner
Revenge, 8	schooner
Liberty, 8	schooner
New Haven, 3	gondola
Providence, 3	gondola
Boston, 3	gondola
Spitfire, 3	gondola
Philadelphia, 3	gondola
Connecticut, 3	gondola
Jersey, 3	gondola
New York, 3	gondola
Lee, 6	galley
Trumbull, 8	galley
Congress, 8	galley
Washington, 8	galley
Gates, 8	galley

Mississippi River, 1778-1779

Morris	ship
West Florida	sloop
Morris	schooner

VI

OFFICERS IN THE CONTINENTAL NAVY AND MARINE CORPS

A list of Revolutionary officers was compiled in 1794. It is "formed from the Minutes of the Marine Committee and Navy Boards, and from the Rolls of the several Vessels; many of the Officers served only for a Cruize" (*Miscellaneous Naval Papers*, March 18, 1794, in the Library of Congress). A previous list had been given out by the Board of Admiralty in September 1781 (*Papers of the Continental Congress*, 37, 473), which is an incomplete register of the officers of that date. The following list has been made up from these two (see also Paullin's *Navy of the Revolution*, Appendix B). A very few unimportant attempts at emendation in spelling, etc., that seemed warranted by other authority, have been made. The names of captains which are numbered comprise those appointed October 10, 1776, in the order of rank; the numbered lieutenants were commissioned October 12, 1776. The same officers generally had earlier commissions, which are also indicated when known; these commissions were superseded in October, 1776. A number of other dates of commission, taken from the 1781 list and other sources, are also given. Annexed to the main list will be found a number of names, not included in either of the old lists, comprising officers commissioned in France and others (see *Journals of the Continental Congress*, April 17, June 6, 1776, June 14, 1777, September 8, 1779; Calendars of *Naval Records* and of *Jones Papers* — indices;

Goldsborough's *Naval Chronicle*, p. 8; Field's *Life of Hopkins*, p. 186); some of them were doubtless never regularly commissioned. To make a wholly complete and accurate list would be impossible.

CONTINENTAL NAVY

Captains and Commanders

Esek Hopkins, commander-in-chief, December 22, 1775.

1. James Nicholson, June 6, 1776.
2. John Manley, April 17, 1776.
3. Hector McNeill, June 15, 1776.
4. Dudley Saltonstall, December 22, 1775.
5. Nicholas Biddle, December 22, 1775.
6. Thomas Thompson, June 6, 1776.
7. John Barry, June 6, 1776.
8. Thomas Read, June 6, 1776.
9. Thomas Grinnell, June 15, 1776.
10. Charles Alexander, June 6, 1776.
11. Lambert Wickes.
12. Abraham Whipple, December 22, 1775.
13. John Burrows Hopkins, December 22, 1775.
14. John Hodge, August 22, 1776.
15. William Hallock.
16. Hoysted Hacker.
17. Isaiah Robinson.
18. John Paul Jones.
19. James Josiah.
20. Elisha Hinman, August 13, 1776.
21. Joseph Olney.
22. James Robinson.
23. John Young.
24. Elisha Warner.

John Nicholson, November 19, 1776.
Samuel Nicholson, December 10, 1776.
Henry Johnson, February 5, 1777.
John Peck Rathburne, February 15, 1777.
Gustavus Conyngham, March 1, 1777.
Samuel Tucker, March 15, 1777.
Daniel Waters, March 17, 1777.
John Green, February 11, 1778.
William Burke, May 1, 1778.
Pierre Landais, June 18, 1778.
Seth Harding, September 23, 1778.
Silas Talbot, September 17, 1779.
John Ayres.
Peter Brewster.
Samuel Chew.
Benjamin Dunn.
John Hazard.
William Pickles.
Thomas Simpson.
John Skimmer.
William Stone.

Lieutenants

1. Peter Shores, July 22, 1776.
2. Robert Harris.
3. Jonathan Maltbie, August 22, 1776.
4. John Brown, June 15, 1776.
5. Ezekiel Burroughs, December 22, 1775.
6. Luke Matthewman.
7. George House.
8. Thomas Albertson.
9. John Baldwin.
10. Simon Gross.

11. David Phipps, August 22, 1776.
12. John Sleymaker.
13. Joshua Barney.
14. Jonathan Pritchard.
15. Adam W. Thaxter.
16. Benjamin Handy.
17. Joseph Greenway.
18. Benjamin Page.
19. Hopley Yeaton.
   Rhodes Arnold, December 22, 1775.
   Jonathan Pitcher, December 22, 1775.
   Benjamin Seabury, December 22, 1775.
   Thomas Weaver, December 22, 1775.
   John McDougal, December 22, 1775.
   Daniel Vaughan, December 22, 1775.
   Joseph Doble, June 6, 1776.
   John Wheelwright, July 22, 1776.
   Josiah Shackford, July 22, 1776.
   William Barnes, August 17, 1776.
   Thomas Vaughan, August 17, 1776.
   Hezekiah Welch, October 19, 1776.
   Patrick Fletcher, November 20, 1776.
   Blaney Allison, December 20, 1776.
   Elijah Bowen, February 5, 1777.
   Robert French, March 25, 1777.
   Robert Martin, April 22, 1777.
   Elijah Hall, June 14, 1777.
   Matthew Tibbs, June 17, 1777.
   John Rodez, August 6, 1777.
   John Fanning, August 10, 1777.
   William Mollison, August 12, 1777.
   Arthur Dillaway, September 19, 1777.
   Joseph Vesey, November 13, 1777.

Silas Devol, January 28, 1778.
Muscoe Livingston, July 27, 1778.
Stephen Gregory, August 4, 1778.
Michael Knies, August 7, 1778.
Samuel Cardal, August 15, 1778.
Peter Deville, August 25, 1778.
Benjamin Bates, December 4, 1778.
Richard Dale, August, 1779.
Alexander Murray, July 20, 1781.
Joseph Adams.
Robert Adamson.
John Angus.
James Armitage.
Josiah Audibert.
Benjamin Barron.
William Barron.
Goerge Batson.
Daniel Bears.
John Bellenger.
Christopher Bradley.
Jacob Brooks.
Philip Brown.
Isaac Buck.
Charles Bulkley.
Edward Burke.
George Champlin.
John Channing.
Seth Clarke.
David Cullam.
James Degge.
William Dennis.
Marie Sevel Dorie.
William Dunlap.

William Dupar.
Joshua Fanning.
Wilford Fisher.
William Gamble.
Nicholas E. Gardner.
William Grinnell.
James Grinwell.
William Ham.
James Handy.
Abraham Hawkins.
John Hennessey.
Stephen Hill.
Christopher Hopkins
Esek Hopkins, Jr.
William Hopkins.
Robert Hume.
Aquilla Johns.
John Kemp.
John Kerr.
Benjamin Knight.
William Leeds.
Edward Leger.
John Lewis.
George Lovie.
Cutting Lunt.
Henry Lunt.
John McIvers.
John Margisson.
Richard Marvin.
John Moran.
William Moran.
William Morrison.
Isaac Olney.

James Pine.
Robert Pomeroy.
David Porter.
William Potts.
Benjamin Reed.
Peter Richards.
James Robertson.
John Robinson.
Peter Rosseau.
Robert Saunders.
John Scott.
Robert Scott.
John Scranton.
Nicholas Scull.
James Sellers.
Daniel Starr.
James Stephens.
John Stevens.
David Welch.
Jacob White.
Richard Wickes.
James Wilson.
Robert Wilson.
Samuel York.

MARINE CORPS

Major

Samuel Nicholas, June 25, 1776.

Captains

Matthew Parke, May 26, 1776.
Andrew Porter, June 25, 1776.
Samuel Shaw, June 25, 1776.

Benjamin Deane, June 25, 1776.
Robert Mullen, June 25, 1776.
John Stewart, June 25, 1776.
Gilbert Saltonstall, June, 1776.
Richard Palmer, July 7, 1776.
George Jerry Osborne, July 22, 1776.
Seth Baxter, October 10, 1776.
James Disney, October 22, 1776.
Joseph Hardy, October, 1776.
Dennis Leary, June 21, 1777.
William Morris, June, 1777.
William Jones, March 4, 1778.
Edward Arrowsmith, October 20, 1778.
William Nicholson, September 6, 1781.
Abraham Boyce.
Isaac Craig.
John Elliott.
Robert Elliott.
John Hazard.
William Holton.
William Matthewman.
Miles Pennington.
—— Rice.
Joseph Shoemaker.
—— Spence.
John Trevett.
Elihu Trowbridge.
John Welch.

Lieutenants

Daniel Henderson, June 25, 1776.
David Love, June 25, 1776.
Franklin Reed, June 25, 1776.

Peregrine Brown, June 25, 1776.
James McClure, June 25, 1776.
William Gilmore, June 25, 1776.
Abel Morgan, June 25, 1776.
Hugh Montgomery, June 25, 1776.
Thomas Pownal, June 25, 1776.
Richard Harrison, June 25, 1776.
Stephen Meade, July 22, 1776.
Nathaniel Thwing, July 22, 1776.
Benjamin Thompson, July 22, 1776.
Alpheus Rice, August 24, 1776.
Jacob White, October 16, 1776.
Thomas Plunkett, December 9, 1776.
William Jennison, February, 1777.
William Waterman, March 4, 1778.
Thomas Elwood, August 24, 1778.
Peter Green, September 25, 1778.
Abraham Vandyke, July 24, 1779.
William Barney.
Henry Becker.
Peter Bedford.
David Bill.
Gurdon Bill.
Benjamin Catlin.
Seth Chapin.
John Chilton.
James Clarke.
James Cokely.
James Connolly.
William Cooper.
David Cullam.
Robert Cummings.
Robert Davis.

Henry Dayton.
John Dimsdell.
Stephen Earle.
Thomas Elting.
Panatier de la Falconier.
Zebadiah Farnham.
William Fielding.
Thomas Fitzgerald.
John Fitzpatrick.
Samuel Gamage.
John Guignace.
Roger Haddock.
James Hamilton.
Jonas Hamilton.
William Hamilton.
John Harris.
Samuel Hempstead.
Samuel Holt.
Benjamin Huddle.
William Huddle.
Robert Hunter.
Hugh Kirkpatrick.
Daniel Longstreet.
Eugene McCarthy.
Richard McClure.
Charles McHarron.
Robert McNeal.
Peter Manifold.
Jonathan Mix.
William Morris.
Alexander Neilson.
James Gerald O'Kelly.
Avery Parker.

Samuel Powars.
Samuel Pritchard.
William Radford.
Jerry Reed.
Nathaniel Richards.
Jabez Smith.
Walter Spooner.
Edmund Stack.
Daniel Starr.
I. M. Strobach.
George Trumbull.
Thomas Turner.
Louis de la Valette.
Zebulon Varnam.
—— Wadsworth.
Samuel Wallingford.
James Warren.
James H. Wilson.
Jonathan Woodworth.

SUPPLEMENTARY LIST

Captains

Isaac Cazneau, April 17, 1776.
Samuel Tomkins, June 6, 1776.
Christopher Miller, June 6, 1776.
Henry Skinner.
John Roach.
Ralph Moor.
Denis Nicolas Cottineau.
Joseph Varage.
Philippe Nicolas Ricot.

Lieutenants

Eli Stansbury, December 22, 1775.
Israel Turner, June 6, 1776.
Mark Dennet, June 6, 1776.
—— Plunkett, July 20, 1781.
Peter Amiel.
Robert Robinson.
John Buckley.
James Linds.
Henri le Meignen.
Pierre Magonet.
Beninge Mischateau.
Armand la Coudrais.
Pierre de Nantes.
Nicolas de St. Valery.

Captains of Marines

John Grannis.
Maurice O'Connell.
Antoine Felix Wybert.
Paul de Chamillard.

Lieutenants of Marines

George Stillman.
Barnabas Lothrop.

VII

CONTINENTAL PRIVATEERS

A list of the private armed vessels to which letters of marque were issued by the Continental Congress has been printed by the Library of Congress in the Calendar of Naval Records of the American Revolution, published in 1906. With the name of each vessel are given the state where owned, the rig, the number of guns and of men, the amount of the bond furnished, and the names of the commander, the bonders, and the owners. The bonds are contained in sixteen volumes of the papers of the Continental Congress (No. 196). The most important of the statistics compiled from them are given below. The numbers of guns and of men in these tables are smaller than they should be, for the reason that in several cases (thirty of the former — eighteen of the latter) the numbers are not stated.

Number of privateers		1697
Ships	301	
Brigs and brigantines	541	
Schooners, sloops, etc.	751	
Boats and galleys	104	1697
New Hampshire	43	
Massachusetts	626	
Rhode Island	15	
Connecticut	218	
New York	1	
New Jersey	4	
Pennsylvania	500	
Maryland	225	
Virginia	64	
South Carolina	1	1697
1776	34	
1777	69	

1778	129	
1779	209	
1780	301	
1781	550	
1782	383	
1783	22	1697

Number of guns, 14,872.   Number of men, 58,400

VIII

CONCORDAT

Agreement between Messieurs John Paul Jones, captain of the Bonhomme Richard; Pierre Landais, captain of the Alliance; Denis Nicolas Cottineau, captain of the Pallas; Joseph Varage, captain of the Stag; and Philippe Nicolas Ricot, captain of the Vengeance; composing a squadron that shall be commanded by the oldest officer of the highest grade and so on in succession in case of death or retreat. None of the said commanders, whilst they are not separated from the said squadron by order of the minister, shall act but by virtue of the brevet which they shall have obtained from the United States of America, and it is agreed that the flag of the United States shall be displayed.

The division of the prizes to the superior efficers and crews of the said squadron shall be made agreeable to the American laws, but it is agreed that the proportion of the whole coming to each vessel in the squadron shall be regulated by the Minister of the Marine Department of France and the Minister Plenipotentiary of the United States of America.

A copy of the American laws shall be annexed to the present agreement, after having been certified by the commander of the Bonhomme Richard, but as the said laws cannot foresee nor determine as to what may concern the vessels and subjects of other nations, it is expressly agreed that whatever may be contrary to them should be regulated by the Minister of the French Marine and the Minister Plenipotentiary of the United States of America.

It is likewise agreed that the orders given by the Minister of the French Marine and the Minister Plenipotentiary of the United States shall be executed.

Considering the necessity there is of preserving the interests of each individual, the prizes that shall be taken shall be remitted to the orders of Monsieur le Ray de Chaumont, honorary intendant of the Royal Hotel of Invalids, who has furnished the expenses of the armament of the said squadron.

It has been agreed that M. le Ray de Chaumont be requested not to give up the part of the prizes coming to all the crews, and to each individual of the said squadron, but to their order, and to be responsible for the same in his own and proper name.

Whereas the said squadron has been formed for the purpose of injuring the common enemies of France and America, it has been agreed that such armed vessels, whether French or American, may be associated therewith by common consent, as shall be found suitable for the purpose, and that they shall have such proportion of the prizes which shall be taken as the laws of their respective countries allow them.

In case of the death of any of the before mentioned commanders of vessels, he shall be replaced agreeably to the order of the tariff, with liberty however for the successor to choose whether he will remain on board his own vessel and give up to the next in order the command of the vacant ship.

It has moreover been agreed that the commander of the Stag shall be excepted from the last article of this present agreement, because in case of a disaster to M. de Varage, it shall be replaced by his second in command and so on by the other officers of his cutter the Stag.

J. P. JONES.
P. LANDAIS.
DE COTTINEAU.
DE VARAGE.
P. RICOT.
LE RAY DE CHAUMONT.

INDEX

INDEX